Karin Weber, MSc
Kye-Sung Chon, PhD
Editors

Convention Tourism
International Research and Industry Perspectives

Pre-publication
REVIEWS,
COMMENTARIES,
EVALUATIONS . . .

"*C*onvention Tourism truly reflects global perspectives with theoretical discussions and case studies. Topical issues related to the convention industry are comprehensive and encompass history, economy, planning and development, marketing, human resources, research issues, and international perspectives. Four case studies add value to the book by providing discussions of critical issues pertinent to different industry players in four regions. The final chapter by Karin Weber and Kye-Sung Chon, editors of this book, expands the discussions to future trends for the convention industry in the twenty-first century and assists readers to better prepare for their future. I recommend this book to advanced undergraduate and graduate students. It will also be very useful to convention industry practitioners."

"*T*his comprehensive book is truly global in its perspective. The text points out areas of needed research—a great starting point for graduate students, university faculty, and industry professionals alike. While the focus is mainly academic, there is a lot of meat for this burgeoning industry to chew on as well."

Patti J. Shock, CPCE
Professor and Department Chair,
Tourism and Convention
Administration, Harrah College
of Hotel Administration,
University of Nevada–Las Vegas

Sungsoo Pyo, PhD
Professor, Kyonggi University;
Visiting Scholar, University of Illinois,
Urbana-Champaign;
Editor, *Journal of Quality Assurance
in Hospitality and Tourism*

More pre-publication
REVIEWS, COMMENTARIES, EVALUATIONS . . .

"*Convention Tourism* brings together an impressive team of contributors to address a discipline that has previously been given little attention in academia. This is especially true with respect to textbooks. This book looks at meetings and conventions as a vehicle for tourism. In this regard, it does a good job of setting forth criticisms of the commonly used acronym MICE (Meetings, Incentives, Conventions, and Exhibitions), to describe this market. The authors also correctly point out that this acronym is technically incorrect. The meeting and convention market is distinctly different than the incentive and exhibition market and deserves the individual treatment that this book provides.

Part one of this book concentrates on building a theoretical framework and discusses many conceptual ideas.

Part two moves into a more practical application of the theory and concepts. It provides specific case studies that illustrate the issues in this industry. Each case study focuses on a different key player in the industry. This focus allows the reader to understand the different goals, objectives, and needs of each player. It also helps define the different roles within the industry. The editors close the book with a discussion of the future of the convention industry. This book is well-conceived and well-executed. It provides an important body of knowledge to the field."

Je' Anna L. Abbott, MHM, JD, MBA
Interim Associate Dean
and Associate Professor,
Conrad N. Hilton College of Hotel
and Restaurant Management,
University of Houston

The Haworth Hospitality Press®
An Imprint of The Haworth Press, Inc.
New York • London • Oxford

Convention Tourism
International Research and Industry Perspectives

Convention Tourism
International Research and Industry Perspectives

Karin Weber, MSc
Kye-Sung Chon, PhD
Editors

The Haworth Hospitality Press®
An Imprint of The Haworth Press, Inc.
New York • London • Oxford

The Haworth Press, Inc., 10 Alice Street, Binghamton, NY 13904-1580.

Cover design by Jennifer M. Gaska.

Interior and exterior convention hall photography courtesy of the Hong Kong Tourism Board.

Library of Congress Cataloging-in-Publication Data

Convention tourism : international research and industry perspectives / Karin Weber, K.S. (Kaye) Chon, editors.
    p. cm.
    Includes bibliographical references (p.) and index.
    ISBN 0-7890-1283-9 (alk. paper) — ISBN 0-7890-1284-7
    1. Tourism. 2. Congresses and conventions. 3. Sales meetings. I. Weber, Karin, 1970-
II. Chon, K.S.

G155.A1 C672 2002
338.4'791—dc21

2002068606

This book is dedicated to the memory
of the late Dr. Martin Oppermann

CONTENTS

PART II: CASE STUDIES

ABOUT THE EDITORS

Karin Weber, MSc, is Assistant Professor at the Hong Kong Polytechnic University. Ms. Weber has been affiliated with the University of Nevada in Las Vegas, and Monash University in Victoria, Australia. Her research has been published in leading tourism and hospitality journals, including the *Annals of Tourism Research,* the *Journal of Travel Research, Tourism Management, the Journal of Travel & Tourism Marketing, Cornell HRA Quarterly*, and the *International Journal of Hospitality Management.* She serves on the editorial board of the *Journal of Travel & Tourism Marketing* and the *Journal of Convention & Exhibition Management* and has contributed research projects to the Professional Convention Management Association (PCMA), Meeting Professionals International (MPI), and the International Association of Convention and Visitors Bureaus (IACVB).

Kaye Chon, PhD, is Chair Professor of Hotel and Tourism Management and is the head of the Department of Hotel and Tourism Management at the Hong Kong Polytechnic University. He was formerly on the faculties of the University of Houston in Texas, the University of Las Vegas in Nevada, and Virginia Tech, in Blacksburg. Dr. Chon is Chief Editor of the *Journal of Travel & Tourism Marketing,* the *Journal of Hospitality & Tourism Research,* the *Journal of Teaching in Travel & Tourism,* and the *Asia Pacific Journal of Tourism Research,* and is current Chairman of the International Society of Travel & Tourism Educators.

Dr. Chon is a past recipient of the John Wiley & Sons Award from the International Council on Hotel, Restaurant, and Institutional Education for lifetime contribution to scholarship and research in tourism/hospitality. His research with the late Martin Oppermann led to the development of a model for convention tourism decision-making that has been widely accepted since its publication in *Annals of Tourism Research* in 1997.

CONTRIBUTORS

Cherylynn Becker, PhD, is Associate Professor of hotel management for Washington State University, teaching at the Swiss Center Campus in Brig, Switzerland. She received her doctorate from Virginia Polytechnic Institute and State University in 1992. Her current research interests focus on the impact of cultural differences in consumer perceptions of quality in hospitality services. Becker's publications have appeared in a number of journals including the *Journal of Hospitality and Tourism Research,* the *International Journal of Hospitality Management, Tourism Analysis: An Interdisciplinary Journal,* and the *Journal of Hospitality and Tourism Education.* She serves on the editorial boards for the *Journal of Travel and Tourism Research* and *Praxis* and the *Journal of Applied Hospitality Management.* Prior to entering academia Becker held management positions in a number of hospitality firms including hotels, restaurants, institutional food services, and private clubs.

Geoffrey I. Crouch, PhD, is Professor and Chair of Tourism Marketing in the School of Tourism and Hospitality at La Trobe University, Melbourne, Australia. Prior to joining La Trobe, he spent six years at the University of Calgary's World Tourism Education and Research Center. He was an elected member of the Board of Directors of the Calgary Convention and Visitors Bureau. Professor Crouch has consulted for the World Tourism Organization and has contributed to several executive programs in destination management for members of the International Association of Convention and Visitor Bureaus (IACVB) and for representatives of the tourism industries in Jordan and India. Most recently he was involved in an evaluation of the effectiveness of the international marketing programs of the Hong Kong Tourist Association. At present he is conducting a convention site selection choice modeling experiment.

Larry Dwyer, PhD, is Director of the Centre for Tourism and Hospitality Research at the University of Western Sydney, Australia. He publishes widely in international tourism research journals, particularly in the area of tourism economics. He has undertaken an extensive number of consultancies for public and private sector tourism organizations in Australia. His consulting work also extends to international agencies, including the World Tourism Organization.

George G. Fenich, PhD, is Professor at the School of Hotel, Restaurant, and Tourism Administration at the University of New Orleans, teaching courses in the school's convention and meeting planning concentration. He spent fifteen years as a practitioner before commencing his academic career in 1985. His PhD, completed at Rutgers University in 1992, focused on convention centers in the United States. He has written numerous articles about meetings and conventions, made conference presentations on the topic, and serves as an editorial board member of the *Journal of Convention and Exhibition Management*. He is a faculty advisor for the Professional Convention Management Association (PCMA) and is involved in grants dealing with the convention industry.

Frank Go, PhD, is Professor and Bewetour Chair of Tourism Management at the Rotterdam School of Management, the Netherlands. Prior to his current post he worked in the United States and was affiliated with universities in Canada and Hong Kong. He was awarded a PhD from the University of Amsterdam's faculty of Economics and Econometrics in 1993. His current research focus is on creating value through relationship marketing, especially within travel, hospitality, conference, cultural, and related industries. He has served as chairman of a number of research consortia, been on the editorial board of several leading tourism and hospitality journals, and authored, co-authored, and co-edited several books.

Robert Govers, MSc, is Senior Lecturer in Travel and Tourism Marketing and Management at Dubai Polytechnic's Business School. Prior to that he was Research Associate for the Centre for Tourism Management at the Rotterdam School of Management in the Netherlands and also served as a Guest Lecturer at the School of Logistics at the Johannesburg Technical College. He earned his MSc in Business Studies from Erasmus University in Rotterdam in 1995, majoring in Marketing Management, and his BSc in Information Management from the College of Technology of The Hague. He has published in the field of tourism and hospitality, quality management, e-commerce in tourism, and tourism research. Through his engagement in a PhD research project that focuses on online destination marketing, using Dubai as a case study, he continues his affiliation with the Rotterdam School of Management.

Yeon-Seok Koo is Executive Director of the Domestic Tourism Marketing Department, Korea National Tourism Organization (KNTO), a statutory organization for Korean tourism. He has been dedicated to convention marketing for seven of his twenty-four years of service for KNTO.

Adele Ladkin, PhD, is a Reader in Tourism at the International Centre for Tourism and Hospitality Research, Bournemouth University, United Kingdom. She is the Deputy Head of Research and Head of the Meetings, Incentives, Conventions, and Exhibitions (MICE) research unit within the School of Service Industries. Her research interests and publications are in the areas of tourism education, career analysis, and labor mobility in the tourism and hospitality industry, and the MICE industry. She is currently Assistant Editor in Chief for the *International Journal of Tourism Research.* She gained an MSc and a PhD in Tourism Management from the University of Surrey, United Kingdom. She is the lead author of an in-depth investigation of the MICE industry for the Travel and Tourism Intelligence Unit, published in 2000, titled *The Meetings, Incentives, Conferences, and Exhibitions Industry: An International Research Report.*

Pier Paolo Mariotti is Editorial Director of *IT,* a magazine aimed at European meeting and incentive planners, for the Ediman Publishing Company. He graduated with a degree in Economics and Business Administration in Verona in 1984. Following studies at the Westminster College, London, he spent the late 1980s in Southeast Asia as a photojournalist and image consultant, specializing in corporate image and destination marketing. He was affiliated for seven years with the Convention Bureau of South Tyrol, where in 1999 he promoted a quality ISO certification project for bureau members. That year he was also involved in the establishment of the Convention Bureau of Turin. Most recently, he collaborated in the planning for an e-marketplace dedicated to the Italian meeting industry.

Donald J. MacLaurin, PhD, is Associate Professor in the School of Hotel and Food Administration at the University of Guelph. He recently completed a three-year assignment as Professor of MICE Management at Nanyang University in Singapore. He has extensive work experience in the tourism and MICE industries with such companies as Hyatt Hotels, British Airways, Tourism Canada, and several prominent tour companies in North America. He holds active memberships in the Council on Hotel, Restaurant, and Institutional Education (CHRIE), and the Professional Convention Management Association (PCMA). Research and consulting interests are focused on the MICE industries. MacLaurin is the author of several publications, the latest of which is a textbook, *Meetings and Conventions: A Planning Guide,* which he authored for Meeting Professionals International (MPI) in 1997. MacLaurin was also a founding member and facilitator of PCMA's learning environment specialist (LES) certification program for the convention services industry.

Vivienne S. McCabe, MBA, is Senior Lecturer in the School of Tourism and Hospitality Management at Southern Cross University, Australia. She has over twenty years' experience in operational management in hotels, health resorts, conferences, and the hospitality sector, and as a partner in a consultancy and training firm. Since joining Southern Cross University, she has been instrumental in the development of a program of study in Convention and Event Management for undergraduates, as well as the master's degree in the same field. She has held lecturing posts at two of Europe's leading hotel and tourism schools, Bournemouth University and Westminster College, and has completed a wide range of consultancy and training assignments for clients in the tourism, hospitality, and conference industry. McCabe is the lead author of the first Australian text on the convention and meeting industry in Australasia, *The Business and Management of Conventions* (2002).

Harald Pechlaner, PhD, is Assistant Professor in the Department of Management, Tourism, and Service Economics of the University of Innsbruck, Austria. From 1993 until 1998 he was Head of the Governmental Tourism Administration of South Tyrol, Italy, and Managing Director of South Tyrol Tourism Board. More recently, he held a visiting professorship at the University of Wisconsin—Stout (1999), a professorship at the Free University of Bozen—Bolzano (2000-2001), and was a visiting research scholar at the University of

Colorado at Boulder (2001). He received his PhD in Social and Economic Sciences at the University of Innsbruck in 1993.

Catherine H. Price, PhD, is Associate Chair and Associate Professor in the Department of Hospitality Management at the University of Southern Mississippi in Hattiesburg. She currently serves as Chair of the Hattiesburg Tourism Commission and is on the Board of Directors of the Area Development Partnership and the Lake Terrace Convention Center Commission. She has over twenty years' experience working in the meeting and convention management industry. In 1981 she established an independent meeting management firm, Price and Associates—The Meeting Company, and a destination management company, Events Extraordinnaire. She continues to provide consulting services to a variety of hospitality and tourism related organizations. Price is the author of *The Complete Guide for Professional Meeting and Event Coordination* and the Professional Convention Management Association's online course *Understanding Your Meeting Customer.* She received a PhD in Convention Management from Virginia Polytechnic Institute and State University in 1993.

Sungsoo Pyo, PhD, is Professor in the Department of Tourism Management, Kyonggi University, Republic of Korea. He is the Editor of the *Journal of Quality Assurance in Hospitality and Tourism.* He is also President of Tourism Systems and Quality Management Research Association in Korea. His research interests include the development of destination quality management systems and the quantitative analysis of various hospitality and tourism systems and optimization.

Julie Spiller, MSc, is a doctoral student sponsored by the London Chambers of Commerce and Industry Commercial Educational Trust (LCCICET) and works for the MICE Research Unit (MRU) at the International Centre for Tourism and Hospitality Research, Bournemouth University. Spiller gained her BSc (Hons) in Human Geography from Reading University, United Kingdom and a MSc in Tourism Management and Marketing at Bournemouth University. Her research interests are the growth and development of the convention industry in the United Kingdom. She is the co-author of an in-depth investigation of the MICE industry for the Travel and Tourism Intelligence Unit published in 2000, titled *The Meetings, Incentives, Conferences, and Exhibitions Industry: An International Research Report.*

Anton M. Vliegenthart is Managing Director of de Doelen Concert and Congress Centre, Rotterdam, a multipurpose venue, which was recently extended with a new congress wing and a five-star Westin Hotel. The new configuration reopened in the fall of 2000, and hosts 650 concerts and 1,000 national and international business events (up to 2,500 participants) per year. Vliegenthart has been working in the convention industry in the Netherlands for the past ten years, and has served as a member of the Board of Directors for the Rotterdam Convention Bureau and as treasurer of the Netherlands Convention Bureau. Furthermore, he was a member of the International Congress and Convention Association's International Educational Committee, preparing the content for the annual meetings industry convention of 1999 (Lisbon, Portugal) and 2000 (Hong Kong, China). He holds a BSc in Political Science from Erasmus University in Rotterdam.

Preface

The human desire to meet and exchange ideas, the basis of conventions and meetings, is as old as humankind. Yet it was only in the twentieth century that an industry which centers on these activities evolved. Even more recent is the increased academic interest in these phenomena—the lack of which long belied their economic significance.

The convention and meetings industry experienced tremendous growth during the past decade and today is truly global in nature. Its origins can be found in Europe and North America. Yet it is the Asia-Pacific region in particular that saw a rapid increase in industry activity since the late 1980s, outperforming the traditional markets and thereby mirroring the shifts in tourism development in general. Spiller, in Chapter 1, highlights some of the key developments in these regions. In this context it is important to note that although the number of destinations vying for the lucrative convention business is steadily increasing, the markets from which business is generated are relatively few and constant. After all, Europe and North America are still host to the headquarters of many international associations and intergovernmental organizations that organize events. Rogers (1998) also notes that the national economies of emerging countries are not yet sufficiently strong to generate the level of corporate business as the traditional players, nor have the former developed the level of market intelligence existent in Europe and North America.

Conventions and meetings represent an important element of the tourism industry. More specifically, they are part of an industry sector which in many regions of the world is commonly referred to as the MICE sector, encompassing Meetings, Incentives, Conventions, and Exhibitions. Other less frequently used terms and acronyms used to describe essentially the same industry sector are MECE (Meetings, Events, Conventions, and Exhibitions), MCE (Meetings, Conventions, and Exhibitions), and CEMI (Conventions, Exhibitions, Meetings, and Incentives).

The use of these acronyms, especially MICE, has been criticized on several grounds. Notwithstanding the likening of such an important industry to "a rodent that makes little contribution to anything" (Anonymous, 1997a, p. 3), the term perpetuates the idea that MICE is one industry rather than four very separate activities. Furthermore, definitions for these individual activities, especially meetings and conventions, vary widely, as noted by Carlsen (1995) and Oppermann (1996a). Ladkin in Chapter 6 elaborates on the problems of definitions and terminology and their implications. She purports that the resolution of conflicting definitions is one of the key challenges the industry will face in the coming years. The focus of this book is on conventions and meetings; neither incentives nor exhibitions are specifically discussed other than with the recognition that they may be a part of both meetings and conventions. Nevertheless, the terms *conventions* and *meetings* and *MICE* are used interchangeably throughout the various chapters—a consequence of much of the present research not being specific regarding which sector is being referred to.

Moving from terminology and definitions to the conceptual boundaries of the phenomenon, conventions and meetings are commonly associated with business tourism. They constitute its most important segment. In the United States 47 percent of business travelers reported that attending a meeting, trade show, or convention was the main reason for their last business trip (Travel Industry Association of America, 1999). McCabe et al. (2000) emphasize that, unlike other tourism areas, the chief activity of conventions and meetings is business rather than leisure. Yet business tourism can involve a substantial leisure element (Davidson, 1994b). In the context of conventions and meetings, Oppermann (1996b) noted that business aspects are only part of the motivational factors associated with attending conventions and meetings. For association conventions, other factors are especially of great importance—an aspect that will be discussed in more detail in Chapter 4, on marketing.

Because the setting for much convention/meeting activity is in major urban areas and the development of the industry is often regarded as a strategy for urban redevelopment, discussion of it is also found in the context of the city/urban tourism literature (e.g., Law, 1993; Murphy, 1997). The construction of large convention centers in particular has become an integral part of many inner-city redevelopment schemes; these structures are built to improve the image of the city while at the same time generating economic benefits for the community. It is the latter possibility that to a certain extent negates concerns that convention centers often operate at a loss, as previous research has clearly indicated (e.g., Fenich, 1998a). After all, convention centers host large conventions, attracting delegates to the locale who spend on accommodation, transportation, food establishments, and also leisure pursuits. It is the spending of the delegates that is substantially higher than in any other tourist category, according to numerous studies assessing this aspect. In addition to delegates and persons accompanying them, convention organizers are also spending money at the destination and, as discussed by Dwyer in Chapter 2, the combined impact of convention delegate and organizer expenditure for a community can be very substantial once the various multipliers come into play.

The rapid expansion of the industry on a global scale is in part due to the expected economic benefits associated with this type of activity. Yet the lack of economic impact data meant that many governments did not recognize the industry as a major benefactor to national economies in the past. In recent years efforts have been made to accurately assess the economic impact of the industry at local, regional, and national levels. However, estimates of the size of the industry vary significantly, as noted by Crouch and Ritchie (1998), highlighting a need for improvement and greater consistency in impact assessment. To that end, Dwyer and Forsyth (1997) developed an economic impact assessment framework for the MICE industry which Dwyer in Chapter 2 further elaborates on in an international context.

In view of the industry's potential economic contributions, it is not surprising that many destinations around the world are actively pursuing opportunities in this sector. Apart from private investments governments have also increasingly taken a more active role in the development of the industry. Support has taken various forms, including investment incentives, tax concessions, developmental loans, training assistance, and marketing campaigns. In Australia, the federal government in 1995 went even further by introducing a national strategy for the MICE industry that was designed to ensure the long-term growth of the industry in the country (Commonwealth Department of Tourism, 1995). However, planning and development initiatives are often hampered by the fragmentation of the industry and the consequent potential for conflict, a point elaborated on by Go, Govers, and Vliegenthart in Chapter 3.

The fragmented nature of the industry, reflected in the multitude of players (e.g., meeting facilities, accommodation, transport, technical support services, marketing entities) also affects the efforts to develop a unified convention destination image. The issue of an attractive image has become more critical than ever due to intense competition. Indeed, numerous studies on convention site selection found that the image factor is of equal or greater importance than the actual facilities (e.g., Oppermann, 1996a,b). This is not surprising, since the lack of a positive image may prevent a particular destination from being included in the decision maker's consideration set. Convention destination marketers, therefore, need to be aware of the importance of individual destination attributes and also the process decision makers go through to arrive at a site for their conventions or meetings in order to devise successful marketing strategies. In recent years, select convention and visitor bureaus, spearheading the marketing effort of convention destinations, have adopted innovative measures to gain a competitive advantage; some of these initiatives are outlined by Crouch and Weber in Chapter 4.

Apart from the destination's infrastructure and its image, the "people" aspect is also a central consideration because the convention industry is essentially a service industry. Consequently, effective human resource management becomes a critical success factor. Yet given the relative youth of the industry, appropriate education and training programs have long been absent, generally lagging behind investments in infrastructure. Issues such as compensation, high staff turnover, and the lack of clear career paths are also affecting employment in the industry and are discussed in more detail by MacLaurin in Chapter 5.

The meeting planner is a key figure in the convention industry. This person is charged with the organization of conventions and meetings, and much of the attention to detail afforded by the planner will bear directly on their success. The trend toward globalization means that the number of meetings and conventions held in foreign countries has risen dramatically in recent years. Consequently, meeting planners must be increasingly familiar with different cultures and aspects that differentiate domestic from international meeting planning. Price and Becker in Chapter 7 detail some of the key considerations in international meeting planning.

As previously mentioned, it is only recently that the MICE industry has received greater recognition as a specialized area of research inquiry. Early studies, especially on conference centers, appeared in the 1970s. However, it was only in the 1990s that a more substantial body of literature emerged, culminating in the introduction of several new textbooks (McCabe et al., 2000; Lawson, 2000; Schreiber and Beckmann, 1999), the inauguration of the *Journal of Convention and Exhibition Management* in 1998, and the publication of numerous articles in both leading tourism and hospitality journals. Yet from a review of the current research, its strong regional focus is apparent. Although often necessary, this focus is not always conducive to creating an awareness of the state of the industry in other parts of the world.

This book aims to provide a more global perspective by discussing and contrasting issues pertinent to the three key destination regions for the convention and meeting industry, namely North America, Europe, and the Asia-Pacific region. In doing so, the contributors draw on a wide range of studies from across the world and consequently provide a comprehensive source of references for researchers and practitioners alike.

The book is divided into three parts. Part I provides a topical overview of issues relating to the convention industry. Spiller offers a historical perspective. Utilizing data from one of the leading international industry associations, she also highlights changes that have taken place in the past decades on a global scale, before detailing industry developments in select countries. Dwyer discusses the economic contribution of the MICE industry. He proposes a framework for the impact assessment of conventions and, in light of this, critically assesses recent economic impact studies that have been conducted throughout the world. Planning and development issues are discussed by Go, Govers, and Vliegenthart, who outline various global considerations before assessing regional initiatives in Europe, North America, and the Asia-Pacific area. Crouch and Weber apply the framework of the "7 Ps" to the marketing of convention destinations in recognition of the industry's significant service content. In addition to a discussion of site selection considerations and decision-making processes, they detail unique approaches that some destination marketing organizations have adopted. MacLaurin analyzes issues and trends that are likely to impact the industry's human resources practices before providing a comprehensive description of education and training programs offered by both industry associations and universities in the three key regions. Ladkin discusses a number of research challenges the industry faces and offers suggestions on how to address them. In outlining the various sources for MICE research, she provides useful references to international industry associations, trade publications, and academic research. The effects of globalization on the convention industry are noted throughout the various chapters, but they become critical in international meeting management, discussed by Price and Becker. They outline planning considerations for international meetings and illustrate them with examples.

Part II contains four in-depth case studies. Each case study focuses on a different industry player from one of the key regions and discusses critical issues pertinent to them. Fenich contrasts the various types of ownership and management of convention centers in the United States. Pechlaner and Mariotti discuss the challenges faced by Mediterranean convention bureaus, with a particular focus on Italy. Pyo and Koo provide an overview of the convention industry of one of the fastest growing players in Asia, the Republic of Korea, while issues and trends faced by convention hotels in Australia are highlighted by McCabe.

Part III is a concluding chapter by the editors, discussing the future of the MICE industry. Weber and Chon highlight major trends in the business, social, technological, and political environment that will impact meetings and conventions in the coming years. They conclude by outlining some of the key issues the industry has to address to ensure its continued growth in the twenty-first century.

Karin Weber
Kye-Sung Chon

PART I:
TOPICAL OVERVIEW

Chapter 1

History of Convention Tourism

Julie Spiller

INTRODUCTION

Montgomery and Strick (1995, p. 4) assert that for as long as there have been people, there have been meetings. They note that "archeologists, in their investigations of ancient cultures, have found primitive ruins that functioned as common areas where people would gather to discuss communal interests, such as hunting plans, wartime activities, negotiations for peace, or the organization of tribal celebrations." Cities, in particular, became focal points for human interaction and commerce (Gartrell, 1992). In ancient Rome, for example, numerous buildings were especially used for holding debates and meetings. The Roman Forum, a public square located in the center of a city, was used for public discussion, judicial matters, and other business. Political debates and historical speeches were held at the Rostra, while meetings of the Senate took place at the Comitium. Many terms used in the convention industry today are based on Latin terms, for example, "conference" stems from the medieval *conferentia* ("to bring together"), and "auditorium" originates from *auditorius* ("place to hear") (Thompson, 1995). However, the foundations for the modern convention industry were laid only in the past two centuries, especially in the United States and in Europe.

The convention industry has experienced tremendous global growth since the 1960s. The aim of this chapter is to provide an insight into the stages of industry development in various parts of the world. First, the origins of the modern convention industry and the impact of economic cycles on its development will be discussed. Then, statistics of the Union of International Associations (UIA) will be drawn upon to illustrate the changes that have taken place in the past fifty years on a global, national, and regional level. Finally, developments at some of the world's key convention destinations are traced.

ORIGINS OF THE CONVENTION INDUSTRY

Developments in the Nineteenth and Early Twentieth Centuries in the United States and Europe

During the late nineteenth and early twentieth centuries, industrialization spread throughout the United States as well as Western Europe. With the growth of industry and commerce, the need for meetings between businessmen and entrepreneurs materialized. Yet as noted by Falk and Pizam (1991, p. 111), meetings were not confined to businesspeople and professionals but also extended to those individuals who would gather to discuss and exchange ideas on political, religious, literary, recreational, and other varied topics. These latter meetings and conventions were greatly facilitated by an extensive network of associations, with many of them requiring attendance at annual membership meetings. The desire to found and join associations is deeply embedded in American culture; it is part of a long and distinguished democratic tradition going back to the Pilgrims and their organized religious meetings (Voso, 1990).

The first convention bureau in the United States was set up in Detroit in 1896. It happened at a time when national trade and professional associations had developed and displayed great interest in bringing their members together at conventions at locations around the country. Initially, hotel management promoted their city or region in addition to advertising their services and facilities for hosting conventions and meetings. Yet as the economic benefits derived from convention business became more recognized by cities, it was businesspeople in Detroit who first employed a full-time salesperson to actively solicit convention business for the area (Gartrell, 1994). This approach proved extremely popular, and other cities quickly followed suit in the ensuing decade. Convention bureaus were established in Cleveland in 1904, in Atlantic City in 1908, in Denver and St. Louis in 1909, and in Los Angeles in 1910 (Rogers, 1998).

The proliferation of convention bureaus in the United States led to the foundation of the International Association of Convention Bureaus (IACB) in 1914. Its primary aims were to facilitate exchange of information about the convention industry among its members and to promote sound professional practices in the solicitation and servicing of meetings and conventions. The increased emphasis on attracting visitors in addition to convention business resulted in the addition of the "V" for "Visitors" in the association's name in 1974, renamed the International Association of Convention and Visitors Bureaus (IACVB) (Schweitzer, 1997). Membership in the IACVB has risen from twenty-eight bureaus in 1920 to approximately 500 bureaus in thirty countries today, representing more than 1,200 professional members <http://www. iacvb.org>.

Europe starkly contrasted to the United States in this period. Rogers (1998) suggests that the Congress of Vienna, held from September 1814 until June 1815, may be regarded as the first truly international conference, with representatives of most of the major world powers of the day being in attendance. Yet Rogers also notes that the few international conferences, mostly political and scientific in nature, that took place during the remainder of the nineteenth and the first half of the twentieth century were too infrequent and insignificant to be regarded as an industry as such. Furthermore, the style of business in those days was simply not conducive to meetings at which views and ideas could be exchanged. Of course, the two world wars taking place in the first half of the twentieth century in Europe also prevented a more rapid development of the industry in the region.

The Convention Industry from the 1950s

The growth of the convention industry since the 1950s is due to a number of factors on both the supply and demand sides. Some of these factors are closely related to factors that supported the growth of tourism in general. For example, the increase in disposable income, the greater propensity to travel, increased leisure time, and improvements in transportation and technology have all facilitated the growth of the convention industry. Lawson (2000, p. 11) suggested numerous factors specific to the convention industry that contributed to its development:

- Expansion of government and quasi-governmental organizations, together with an increasing need for meetings between the public and private sectors
- Growth of multinational corporations and pannational agencies, necessitating more interdepartmental and interregional meetings
- Developments in association interests, cooperatives, professional groups, and pressure groups
- Changes in sales techniques, use of product launches and sales promotion meetings
- The need to update information and methods through in-company management training, continuing professional development, and attendance at ad hoc or scheduled meetings
- Development of subject specialization—conferences enable an expert to pass on information to a large number of others peripherally involved
- Health insurance requirements leading to the introduction of executive conference centers in which "hard work" and "hard play" could be offered as an integrated package.

Resulting from the greater demand for conventions and meetings and in view of the industry's potential economic benefits, many destinations around the world invested heavily in infrastructure development. National and local convention bureaus actively promote destinations' facilities and other attributes that influence the site selection process. Furthermore, industry representation and coordination through international, national, and regional associations have also improved significantly (Lawson, 2000).

Today, the convention industry is regarded as one of the most buoyant sectors of the tourism industry. It is least responsive to price changes and helps to reduce "peak-trough" seasonal patterns (Oppermann, 1996b). The convention industry has the potential to attract high-spending visitors who often stay longer at and make repeat visits to a destination. Furthermore, it is seen as prestigious to host international conferences, with tourism authorities throughout the world being keen to attract convention visitors to their destinations. Yet it is also important to consider the effects of economic conditions on the growth of the industry to truly understand the development of the sector.

IMPACT OF ECONOMIC CYCLES

Both global and national economies experience periods of economic prosperity and decline, with potential positive and adverse impacts for the convention industry respectively. During a recession, the corporate sector often reduces expenditure on conferences and meetings. Attendance at association gatherings may also fall due to association members either being unable or unwilling to pay for the costs associated with attendance, especially if they receive no sponsorship. For example, the number of Americans attending conferences fell dramatically as a result of the recession in the United States in 1979 (Lawson, 1982). The recession of the early 1990s severely cut the budgets of conference organizers. According to Duarte (1992), convention expenditure in the United States fell from US$15 billion in 1989 to US$11 billion in 1991, while corporate meeting attendance dropped from 58.4 million to 49.6 million delegates during the same period.

Following the Gulf War in 1991, the global economy slowly began to recover in 1993. This economic upturn was reflected in the convention industry by 1996. A survey of 200 corporate buyers showed that 90 percent of conference organizers expected their budget to increase or at least stay the same in the coming years (White, 1996). In 1998 economic indicators pointed to a global economic downturn, resulting from the 1997 Asian financial crisis. Recessionary conditions lead to increased financial restraint by both businesses and individuals. "When interest rates rose in 1998 in the UK the consumer, in a way, anticipated the harder times, by ratcheting spending" (Brummer, 1998, p. 28). This had a detrimental effect on the convention industry. Fewer bookings occurred, leaving spare capacity unsold, which, in turn, resulted in a reduction in prices and profit levels. However, large international meetings are often organized between two and four years in advance so that the true impact of any downturn may not be witnessed for some years in the future.

GLOBAL DEVELOPMENTS

The Union of International Associations (UIA) is an international industry association that has collected statistics on meetings and conventions for more than forty years. Using strict criteria for data collection, it is widely regarded as the industry's most authoritative source, despite some limitations that are outlined in Chapter 6. The following discussion is based on UIA figures and provides an insight into the shifts that have taken place from 1954 to 1999. In perusing these figures, it is important to keep in mind that they refer to international association meetings only. Consequently, they do not take into consideration national and regional conference activity, or the corporate sector, which, according to Lawson (2000), accounts for the vast majority of the industry. Nevertheless, international conventions, while relatively small in total numbers, are the premier events of the MICE industry, as asserted by Fenich in Chapter 8, and generate considerable economic benefits for host destinations (Dwyer, Chapter 2).

Global Distribution

Table 1.1 provides an overview of the share of the international conference market held by the various continents during the past forty-five years. The trends observed by Oppermann (1996a), based on the assessment of statistics until 1993, appear unabated. In 1999, Europe remains the continent hosting the majority of international conferences. Yet its share continues to decline, from 74 percent in 1954 to 61 percent in 1992 to 57 percent in 1999. Simultaneously, the number of international conferences hosted by Asian countries has

TABLE 1.1. International Congresses by Continent, 1954-1999 (% of Total Market Share)

	1954	1968	1974	1982	1992	1999
Europe	74	70	65	65	61	57
North America	11	13	14	14	14	16
South America	8	5	5	5	6	5
Asia	4	8	9	11	12	13
Africa	3	3	4	3	5	5
Australasia	1	1	3	3	2	4

Source: Provided by UIA Congress Department in 2001; compiled from *International Congress Calendar* archives and *Yearbook of International Organizations.*

been increasing, from 4 percent in 1954 to 12 percent in 1992 to 13 percent in 1999. An upward trend can also be noted for Australasia, particularly in the 1990s, even though its increase is not as dramatic as Asia's. North America's share of international association meetings has been fairly stable in the past decades at around 15 percent, ranging from 11 percent in 1954 to 16 percent in 1999.

Top Convention Countries

Europe's dominance in the international conference market is also reflected in the top ten countries for international conferences, presented in Table 1.2. The United States, France, the United Kingdom, and Germany represent the most popular destinations for international conferences for the time period examined. As already noted by Oppermann (1996a), fluctuations in rankings occur mainly for lower-ranked countries. Furthermore, special events being held in a particular country appear to have a positive influence on its ranking. Rockett

TABLE 1.2. Top Fifteen Countries for International Congresses, 1954-1999

1954	1968	1974	1988	1992	1999
France	France	United States	United States	United States	United States
Switzerland	United States	United Kingdom	United Kingdom	France	France
United States	Germany	France	France	United Kingdom	United Kingdom
Italy	United Kingdom	Switzerland	Germany	Germany	Germany
United Kingdom	Switzerland	Italy	Italy	Spain	Italy
Germany	Italy	Germany	Australia	Netherlands	Netherlands
Netherlands	Belgium	Belgium	Netherlands	Italy	Australia
Brazil	Austria	Austria	Switzerland	Belgium	Spain
Belgium	Netherlands	Israel	Belgium	Switzerland	Belgium
Austria	Spain	Canada	Spain	Japan	Austria
Canada	Czechoslovakia	Netherlands	Japan	Austria	Canada
Spain	Japan	Spain	Finland	Canada	Japan
Denmark	Mexico	Czechoslovakia	Canada	Denmark	Switzerland
Norway	Czechoslovakia*	Sweden	Austria	Finland	Finland
Sweden	Denmark*	Japan	Sweden	Sweden	China

Source: Provided by UIA Congress Department in 2001; compiled from *International Congress Calendar* archives and *Yearbook of International Organizations.*
*Indicated from city rankings (i.e., Prague, Czechoslovakia, and Copenhagen, Denmark)

and Smillie (1994) illustrate this with Spain, which improved its ranking dramatically in 1992. In that year, Spain hosted the Summer Olympics in Barcelona, had the Cultural Capital of Europe (Madrid), and held the World Exposition in Seville.

Top Convention Cities

Western European cities dominate the ranking of top convention destinations, with Paris occupying consistently the first rank since 1954 (Table 1.3). As in the case of host countries, the greatest fluctuations are evident in the lower ranks, with the top three convention cities remaining relatively stable over the time period under review. Law (1993) notes that many world organizations, such as UNESCO and the OECD, have their headquarters in cities such as Paris, London, Geneva, and New York. Cities such as Brussels and Strasbourg are home to important supranational continental organizations (e.g., European Economic Community). Capital cities, of course, also fre-

TABLE 1.3. Top Fifteen Cities for International Congresses, 1954-1999

1954	1968	1974	1988	1992	1999
Paris	Paris	Paris	Paris	Paris	Paris
Geneva	Geneva	London	London	London	Brussels
London	London	Geneva	Madrid	Brussels	Vienna
Rome	Brussels	Brussels	Brussels	Vienna	London
Brussels	Strasbourg	Rome	Geneva	Madrid	Singapore
New York	Vienna	New York	West Berlin	Geneva	Berlin
Vienna	Rome	Vienna	Rome	Amsterdam	Amsterdam
Amsterdam	New York	Washington	Sydney	Singapore	Copenhagen
Copenhagen	Mexico City	Berlin West	Singapore	Washington	Sydney
The Hague	West Berlin	Dublin	Washington	Barcelona	Washington
Munich	Tokyo	Mexico City	Vienna	Copenhagen	New York
Zurich	Prague	Zurich	New York	Strasbourg	Helsinki
Stockholm	Washington	Budapest	Strasbourg	Hong Kong	Budapest
Liege	Madrid	Montreal	Amsterdam	Budapest	Hong Kong
Washington	Copenhagen	Prague	Seoul	Prague	Strasbourg

Source: Provided by UIA Congress Department in 2001; compiled from *International Congress Calendar* archives and *Yearbook of International Organizations.*

quently host the headquarters of large corporations that hold international conferences.

The strong position of the United States in terms of overall market share does not translate into an equally strong representation among the top convention cities. It is only Washington that has been consistently positioned in the top fifteen convention cities in the years assessed, though mainly in the lower ranks, while New York City did not feature in the top fifteen in 1992 at all. The emergence of Asian cities is also evident. Singapore, not among the top fifteen in the first three years under review, has been in the top ten convention cities since 1988, steadily climbing at each interval. More recently, Hong Kong has emerged in the rankings. Finally, the positive effect of special events is also evident at the city level. Oppermann (1996a) points to the fact that Seoul and Barcelona entered the ranking only when they hosted the Summer Olympics in 1988 and 1992 respectively. The same holds true for Mexico City, the host of the Summer Olympics in 1968.

Despite the universal factors noted previously that are still shaping the industry today, the pace of development has varied greatly among the various world regions in the past fifty years. The following section will shed light on the industry developments in the United States, Europe, and the Asia-Pacific region.

REGIONAL DEVELOPMENTS

United States

The United States is the leading country with respect to hosting conferences organized and/or sponsored by international organizations <http://www.uia.org> and international meetings by associations <http://www.icca.nl>. The number of large national conferences, both with international and solely domestic participation, is, however, much greater. The growth in the number of conventions and meetings was facilitated by the increase in supporting infrastructure, especially the construction of convention centers. By the end of World War II, very few convention centers existed, mainly in major cities such as New York and Chicago (Graveline, 1984). During the 1970s and early 1980s over 100 convention centers were built (Listokin,

1985). Var, Cesario, and Mauser (1985) noted that before 1960 only about two dozen North American cities actively bid for convention trade, but the number had increased to more than one hundred by 1985. By 1996, the number of convention centers had reached more than 500 (Nelson, 1996). Yet it is not only the number but also the increase in size of convention centers that is worth noting. In 1970, there were 6.7 million square feet of convention center space, which by 1990 had increased to 10 million square feet (Sanders, 1992). Yet the projected added exhibit space from expansions to existing facilities and new facilities from 1999 until 2004 is greater than the total convention center space in 1990 (Anonymous, 1998).

Zelinsky (1994) provided a detailed comparison of the ranking of U.S. convention sites in 1964-1965 and 1990-1991, based on the estimated number of international and national convention participants. This comparison pointed not only to the dramatic increase in the number of conventions and estimated participants, particularly in metropolitan areas, but also to the significant changes in the ranking of these cities. He further noted that the ranking of a city is neither influenced by the size of its population nor its hinterland population. In recent years, several authors (e.g., Braley, 1996b; Dobrian, 1998; Korn, 1998; Shure, 1998) have commented on the increased interest in hosting conventions in second-tier cities rather than first-tier cities and identified potential reasons for this trend. The improved economic conditions in the United States in recent years resulted in record levels of business and leisure travel. Consequently, hotel occupancy and room rates surged. The upward pressure on rates and availability in major cities led many associations to consider second-tier cities. These cities offered not only more competitive packages in terms of price and availability, but also greater flexibility. The latter is evident in less stringent contract clauses and a greater willingness to cooperate with the association, for instance, in accommodating the specifics of the event or in promoting the city to association members (Shure, 1998). In particular, the efforts of these second-tier cities' convention and visitors bureaus have been cited by many meeting planners as a contributing factor (Dobrian, 1997). At the same time, the infrastructure in these cities improved tremendously, with new state-of-the-art convention centers being built, existing centers being expanded, and hotel inventory being added (e.g., Lenhart, 1998a). The investment in infrastructure was in many instances attributable to cities looking for a competitive edge in the stagnant economy of the late 1980s and the early 1990s, a time when there was much public finance available for infrastructure projects. There are, however, some potential drawbacks to second-tier cities (Benini, 1997), including limited air service, the need for greater promotion to association members, and lower service quality.

Europe

Growth in the convention industry in Western Europe began slowly during the 1960s. Several international organizations were established in the 1960s that would influence industry developments in the following decades, including the International Congress and Convention Association (ICCA) in 1963, the European Federation of Conference Towns (EFCT) in 1964, and the International Association of Professional Congress Organizers (IAPCO) in 1968. EFCT, in particular, was established to promote Europe as a conference destination, and to advise and assist meeting planners in the selection of destinations and venues. It has become a major force in lobbying issues to the European Union and emphasizing the economic significance of the industry. Today, thirty-five countries are members of the EFCT <http://www.efct.com>. EFCT was also instrumental in the creation of the European Meetings Industry Liaison Group (EMILG) in 1995. A joint initiative with IAPCO, ICCA, and Meeting Professionals International (MPI). EMILG seeks to address matters impacting the industry in Europe by way of discussion with and representations to political entities.

The opening of Eastern Europe following the fall of the Berlin Wall in 1989 saw several new convention destinations emerge. For example, Hungary was placed fifteenth in the country rankings in 1999, and its capital, Budapest, ranked fourth in terms of convention cities, with Prague, the capital of the Czech Republic, following in sixteenth position, based on statistics by ICCA. ICCA is the other major industry association apart from UIA that collects data on the international convention and meetings market, though its criteria for data collection differ markedly from those of UIA (see Chapter 6). Consequently, the two are not directly comparable but rather serve to provide a different insight.

The outlook for Europe's convention industry can be regarded as positive, despite its relative maturity and challenges to its status, especially from Asian destinations. Davidson (1998) provides several reasons for this optimism. Of particular importance is the fact that 80 percent of all conferences held in Europe are domestic (CEC, 1996). The existence of the European Union, promoting trade—movement of goods and services among European countries—facilitates convention organizers' desire to rotate convention destinations on an annual basis. The introduction of the Euro in 2002 has simplified this process even more due to a greater ability to compare relative prices. Furthermore, the availability of high-speed rail links, such as the Eurostar and the TGV, and the immense competition between low-cost airlines promotes greater movement of individuals throughout Europe. Nevertheless, there is some concern that demand may not keep pace with increasing convention center supply, with the number of convention centers of international standard approaching almost 300 in 1995 (CEC, 1996). This concern has been especially voiced in the United Kingdom, France, Germany, and Spain.

United Kingdom

In the United Kingdom, seaside and inland resorts have been regarded as the main providers of conference facilities until recently (Law, 1993). High-profile political parties and trade unions traditionally held their conferences there. Resorts such as Blackpool, Brighton, Bournemouth, Torquay, Harrogate, and Llandudno began to develop conference business in the period between the two world wars in an effort to prolong the short summer season. Yet in view of the continued development of the industry, the standard of many of the existing venues was deemed inadequate, resulting in the construction of purpose-built facilities in Brighton in 1977, in Harrogate and Llandudno in 1982, and in Bournemouth in 1984.

U.K. government policies during the 1980s promoted economic regeneration, particularly in deprived areas. Government finance was provided to help fund large developments, such as convention centers, with the aim of creating jobs and boosting local economies. As a result, the 1980s were an era of construction of large, publicly funded convention facilities (Spiller and Ladkin, 2000), including the North Wales Conference Centre and the Royal Centre, Nottingham (1982), the Bournemouth International Centre (1984), the Newport Centre (1985) and the Barbican Centre, London (1986). The construction of convention centers continued throughout the 1990s. The International

Convention Centre in Birmingham opened in 1991, built at a cost of £180 million, followed by the opening of the Edinburgh International Conference Centre in 1995 at a cost of £38 million, and the Millennium Conference Centre in London in 1997 at a cost of £35 million (Rogers, 1998). In addition to purpose-built convention centers, numerous venues opened across the United Kingdom in the 1990s that have capabilities to stage large conventions.

Yet it is not only large purpose-built convention centers that support the growth of the convention industry but also the establishment and upgrading of other facilities such as hotels (especially for the corporate market), facilities at universities, and alternative venues. The increased use of alternative and unusual venues such as stately homes and castles for meetings of the corporate market in particular has also been noted by several authors (Callan and Hoyes, 2000; Leask and Spiller, 2001). The combination of improved infrastructure, well-established convention bureaus representing the major cities, and the greater recognition of the value of the industry by local authorities has led to the competition among U.K. towns and cities for the lucrative conference business becoming more fierce than ever. This is exacerbated by the fact that the once-dominant position of the United Kingdom in the international arena is being challenged by new international destinations. Overseas convention destinations, rather than those in the United Kingdom, are often chosen as they offer similar or better technical support in terms of modern conference facilities and telecommunications. In addition, flight times and prices have decreased substantially, thus making it easier and cheaper to go abroad. Many overseas countries now have a competitive edge over the United Kingdom.

In 1999, about 450,000 conferences were held in the United Kingdom, valued at £1.5 billion, down from more than 500,000 conferences in 1996, valued at £2.3 billion (Leask and Spiller, 2001). The most important locations for meetings are London and Central England (Tourism Research and Marketing, 1999). London remains the dominant convention destination due to its status as one of the world's financial centers, the location of numerous corporate headquarters, its extensive and excellent infrastructure, and ease of access.

Asia-Pacific Region

The World Travel and Tourism Council (WTTC) predicts that the Asia-Pacific share of global international visitor arrivals will increase from 11.5 percent in 1990 to 15.3 percent in 2000 and 20.3 percent in 2010 (Muqbil, 1997). By 2010, intraregional travel will account for 80 percent of all visitor arrivals in Asia-Pacific countries. Yet it is not only Asia's tourism industry at large that has grown rapidly; its convention sector has also shown stronger-than-average growth. Major growth in the Asian convention industry took place during the 1980s. Hunt (1989) asserted that Asia's convention industry grew by 73 percent during the 1983-1987 period, compared with world growth of 51 percent. This figure, however, is qualified by reference to problems in data collection resulting from inconsistencies in definitions and the lack of accurate records by many venues—problems that persist today. Nevertheless, the growth of the industry in Asia has been substantial, with several factors accounting for the tremendous increase in the number of conventions and meetings.

Muqbil (1997) cites the success of regional economies, at the time averaging growth of between 6 percent to 8 percent per year, as a primary driving force. Of course, in the wake of the Asian financial crisis in 1997, many countries experienced serious setbacks. Yet signs of recovery are appearing, with intraregional and international trade expected to rise once again, facilitated by multilateral agreements such as Asia-Pacific Economic Cooperation (APEC) and the Association of Southeast Asian Nations (ASEAN) Free Trade Area. Many multinational corporations that are based in developed nations have expanded and continue to expand into Asian markets, with the establishment of factories and regional offices necessitating meetings. Similarly, international associations are increasingly including Asian destinations in their roster of annual convention destinations, with large annual conventions being held in Asia by medical associations and global clubs such as the Rotarians and the Lions.

Major infrastructure developments facilitated the growing demand. Today numerous world-class convention centers exist in the region, including the Singapore International Convention and Exhibition Centre (SICEC), the Hong Kong Convention and Exhibition Centre (HKCEC), the Queen Sirikit National Convention Center in Bangkok, the Tokyo International Forum, and the Sydney Convention and Exhibition Centre. In addition, international standard hotels, both chain and independent properties, are being built with modern meeting facilities; existing properties are upgrading theirs. It is not only major cities that have invested in convention infrastructure but also resort cities across the region (Muqbil, 1997). Convention facilities in Asia offer a high level of service, relatively low prices, and state-of-the-art technological facilities. At the same time easy access is facilitated by modern airports serviced by all the major international airlines and good local transport systems at the major convention destinations.

Carlsen (1999) points out that the infrastructure developments were complemented by the implementation of significant policy, planning, and marketing initiatives in the region during the past decade. For example, the former Australian government developed a national strategy for the industry (Commonwealth Department of Tourism, 1995) to capitalize on potential opportunities arising from the 2000 Sydney Olympic Games. Japan declared thirty-five cities to be convention cities and enacted legislation that makes the promotion of meetings a national priority (Hill, 1997b). The Asian Association of Convention and Visitor Bureaus (AACVB) implemented the "Convene in Asia" campaign in 1995.

An in-depth assessment of the development and key issues of the convention industry for one of the new key players in the region, South Korea, is provided in Chapter 10. Therefore, a historical account of the development of the convention industry will be provided here from another key player in the Asia-Pacific region, namely Australia.

Australia

Australia experienced tremendous growth in its MICE sector in the past two decades. In a landmark study carried out in 1976, Cooper analyzed the economic impact of the meetings and convention industry in Australia. Cooper (1999) recently contrasted the predictions he made in 1976 of the anticipated size of the industry in 1993 with the actual characteristics of the industry in that year. His results suggested that the dollar value of the convention sector as estimated in 1976 (after correction for inflation) was about 73 percent of the actual figures for 1993, with growth clearly being stronger than it appeared possible more than twenty years ago.

Cooper's (1976) study was also important in that it laid the foundation for the development of the Sydney Entertainment and Exhibition Centre, although it was only in the late 1980s that purpose-built convention centers opened in Australia's key convention destinations (Sydney in 1988, Melbourne in 1990, Adelaide in 1987, and Brisbane in 1995). More recently, convention centers have been built in regional centers, such as Cairns (Queensland) and Albury (New South Wales), and plans are in place for the construction of convention centers in Alice Springs, the Gold Coast, and Perth. In addition to convention centers, a proliferation of meeting facilities in five-star, four-star, and three-star hotel properties has occurred, as noted by Carlsen (1999). He also points to the significant number of alternative venues to demonstrate the country's infrastructure capacity. In 1996, Australia's federal government commissioned the Bureau of Tourism Research (BTR) to carry out a survey of the country's MICE infrastructure (venues, accommodation, transport, and other support services) to identify hindrances to growth and establish forecasts (BTR/TFC, 1998). The report voiced concern about the adequacy of Australia's MICE infrastructure at the time and for the future in view of anticipated market growth. However, in the years since, it appears that concerns are now greatest about the increased competition, on both a national and international level, resulting from the increase in the number of convention facilities in Australia and in the Asia-Pacific region (Muqbil, 1997; Weber and Ladkin, 2001).

The growth of the industry has been greatly facilitated by government support which has taken many forms, including developmental loans, investment incentives, tax concessions, training assistance, and promotional and marketing campaigns (Cooper, 1999). In 1995, the national strategy for the meetings, incentives, conventions and exhibitions industry was launched—a long-term growth strategy for the industry that also aimed to capitalize on the opportunities presented by the 2000 Sydney Olympics. However, due to a change in government, the strategy was withdrawn in early 1996.

The Sydney 2000 Olympics had a significant impact on the Australian MICE industry. In the lead-up to the Sydney Olympics numerous entities decided to hold meetings and conventions in Australia either prior to, during, or immediately after this megaevent. The success of the Olympics and the Australian Tourist Commission's (ATC) various promotional campaigns have further contributed to Australia maintaining its top position in the Asia-Pacific region since 1996, ahead of Japan <www.icca.nl>. Ladkin and Spiller (2000b) note that the increase in convention and meeting activity in the years leading up to and immediately following the Sydney Olympics is similar to that experienced by Atlanta, Georgia, the host of the 1996 Summer Olympics. In 2000, the industry is estimated to be worth AU$7 billion and it is estimated that in 2010 the industry will be worth an estimated AU$10 billion (Johnson et al., 1999).

CONCLUSION

This chapter has provided an overview of the development of the convention industry on both a global and regional basis, utilizing UIA statistics. While the convention industry is expanding and becoming increasingly competitive on a global scale, some continents, namely North America and Europe, are reaching maturity. An increasing concern exists in these regions that an oversupply of facilities will become a significant threat to their convention industries. Murray (1995) suggests that too many purpose-built convention centers are being constructed. The abundance of convention centers comes at a time when many associations are facing tighter budgets; with mergers constantly on the agenda, the number of corporate and association events is decreasing. This creates a situation in which buyers are in a position to bargain for lower rental rates (Nelson, 1996). This may in turn lead to the closure of some of these facilities.

Growth is likely to continue in the Asian convention industry, which is still in its infancy. Increasing competition will stem from newly emerging convention destinations. For example, there has been a shift in demand from traditional beach resorts to more exotic, cultural, and activity-based destinations. In general, the competitive situation in the Asia-Pacific region in the next few years will be strongly affected by the developing Chinese convention industry, the renewed marketing activity from Japan, and the competent marketing and professionalism of the Australian and New Zealand industry (Muqbil, 1997).

As stated by Lawson (2000, p. 220) "arguably the greatest challenges facing the industry in the next decade and beyond are likely to be concerned with maintaining growth and sustaining the benefits of investment." The development of a national policy on business tourism or the conference sector might be an effective mechanism to move the sector toward a more profitable future. The convention industry is a dynamic industry. It has experienced significant changes over its relatively short lifetime. The next decade may see even greater changes as some destinations experience tremendous growth, some stagnate, and others decline.

Chapter 2

Economic Contribution of Convention Tourism: Conceptual and Empirical Issues

Larry Dwyer

INTRODUCTION

The convention industry is globally recognized for its valuable economic contribution to tourism destinations. It also has significant growth potential. Major economic impacts of the industry are its contribution to employment and income, at both national and regional levels. Convention tourism is also associated with a range of other benefits (and costs) of a more intangible nature. Intangible benefits include associated social and cultural benefits to the destination, the exchange of ideas, the cultivation of business contacts, the provision of forums for continuing education and training, and the facilitation of technology transfers (Dwyer and Forsyth, 1997; Dwyer, Mellor, et al., 2000).

Despite the acknowledged economic significance of the convention industry as a special tourism market (Dwyer and Mistilis, 1997; Muqbil, 1997), the sector has attracted little research from economists. Although some discussions have suggested that the convention sector is a "high-yield" tourism market and an important generator of foreign exchange, income, and employment, as well as a means of growth for in-house conference facilities, little hard data are available upon which to estimate the precise magnitude of these effects. This is unfortunate because decisions about resource allocation by both private and public sector stakeholders greatly depend on accurate information regarding potential gains. Substantial resources are allocated to the convention industry with the expectation of economic gains (Carlsen, 1999; Muqbil, 1997). Information on economic impact is essential to determine the appropriate extent of government support through initiatives such as development loans, investment incentives, tax concessions, training assistance, and promotional and marketing campaigns (Cooper, 1999). In the absence of accurate data on the industry's economic significance, destinations may underallocate or overallocate resources to the convention industry, resulting in reduced net economic benefits.

This chapter highlights issues relevant in estimating the economic contribution of the convention industry. It sets out the steps involved in economic impact assessment of the convention sector from the perspective of the host destination. Conceptual and empirical issues pertinent to each step are discussed, and gaps in the research literature are identified.

ESTIMATING THE ECONOMIC CONTRIBUTION OF CONVENTIONS

The technique for estimating the economic contribution of a particular convention, or the convention sector to a host destination, is based on the method established for estimating the economic contribution of special events. Substantial literature now exists detailing the appropriate methodology of event assessment (Burns, Hatch, and Mules, 1986; Burns and Mules, 1989; Crompton, 1999; Getz, 1994). An economic impact framework based on the method of event assessment but explicitly addressing the convention sector has been developed by Dwyer and Forsyth (1997) and Dwyer, Mellor, et al. (2000).

Some researchers estimate the total expenditure associated with a convention to indicate its economic significance (Braun, 1992; Convention Liaison Council, 1993). This amount, the gross expenditure (GE), encompasses all purchases of final goods and services linked with the convention from the various interested parties—delegates, accompanying persons, other convention participants, organizers, and sponsors—regardless of its origin. Tourism operators and other businesses are interested in gross expenditure since it comprises their total sales revenue resulting from the convention. At the same time, GE also provides a measure of the importance of conventions compared to other modes of business activity. However, gross expenditure cannot be used to estimate economic impacts since it includes all convention-related expenditure, not just "new money" injected into the destination.

Dwyer, Mellor, et al. (2001), in a review of economic impact studies carried out in Australia in the past decade, discussed a number of additional concerns. These concerns relate to individual studies and to the comparability of studies. They noted the following:

1. Studies of convention-related expenditure differ in methodology, scope of analysis, data collection methods, and accuracy of expenditure surveys.
2. The expenditure data for conventions tend to be of an aggregate nature, covering several conventions in a given location in some defined period of time. Hence, attendance and expenditure data for particular conventions often cannot be determined.
3. Some of the published estimates are clearly inaccurate or else are based on assumptions that do not appear to be justifiable. Consequently, much of the data is not directly comparable.
4. Studies have focused on conventions in major metropolitan areas, thus providing little information on convention-related expenditure in regional areas. Existing studies also are not of sufficient accuracy to justify generalizations about expenditures by type of convention.

While no formal review of studies conducted in other countries has been undertaken at this point, it is reasonable to suspect that the problems of inaccuracies and incomparability of studies also exist in other major international convention markets. To address this problematic situation, the following framework for the assessment of the economic impact of conventions is proposed.

CONVENTION IMPACT ASSESSMENT FRAMEWORK

The estimation of the economic impact of a particular convention involves the following four steps:

1. Estimate the in-scope expenditure of convention participants and accompanying persons;
2. Estimate the in-scope expenditure of convention organizers, associations, and sponsors;

3. Allocate total in-scope expenditure to particular industries; and
4. Apply multipliers to total in-scope expenditure to estimate the contribution to regional income and gross regional product.

Various assumptions and judgments must be made at each step.

Expenditure representing an injection of "new money" into an area is commonly referred to as "in-scope expenditure" (Burns and Mules, 1989). The term "in-scope visitors" refers to those delegates and accompanying persons, organizers, and sponsors who would not otherwise have come to the destination had the convention not been held, i.e., visitors for whom the convention is the main reason for the trip. Injections into the host economy arise from expenditure by in-scope visitors to the convention, expenditure by organizers that originates outside the destination, and government, corporate, and association sponsorship which entails a flow of funds into the region. Only in-scope expenditure is relevant in estimating the convention's economic impacts.

In-Scope Expenditure Estimation—Convention Participants and Accompanying Persons

There are several major determinants of in-scope expenditure.

Number of Delegates and Accompanying Persons

An obvious association exists between the number of visitors and their total injected expenditure. For a given average daily expenditure per visitor, the more visitors there are, the greater the in-scope expenditure will be. The number of persons accompanying convention delegates can be quite substantial. According to a study of the convention sector in Adelaide, Australia (KPMG, 1993), every international convention delegate had 0.175 persons accompany him or her on the trip, which is very close to the estimate of 0.16 persons reported by a survey of convention visitors to Tasmania (Tasmanian Convention Bureau, 1996). In contrast, in Singapore the average travel party size for association meeting delegates in 1999 was 1.67 persons (Singapore Tourism Board, 2000). It is estimated that accompanying persons add around 15 to 20 percent to convention-related expenditure in Australia (Dwyer, Mellor, et al., 2000a).

Types of Delegates and Types of Conventions

There is some evidence that convention visitors spend more per day than the "average" visitor to a destination. For example, the Singapore Exhibition and Convention Bureau (SECB) found that per diem expenditure of association meeting delegates, about S$300 in 1999, is about three times as much as that of "average" tourists (SCEB, 2000). However, in several studies the average daily expenditure of convention visitors has been exaggerated by dividing the average total delegate expenditure for the entire visit to the destination by the number of conference days only (KPMG, 1993; Perth Convention Bureau, 1994). The appropriate statistics to employ, for purposes of economic impact analysis of any given destination, is average total delegate expenditure over all days spent at the destination.

Some evidence also suggests that different types of conventions generate different levels of average daily expenditure. System Three (1998) distinguished four types of conferences—corporate, association, academic, and other (including public sector and government bodies, charities, religious organizations, political parties, and trade unions). Corporate conferences generated the highest daily average expenditure, followed by academic, association, and other conferences. Grado, Strauss, and Lord (1998), assessing the economic impacts of conferences and conventions in the United States, found different average expenditure levels according to type of convention—business/professional, academic, heritage related, and special interest. Research conducted in Sydney, Australia, found that medical conferences tend to be associated with higher average daily spending per delegate followed by corporate and association conferences (Sydney Convention and Visitors Bureau, 1996, 1997, 1998).

The spending behavior of delegates also appears to be related to their origin. Studies undertaken in Australia reveal different spending patterns of convention visitors depending on origin markets. Dwyer, Mellor, et al. (2001), in a review of several studies, found that the average daily spending of interstate delegates to conventions held in Australia was lower, on average, than the average daily spending of delegates from overseas. Data are too sparse to permit generalizations at this time. Further research is needed on the development of an appropriate typology for categorizing conventions. Once that is achieved, estimates of delegate expenditure by type of convention can be undertaken to determine if there are trends in aggregate expenditure levels associated with conventions of different types.

Trip Duration

For a given level of average daily expenditure, the greater the duration of stay at the destination, the greater the injected expenditure. Conventions differ in their duration. In Las Vegas the estimated average duration of conventions was four days in 2000 (LVCVA, 2000). In Hong Kong, conventions lasted on average for three days, with convention delegates' average length of stay in the city being 5.5 days in 1999 (HKTA, 2000). In Singapore, association meeting delegates spent an average of 5.18 days in the city in 1999 (Singapore Tourism Board, 2000). Convention visitors to Melbourne, Australia, spent on average 4.6 nights in the city, with international delegates staying longer than domestic ones. The former's length of stay in Australia, including their stay in Melbourne, averaged 9.2 nights (CRC, 2000). The duration of stay thus depends upon both the conference duration and the attractiveness of pre- and postconference tour opportunities.

The importance of pre- and postconvention tours has been highlighted by two studies conducted in Australia. About 25 percent of the spending of interstate delegates and almost 50 percent of spending by international delegates to Western Australia occurred either before or after the conferences attended (Perth Convention Bureau, 1994). Surveys conducted in Tasmania indicated that, on average, about 60 percent of conference-related spending occurred prior to or following a conference (Tasmanian Convention Bureau, 1996). It is clearly evident that the expenditure associated with conventions will be greater to the extent that delegates take pre- and postconventions tours. Pre- and postconvention touring also has the potential to disperse the economic impacts of this sector more widely throughout the destination.

Costs at the Convention Destination and Other Destinations

For any given convention, the higher the prices locally, the more expenditure will be injected into the host destination. Studies indicate that delegates to conventions held in Sydney spend more per day than on conventions held in other Australian capital cities (Dwyer, Mellor, et al., 2001). Yet if a destination develops a reputation for high prices it may adversely affect its capacity to attract conventions in the long term. Consequently, there is substantial pressure on convention destinations to maintain their international price competitiveness (Dwyer, Mistilis, et al., 2001; Go and Govers, 1999).

The value a country derives from convention visitors extends beyond their direct expenditure in the country. Convention delegates must be asked to report all expenses incurred by themselves and accompanying persons in or traveling to a country, including all amounts paid before leaving home and all amounts charged to credit cards. Air tickets purchased from national carriers (international and domestic) must be considered, as well as the country's component of fully inclusive prepaid package tours. Thus, only part of the international airfare and prepaid package tour costs are attributable to the particular country, and assumptions about the country's component of these items have to be made to derive at a final estimate of the in-scope expenditure.

The treatment of international airfares has been inconsistent in assessments of the economic significance of the convention industry. Johnson et al. (1999), in a study for the Bureau of Tourism Research (BTR) on the economic contribution of conventions to Australia, correctly included expenditure on international airfares and international packages when the majority of this expenditure was received by an Australian business. It established that average total expenditure of international delegates (including airfares and packages) was AU$5,944. In contrast, the earliest study on the industry's economic impact by the Australian Tourist Commission (ATC) (1990) excluded international airfares from expenditure items. Dwyer and Forsyth (1997) argued that this exclusion appeared unjustified. They point out that the ATC report itself estimated that about 40 percent of all delegates to Australia in 1990 used Qantas, the country's international carrier. Consequently, the revenue earned by Qantas would have been about 40 percent of the average cost of an airfare of AU$2,445, amounting to over AU$950 per delegate on average and a contribution of over AU$60 million to Qantas's turnover.

Domestic airfares also require particular consideration. Only a proportion (unknown) of expenditure on domestic airfares will flow to any particular region. Attributing airfares to any one region within a country is problematic given the inherent nature of domestic services. Yet all delegate expenditure on domestic airfares was incorrectly included in several studies ascertaining conventions' economic contribution to one Australian state, New South Wales (SCVB, 1997, 1998, 1999). Moreover, some expenditure estimates included domestic airfares for international delegates but not for interstate delegates (SCVB, 1996, 1997). It is not appropriate for it to be included for either, since it is not known where the expenditure will flow.

Additional Considerations—Switched
and Transferred Expenditures

It is important to account for delegates who would have visited the destination even if the convention had not been held. Their visit cannot be attributed to the convention. For example, the Melbourne Convention Delegate Study (1999) established that about 30 percent of delegates would have visited Melbourne, Australia, even if they had not attended a convention (CRC, 2000). Consequently, the expenditure of these visitors should be excluded from estimates of in-scope expenditure. Such a "time-switching effect"—visitors changing the timing of their visit to a destination to coincide with a convention—however, gives rise to a further complication since these visitors may stay longer and spend more than they otherwise would have. In such cases the incremental expenditure must be regarded as injected expenditure associated with the convention. Visitor expenditure surveys can reveal this type of information (Getz, 1994).

Residents of the host destination may spend less on purchases of goods and services during a convention. For example, they may be less inclined to dine out due to perceived crowding of restaurants or traffic congestion. Visitors may also occupy rooms or airplane seats that may have been filled otherwise. In addition, a convention may also cause some residents to leave the area for all or part of its duration. The convention destination thus suffers a loss of sales revenue that would otherwise have accrued to local businesses.

The extent to which a convention held locally causes residents to spend their money elsewhere or to reduce the amount which they otherwise would have spent, can be determined only from surveys. Since those who do reduce their expenditure by a certain amount during the period of the convention may compensate by spending the same amount following the convention, only the proportion of the reduced expenditure that goes into additional savings shall be counted. In like manner, the degree to which a convention held in a location deters visitation from nonconvention visitors is also difficult to estimate with precision, especially as a proportion of those intending visitors may simply "switch" their visits to another time. Once again, any estimates will be only as accurate as the survey technique allows.

Finally, the issue of transferred expenditure must be discussed in this context. Residents of the host destination who attend a convention presumably would have in its absence spent the same amount on other goods and services. Specifically, they may transfer expenditure from one location to another (e.g., purchases of food and beverages) and/or from one expenditure category to another (e.g., purchase of convention registration instead of clothing items).

In-Scope Expenditure Estimation—Convention Organizers, Associations, and Sponsors

Expenditures by organizers, associations, and sponsorship funds also represent an injection of "new money" into the destination. It must be considered in conjunction with convention visitor expenditure in estimating the total in-scope expenditure associated with a convention. Unfortunately, organizer/association/sponsor expenditure is often omitted in convention impact assessment. Yet the omission of this particular category will result in an underestimation of the industry's economic impacts.

Expenditure by convention organizers depends on the revenues they receive. The revenues received can be divided into the following types, according to their source: delegate registration fees, corporate sponsorship, government sponsorship, and sponsorship from associations. Delegate registration fees are typically respent at the destination by convention organizers on items such as the hiring of the convention venue, equipment, various business expenses, catering, and social programs. To avoid double counting, registration fees are best treated as revenue to the convention organizer that is subsequently reinjected wholly or in part into the destination economy rather than convention visitor expenditure. In the past, some studies have included registration fees in delegate expenditure estimates (e.g., System Three, 1998), whereas other delegate expenditure estimates exclude registration fees (e.g., SCEB, 2000). A recent study in Australia included the component of the registration fee spent by the organizers on food and beverages for delegates during the conference, yet ignored all other costs covered in the registration fee (Tasmanian Convention Bureau, 1996). The substantial amount of organizer expenditure, over and above delegate registration fees, has been recognized only in a few studies to date. In Queensland, Australia, it was found to represent an additional 7 percent of expenditure beyond that of convention delegates (Queensland Travel and Tourism Corporation, 1997).

Sponsorship from local sources or from within the state should be regarded as transferred expenditure unless there are reasons to believe that an additional injection of funds has occurred. If local convention sponsorship is not forthcoming, it is likely that these funds are used to sponsor an alternative event or are allocated to another expenditure activity at the destination.

Allocation of Total In-Scope Expenditure to Particular Industries

Total in-scope expenditure is the aggregate of in-scope convention visitor and in-scope convention organizer/sponsor expenditure. The pattern of expenditure of convention visitors and organizers, as well as its volume, is of key relevance to the economic impact assessment of conventions since different industries have different types of linkages with others in the economy, and hence different multiplier effects. In-scope expenditure can be allocated to individual industry sectors on the basis of expenditure surveys of convention visitors and organizers.

According to Dwyer and Forsyth (1997), there are several key industry categories that capture the main types of convention-related expenditure. These are accommodation, transportation, shopping, food and beverage, entertainment, and organized tours. They also note that conventions are closely linked to expenditures on business services such as professional conference organizers, catering services, specialized technical support, and advertising, with convention organizers likely to allocate a high proportion of expenditure to these services. The business service sector is generally associated with a higher multiplier than other industry sectors. Johnson et al. (1999) investigated the type of businesses that benefited most from convention-related expenditure in Australia. In descending order they were convention organizers and, in turn, those businesses that provided services to them: meetings venues; caterers and professional conference organizers; accommodation venues, particularly establishments recommended to delegates; domestic airlines; food and beverage outlets; and international airlines. These businesses receive around three-quarters of convention-related in-scope expenditure in Australia.

Application of Multipliers to Total
In-Scope Expenditure

The application of input-output multipliers represents the final step in the economic impact assessment of conventions. The aim is to determine the total effect on output, household income, value added, and employment of the direct spending and respending associated with conventions. Output multipliers measure the effects of an exogenous change in final demand on the output of industries in the economy. Income multipliers establish the income earned by households because of new outputs. Value added at factor cost due to the change in output (i.e., wages, salaries, and supplements earned by households plus gross operating surplus of business) is measured by value-added multipliers. Employment multipliers relate the employment generated as a result of increased output. Several studies assessing the economic impacts of conventions have used output multipliers (Braun, 1992; Convention Liaison Council, 1993). However, the use of income or value-added multipliers is recommended, because they avoid the double counting of changes in economic activity associated with the output multipliers (Dwyer, Mellor, et al., 2000; Mules, 1999).

According to Archer (1982), multipliers can be decomposed into their various effects, namely initial, production induced, and consumption induced. Type II multipliers are relevant for assessing the economic impacts of convention-related tourism. They take into account both production-induced and consumption-induced effects, in contrast to Type I multipliers that exclude consumption-induced effects (Hunn and Mangan, 1999; Mules, 1999). Dwyer, Mellor, et al. (2000) further elaborate on the applicability of multipliers. They note that the estimation of consumption-induced effects using input-output tables assumes that those earning the extra income were not previously employed. Since these workers would have at least been receiving unemployment benefits, not all of their consumption represents a net addition to final demand. Thus Type II multiplier values represent an upper bound to the level of increased economic activity resulting from the increased expenditure due to the convention, while Type I multipliers can be considered the lower bound. Actual economic impacts will more closely approach Type II multiplier values. At times, input-output models yield very high and apparently unrealistic multipliers, for example, Grado, Strauss, and Lord's (1998) use of a multiplier of three in estimating the economic impacts of conventions in the United States. Consequently, one must be mindful of the caveats that are attached to the use of input-output multipliers (Dwyer, Forsyth, et al., 2000).

In-scope expenditure allocated to each industry (accommodation, transportation, etc.) can be multiplied with the relevant multiplier value to yield value-added generation estimates, both at an aggregate level and by industry segment. The size of the multipliers will vary according to the region under study. It will reflect the different input-output tables estimated for different regions. Consequently, the increment to household income or value-added in the region will vary, with the pattern of in-scope expenditure by visitors and organizers and its subsequent allocation to particular industries being the main determinants.

The increment to employment resulting from convention-related expenditure can be estimated by applying employment multipliers based on input-output tables. However, as noted by Dwyer, Mellor, et al. (2000), use of these multipliers tends to exaggerate the amount of employment generated. Employment generation models based on input-output tables assume a constant proportional relationship between sales turnover and the level of employment. However, different firms, according to the nature and scale of their business, have different marginal propensities to employ labor in the context of increased sales. In some firms, staffing levels may be relatively insensitive to changes in turnover, while other firms may seek better utilization of those currently employed (e.g., provision of overtime, weekend work). Thus, the use of employment multipliers based on input-output tables is problematic.

Leakage

It is also important to recognize that not all in-scope expenditure will be retained within the region hosting the convention. Depending on the size of the region, a proportion of the in-scope expenditure will be spent on goods and services sourced outside the region. Hence, it "leaks out" of the region, thereby reducing the multiplier effects. In general, regions have a higher propensity to import goods than a nation as a whole because they are more specialized and less self-sufficient, giving rise to greater leakage. However, leakage would not be an issue from a national perspective if other regions in the country address the import needs of a particular region. In such cases, the nation would still be capturing all convention-related expenditure.

The payment of taxes to the federal or state government and payments for imports represent the two major types of leakage out of a regional economy. Federal and state taxes can be regarded as leakage because they represent income accruing to residents of the region that is not available for respending in the region. Of course, the government receiving the tax may spend it in the region, but this depends on its macroeconomic policy stance (Dwyer, Forsyth, et al., 2000). Expenditure on imports to the region is considered a leakage of income out of the host region, as such expenditure generates new output and income in other regions, although possibly still within the national economy.

In the past, researchers have neglected to investigate the distribution of convention-related expenditure by convention visitors and its impacts on subregions of an economy—an issue related to leakages. Very little is known about the extent to which the convention sector benefits regional economies outside the major convention destinations. Mistilis and Dwyer's (1999) study is an exception. They used hitherto unanalyzed data from the Australian Bureau of Statistics on expenditure by convention visitors to Australia. These data were used to compare the amount of convention-related expenditure injected into urban and nonurban areas. They found that expenditure by interstate visitors was evenly distributed between urban and nonurban areas, but that expenditure by international visitors is confined mainly to capital cities and tourism gateways. There is clearly a need to direct more attention to the development and promotion of pre- and postconvention touring, especially for international delegates. The study results also indicate that the distribution of convention-related expenditure is an important issue deserving further investigation.

OTHER ECONOMIC IMPACTS

Several other types of economic impacts are not taken into account in traditional economic impact assessment. These are impacts that result from expenditure injections associated with conventions, but are not directly related to the in-scope expenditures of visitors, organizers, and sponsors. These "other" economic impacts of conventions include: new business development, induced investment, net benefits/costs to local communities, and the long-term benefits to tourism promotion of the destination. Unfortunately, these types of impacts tend to be neglected in studies regarding the economic significance of conventions due to the greater difficulty in measuring them. For example, impacts such as new business development are, in principle, quantifiable, yet they are difficult to measure in practice. Because increased business activity is already reflected in the increased in-scope expenditure, it should not be counted again.

Induced investment constitutes another source of injected expenditure that has multiplier effects. Regardless of the balance between private and public sector expenditure, investment sourced from new money has multiplier effects on income and employment. Operating losses from excess capacity in the convention sector must be accounted for in an overall assessment of the economic contribution of conventions to a tourism destination. Any such losses will offset the gains from the expenditure injections. Although researchers have discussed such impacts in the context of special events (Crompton and McKay, 1994; Delpy and Li, 1998), very little attention has been devoted to a consideration of their importance in the convention industry. Similarly, the impact of conventions on future tourism flow to a destination requires further exploration.

In addition to these other types of economic impacts, there are always particular benefits and costs associated with a convention that cannot be quantified in an objective way. These types of impacts on local communities, which include the social, cultural, and environmental impacts of convention tourism, may be positive or negative. They require a cost-benefit analysis to account for them appropriately. Although some attention has been paid to these types of benefits and costs in the assessment of special events (Burns and Mules, 1989; Crompton 1999), they tend to be treated very superficially or else neglected altogether in economic impact studies of the convention industry.

CONCLUSION

This chapter proposed a framework for the economic impact assessment of conventions. It outlined the four steps required in evaluating a convention's economic contribution. Conceptual and empirical issues relevant to each step were discussed, and gaps in the research literature identified. The discussion highlights the different approaches taken to establishing conventions' economic contributions, not only across different countries but even within one country.

The economic evaluation of conventions presents certain challenges but is crucial to the decision making of private and public sector stakeholders for the efficient allocation of scarce resources. Sound decisions regarding such resource allocation will depend upon the adoption of best-practice methods of assessing all of the various economic impacts of conventions, including those not covered by traditional economic impact analysis.

Chapter 3

Planning and Development Issues for the Convention Industry

Frank Go
Robert Govers
Anton M. Vliegenthart

INTRODUCTION

The convention industry's evolution is driven by the interplay of three important developments. First, there is the trend toward globalization, reflected in the relentless convergence of economies, infrastructures, and communications. Second, the rise of human mobility expressed in particular by the rise of travel and tourism. Presently, the mass travel market is undergoing a fragmentation of traditional categorization or grouping of almost anything, leading to "individualization." Third, the realization among decision makers at the municipal level that the convention industry is an integral part of and contributes significantly to regional economic development has caused cities and businesses to invest in facility planning and development. It has also resulted in universities conducting dedicated research, and a growing number of educational institutions offering a specialized curriculum that focuses on the convention industry. The further development of the dynamic MICE industry depends upon the adaptation of a strategic approach to planning and development within the broader travel and tourism sector context.

This chapter examines significant planning and development issues in the meetings and conventions industry, particularly the environmental factors that impact on supply, demand, and the interfacing between actors. Planning and development issues pertinent to the convention industry in general will be discussed before outlining specific global factors that are likely to impact the industry in the coming years. An overview of regional planning and development initiatives is provided in conclusion.

PLANNING AND DEVELOPMENT ISSUES FOR THE CONVENTION INDUSTRY

The essence of formulating and implementing plans is to attain objectives. In this regard, three relevant dimensions of planning and development can be distinguished (Go, 1997). First, whether formal or informal, rational or irrational, planning and development proceed through a number of stages. At each stage, decision making is driven by myriad variables, including shifts in demand, supply, and capability. The dimension that considers how plans are developed and implemented suggests that a *process* must be at work. Second, the notion of *development* indicates that the process should yield some *output* or *product.* Such output of developmental activity is a course of action to be followed by meeting planners who achieve organizational goals without jeopardizing their professional integrity. The developmental dimension of the meetings and conventions industry is therefore concerned with the *content* of trade and tourism, including the organization of the meetings that people attend. Finally, to achieve goals it is necessary that both plans and developmental activities fit national and international *contexts.* This dimension is concerned with the planning and developmental *context*—that is, the analysis of the dynamism of networks in the context of the national and supranational competitive space. The contextual dimension of the meetings and conventions industry is concerned with the reflection of issues, "that actors can operationalize to handle the problems stemming from this dynamism" (Go and Appelman, 2001, p. 183).

As organizations schedule and book major conventions several years in advance, it should be obvious that planning and development is extremely important to the industry. Most of the world's meetings and conventions take place at or near nodes, where routes intersect, which implies that the industry is very dependent on the communications and transportation infrastructure and changes that occur within it. In particular, economic, technological, or political changes in the system can have a significant impact on infrastructure development and convention centers. For example, an issue that warrants the attention of planners and developers is the emergence of more, cheaper, and improved methods of telecommunication. The "annihilation of space by time" (Harvey, 1985, p. 37) or the "death of distance" (Cairncross, 1997) has changed the communications context dramatically. It raises significant issues such as:

- Does a better and cheaper communications system diminish the significance of physical spaces and particularly convention centers?
- How should convention facilities and destinations be planned, developed, and used to facilitate the optimal circulation of knowledge and skills capital in the broad sense?
- Is the role of the convention industry being reshaped by the convergence of technology? If so, how and to what extent?
- Should the convention industry reposition itself to demonstrate its value-adding capacity in the emerging context?

Conventions and meetings around the world generate expenditures and stimulate the economic development process at the international, national, regional, and destination level. It is therefore important to note several significant differences that arise as a consequence of interaction among such levels and impact the planning and development process.

First, the world's key markets are at different socioeconomic stages. For example, the European market is mature, whereas the Asian market is still emerging. It implies different opportunities and challenges requiring distinctive approaches to the planning, development, and management of the convention industry.

Second, in the future, international trade and tourism are likely to give impetus to both the convergence and divergence of trade and tourism development. Day (1990) observed that consumer needs and lifestyles simultaneously have become more global and more indigenous. As a result the simultaneous homogeneous and individualized market has caused the emergence of a complex and diverse market environment. It implies that organizations must become more flexible to cater to the shifts in demand and create added value. Despite the trend toward globalization and greater convergence, the different cultural traditions on the national, regional, and destination levels will continue to present a significant gap in cross-cultural communications. Such diversity is deeply ingrained within cultural values and therefore very difficult to change. Due to globalization and individualization the different cultures and styles of meetings and convention "actors" will increasingly impact the planning and developmental process (see also Chapter 7).

Third, there are significant differences between the corporate cultures of public and private organizations. The planning and development of meetings and conventions is dependent, among others, for financing purposes, on the involvement of myriad private sector actors (hotels, food service, catering, beverage operations, etc.) and public or semipublic actors (government, transportation, etc.). The public and private differences in values raise considerably the potential for conflict. The exploratory analysis that ensues focuses on two levels of analysis: a global assessment and a regional assessment, concluding with a comparative appraisal.

GLOBAL FACTORS IMPACTING
PLANNING AND DEVELOPMENT

Globalization

The core business of the convention industry is to serve the diverse meeting needs of people, both at the national and international level. The thrust toward globalization is a logical consequence of economic and political trends, in which national borders are vanishing and act less as a barrier to the growth of trade and tourism. The emergence of supranational institutions, such as the integration of Europe and the expansion of the European Union to include countries in Eastern and Central Europe shall raise the complexity and need for decision making. It should increase the number of conventions that will be held by business, political, and nongovernmental organizations. To date, convention industry-related research has been largely confined to the functional nature of the business. The rapid growth in the Asia-Pacific region and other non-Western societies will increase spatial interaction between communities with different cultural backgrounds. It will require greater insight into cross-cultural issues (Hofstede, 1984) that arise from face-to-face interaction between multinational groups. Meeting planners could contribute to avoiding potential conflict if they comprehend the cross-cultural issues (see Chapter 7).

Expanding operations globally is increasingly seen as a key to consolidating one's market position and strengthening one's communication chain. The Internet is likely to advance the quest for comparison, learning, and stimulation of face-to-face meetings. Paradoxically, Porter (1998, p. 77) recognized that an enduring competitive advantage in a global economy lies increasingly in local "knowledge, relationships and motivation that distant rivals cannot match." Within a globalized society organizations should become "more and more part of their environment both ecologically and socially to capitalize on the pivotal potential of the value chain" (Go and Appelman, 2001, p. 187).

Fragmentation

The convention industry is rather fragmented in nature. It is comprised of many different elements, including meeting venues, hotel accommodation, food and beverage services, entertainment, technology support, transport, conference interpretation, sponsorship, exhibition management, and marketing. Each element is characterized by its own specific attributes that must be combined and managed expertly to serve the different target markets, such as the association sector and the corporate market. An issue of growing importance will be to identify ways to achieve scale economies while serving diverse market needs and maintaining the identity of individual partner organizations.

In general, there is presently little cooperation between the various branches that are part of the industry. One result is that the "industry" is unable to speak with a united voice. Another result is that there is little, if any, cooperation between the associations of different countries; ignorance of one another's initiatives and activities is not unusual. There is, therefore, a clear need for both qualitative studies and quantitative indicators in which the multifaceted nature of internationalization processes of both enterprises and institutions can be tracked. The topic of internationalization and of competitive institutions deals with the question of the international coordination of activities and can be considered a prime management research problem. For instance: How can joint decision-making processes be applied to present a unified convention destination identity to (potential) clients?

Potential for Cooperation and Conflict

International trade and tourism have given an impetus to a convergence-divergence paradox (Go, 1997). As convention destinations become increasingly integrated into the global communications and transport network, alliances, partnerships, or other cooperative efforts with other travel and tourism players have become increasingly a marketing tool in the convention industry (Jusko, 1994; Selin, 1993). For example, the Netherlands government recently initiated at the policy level a partnership between the National Congress Bureau (NCB) and the National Tourist Office (NTO), primarily for purposes of efficiency. Both organizations have a distinct purpose and serve different target markets. It is therefore essential to maintain their respective identities. However, it is quite possible and would be logical to pool, where possible, certain "back office" tasks so as to achieve scale economies. For example, joint research efforts would provide both organizations with insights into the travel motivation of business travelers and conference delegate spending in tourist destinations at reduced costs. Similarly, they could also jointly fund research to develop the use of Internet marketing, identify competing products, based on methods and techniques using factual data of consumers' buying behavior (Waarts, 1996).

Although partnerships between airlines, hotels, and car rental firms offering fly-and-drive packages have been in place since the early 1980s, the pursuit of network partnerships between the convention industry, national and city tourism organizations, and airlines is an area in which unnecessary rivalry still exists. At the same time a lack of internal resources, an increase in competition knowledge, and dependency on information technology networks make a straightforward organic growth very difficult for many convention organizations. Being "complementary" in nature, convention organizations need transport, hotel, attraction, and public sector organizations to "produce" value-added convention services. At the same time, clients want flexibility. Therefore, convention centers and destinations have but little choice; they must bring together the building blocks and form an alliance upon which the performance of their own organization depends. In summary, in a network economy, a "decision-making" team rather than a "command" approach is more likely to gain and maintain a competitive advantage.

Technology

Future convention industry expansion will move beyond brick-and-mortar upgrading and the expansion of capacity and connections to transportation nodes, such as the high-speed international trains in Europe. Specifically, convention organizations will shift their attention increasingly to the communications sector and conversely well-established media corporations will become increasingly involved in the convention industry. The emergence of computer-based systems linking several industry sectors, such as intermediaries and airlines, is cited by Leiper (1990) as an example of transindustry cooperation. Here the contextual issue arises: if and to what extent will the convergence of electronic communications and physical convention facilities impact transaction costs and lead to changes in distribution channels as a result of the Internet and emerging business networks (Go and Govers, 1997; Oppermann, 1994)? Emerging insight into both physical and electronic spaces seems to reveal that hitherto unexamined transaction costs are inextricably connected to the efficiency and inclusiveness made possible by electronic communications (Govers, Go, and Jansen-Verbeke, 2000).

The results of a recent benchmark study (Yuan et al., 1999) show that the directors of many U.S.-based convention and visitors bureaus (CVBs) have not recognized the potential of the Internet and intranet to support and enhance the various functions within their organization. Yuan et al. point to a potential crisis that CVBs will confront in the near future, which can be avoided only by identifying the real barriers limiting the use of Internet technology and developing strategies designed to enhance the intellectual capital within the CVB organization.

The increasing importance of information and communication technology (ICT) and the corresponding organizational transformation as a driver of change has become a point of attention. In this sense it is mandatory to observe that it is not technologies themselves that drive change, but the manner in which such technologies are organized to fit successfully into the daily lives of consumers and employees that determines the success of new technology (Go and Appelman, 2001; Lash and Urry, 1994). It is therefore important to monitor the reactions of consumers and employees to new technology. Since 1997, the International Federation of Information Technologies in Tourism (IFITT) rewards tourism destinations at the annual Conference on Information and communication technologies in tourism for the best Web site. The evaluation criteria include ease of use; joy of use (entertainment); content (information, education, etc.); design and creativity (innovative, agreeable presentation, etc.); interactivity; transaction support (reservations, billing, etc.); and added value. Jung and Baker (1998, pp. 95-96) also compared other design criteria from different sources and observed agreement in the literature concerning the following elements: content (information); transaction support; interactivity (communication); and added value (for instance, in the form of entertainment).

Greater Competition—Greater Importance of Destination Image

The increased investment in convention facilities around the world provides meeting planners with more options regarding destinations that may be included in their consideration set, ultimately leading to greater competition in the convention industry. The rising level of competition coupled with rising costs and a lack of resources is likely to lead to a shift from "stand-alone convention sites" to the competition between "multipurpose destination organizations" integrating with other complementary activities. Therefore, the notion of convention destination image (Oppermann, 1994) will become an increasingly important issue.

Conceptually, image may be referred to as a "set of attitudes based upon evaluations of cognitive, affective and conative aspects that determine customer behavior" (Pruyn, 1994, p. 148). Convention destination image might be defined as the sum of beliefs, ideas, and impressions that meeting planners and other stakeholders have of a convention destination (Kotler, Haider, and Rein, 1993). It represents a simplification of a large number of mental associations and pieces of information connected with a place. The image of convention destinations and facilities is important and should be of concern to convention industry marketers to resolve issues such as:

- How do meeting planners and other stakeholders perceive our destination and facilities relative to the competition?
- How can researchers best identify, measure, and control a convention destination's image to attract clients and make them return?

- What does brand image mean with regard to a convention destination?

LeBlanc (1992) supports the notion of destination image research as a form of service quality measurement, because both quality and satisfaction are concerned with the difference between expectations and perceptions. The study suggests a significant relationship between perceived quality and image, and by extension confirms the significance of the image factor. It also pinpoints the relevance of applying the importance performance analysis technique to measure the competitiveness of international conference destinations (Go and Govers, 1997; Go and Zhang, 1997) and benchmark performance.

Subsequently, based on an inventory of the attributes that categorize the relevant characteristics of convention destinations, the performance could be measured for each relevant attribute. It should be possible to develop a user-based system for conventions and meetings following, for instance, Morgan (1999) who developed a rating system for beaches. Some reservations about applying such a multiattribute information processing paradigm seem to be in order, however, at least from an experiential goods perspective. Leemans (1994, p. 210) puts it this way: "there are emotion-laden goods and services for which the consumption experience is an end in itself." Although Leemans examined books as a "hedonic" product, it would not be far-fetched, at least from a content perspective, to imagine convention service to fit in the same category. Both products are experienced by clients, which implies, according to Leemans, that "factual information on objective and often physical characteristics of single items are much less important than the image (a nonphysical attribute) that is built around items" (1994, p. 210).

Broader Context of Quality of Life in Cities

The convention industry has a direct impact on the quality of life for residents. If a convention destination is well planned and well managed, it will be able to attract visitors and create jobs, income, and tax revenues. The convention industry is too important to local communities to be left in the hands of "outsider" professionals (McNulty and Wafer, 1990). Moreover, there is growing desire for local participation on the part of convention and visitors bureaus. For example, the Amsterdam Convention and Tourist Board has been actively involving its local stakeholders in a participatory decision process. In particular, a knowledge network has been established in Amsterdam and plans are underway to explore opportunities and establish priorities for further collaboration with stakeholders both within the municipality and in its surrounding region.

The planning, development, and sustenance of comprehensive and competitive convention sites require substantial investments, which generally only the dominant nodes in the global city network can finance. The probability of return on such investment for large metropolitan areas can be substantial (Catin, 1995). The development of a variety of cultural, educational, and convention facilities often results in the augmentation of productivity at the local level. Apparently, the combination of residing in, working in, and experiencing the cultural climate is an irresistible factor that attracts many people to metropolitan areas. Consequently, it will be an important incentive for metropolitan areas to apply policy that combines both the economies of scale in production and cultural diversity, that, among others, arises from the offering of a range of arts, social, and educational activities. In this sense, convention facilities contribute to a polycentric structure supporting both business and cultural community activities and have become an important element of city life across the world. Currently, a growing number of cities are involved in the process of either building new convention centers, or expanding and/or renovating existing ones. The number of convention centers is likely to increase in the future due to the contribution that convention centers make within the broader context of quality of life in cities.

Lack of Comprehensive Research

Any industry's economic significance is only as good as its data. The diversity and noncumulative nature of research has resulted in "a jigsaw puzzle without a picture to refer to." If the convention industry's interests are to be seriously considered in policymaking, the current system of collecting, organizing, and disseminating data requires improvement so that planning and development can be more effective. Research issues and challenges for the convention industry are discussed in depth in Chapter 6.

REGIONAL PLANNING
AND DEVELOPMENT INITIATIVES

This section will offer insights into how strategic issues have influenced the status of the convention industry on a regional basis. Table 3.1 reveals the changes in market share by continent during the past decade. The numbers of meetings for the top convention countries for the period from 1991 to 1999 are shown in Table 3.2, while Table 3.3 lists the number of meetings for major convention cities.

Europe

Europe has always claimed more than half the market for international meetings (see Table 3.1), with an equally strong representation among the top convention cities (see Table 3.3). Not only does Europe have a stronghold but also, after some years of stagnation, it is again taking its share of market growth. The Boston Consulting Group would typically describe this as a "Star" product, with a high market share in a growing market. Therefore, the European market seems to be concentrating on how to reap maximum benefits from this strong competitive position. Proven techniques to maintain such a strong competitive position are achieving economies of scale and sharing technological resources through international partnerships. For example, the European Travel Commission (ETC) has pooled thirty countries across the continent and recently launched a comprehensive Web site <www. visiteurope.com>, providing a much needed gateway that attracts non-Europeans to visit the continent. In an effort

TABLE 3.1. Number of International Conventions per Continent, 1991-1999

	1991-1992	1993-1994	1995-1996	1997-1998	1999
Europe	62	59	59	59	58
Asia	14	17	19	17	17
North America	12	12	10	10	11
South/Central America	7	6	5	6	5
Australia/Pacific	3	4	4	5	7
Africa	2	2	3	3	3

Source: <http://www.icca.nl>.

TABLE 3.2. Number of International Meetings per Country, 1991-1999

	1991-1992	1993-1994	1995-1996	1997-1998	1999
United States	466	489	427	456	200
Spain	314	241	239	303	156
United Kingdom	350	369	357	364	153
Germany	365	334	257	309	149
France	340	345	289	280	129
Italy	225	251	240	261	113
Australia	115	154	195	238	103
Finland	130	116	148	160	100
Netherlands	250	243	270	239	97
Japan	219	241	254	203	90
Canada	169	196	145	156	79
Austria	161	156	171	161	78
Sweden	126	127	132	173	75
Brazil	96	89	64	93	73
Hungary	102	92	118	83	71
Norway	88	105	95	101	64
Denmark	133	140	181	152	61
Switzerland	137	110	119	122	53
Belgium	144	133	132	135	50
Republic of Korea	63	54	60	87	48

Source: <http://www.icca.nl>.

to make its Web site a household name in the United States, one of its key markets, the European Travel Commission spent US$1.25 million on a television advertising campaign in five U.S. cities and an auxiliary print campaign in three of those. While the jury is still out, the introduction of the Euro in 1999 may have benefited the convention industry. It resulted in the expected reduced costs of currency transfer and greater convenience for travelers, but unexpectedly benefited the convention industry in another way. In many countries, the U.S. dollar was worth 30 percent more, at the end of 2000, than it was in 1999 when the Euro was inaugurated. Consequently, Europe's competitive position improved significantly (Teale, 2001).

TABLE 3.3. Number of International Meetings per City, 1991-1999

	1991-1992	1993-1994	1995-1996	1997-1998	1999
Vienna	112	100	113	121	63
Copenhagen	70	83	134	109	50
Madrid	100	80	75	122	48
Budapest	80	78	94	66	46
Helsinki	48	45	63	77	42
Stockholm	56	63	77	93	41
Berlin	92	98	49	55	40
Seoul	44	38	46	63	40
Barcelona	82	71	85	93	39
Sydney	45	47	56	77	38
Amsterdam	91	91	100	99	37
Rio de Janeiro	36	41	28	38	36
Edinburgh	30	46	61	70	35
Paris	119	117	97	97	33
London	78	67	77	87	32
Prague	48	43	67	65	30
Hong Kong	55	53	80	56	29
Rome	32	28	44	56	26
Singapore	61	51	73	65	25
Vancouver	23	27	27	38	25

Source: <http://www.icca.nl>.

Asia

Following the Asian financial crisis, competition in the region grew even fiercer, making it even more important for the industry to compete on the basis of key success criteria and a better understanding of clients' expectations. Go and Govers (1997) applied the importance-performance technique (I/P analysis) to measure the competitive strength of international conference destinations, with a particular focus on Asia. Based on fifty-one questionnaires completed by conference organizers in the region, the importance of seven convention destination attributes was established. Subsequently, respondents were asked to rate the performance of eleven Asian convention destinations on these attributes.

The results, presented in Table 3.4, indicate that respondents perceive Singapore and Hong Kong as the two most competitive conference destinations in Asia. They are followed by a "second tier," comprised of four convention destinations, namely Tokyo, Bangkok, Kuala Lumpur, and Taipei. In the "third tier" of Asian convention destinations Beijing is perceived to have a marginal lead over Shanghai, followed by Seoul, Jakarta, and Manila. Due to a small sample size, these results should be treated with some caution. However, the findings of this study generally support the results of previous research and do emphasize the significance of issues such as the capacity of facilities, quality of service, accessibility, price, and image. The respondents rated these basic attributes as either very important or quite important. The management of CVBs in Asian conference and meeting destinations will need to ensure that the expectations of meeting planners and conference delegates are not only met but exceeded. The top performer in Asia, Singapore, is apparently very conscious of both the importance of and its high performance on

TABLE 3.4. Performance Ratings for Asian Convention Destinations

Destination City	Attributes Affecting Competitiveness							
	Facilities	Accessibility	Service	Attraction	Price	Climate and Environment	Image	Overall
Singapore	4.29	4.36	4.07	3.46	2.93	3.64	4.21	4.18
Hong Kong	4.25	2.91	3.75	3.88	2.31	3.44	4.19	4.00
Tokyo	4.09	3.27	4.09	3.60	1.64	3.55	4.00	3.89
Bangkok	3.15	3.31	3.54	3.92	3.54	2.23	2.92	3.50
Kuala Lumpur	3.00	3.18	3.18	3.18	3.27	3.00	2.91	3.25
Taipei	3.09	3.27	2.73	2.82	2.55	2.64	2.91	3.13
Beijing	2.39	2.69	2.39	3.39	3.08	3.00	2.92	3.00
Shanghai	2.67	2.50	2.58	2.75	2.42	3.67	2.92	2.89
Seoul	2.90	2.90	2.80	2.80	2.50	2.60	2.60	2.88
Jakarta	2.82	3.09	2.91	2.91	3.27	2.73	2.64	2.75
Manila	2.90	2.50	2.80	2.70	3.20	2.50	2.50	2.57

Note: All variables were measured on a five-point scale with 1 indicating a poor performance and 5 indicating an excellent performance.

these factors. It lists accessibility, infrastructure, facilities, accommodation, service, affordability, safe environment, tourism appeal, and track record as the reasons that organizers should choose Singapore as their convention destination <www.meet-in-singapore.com.sg>.

Regardless of the various initiatives of the Asian Association of Convention and Visitors Bureaus, many individual Asian convention destinations had to step up their own marketing activities to address the increased competition due to the shrinking market, especially following the Asian financial crisis. Some examples of the MICE campaigns include Hong Kong's "Convention Ambassador Program" (ongoing since 1998), Malaysia's "2001—Year of Conventions," and Indonesia's "Bridge for Success, Convene in Indonesia" (ongoing since 1998). While Singapore's "Global Meet 2000" is a three-year campaign "to reaffirm Singapore's position as a MICE capital," Australia's MICE campaign had as its goal the generation of AU$100 million in 2001 through business events (PCVC, 2001).

However, what developmental actions might a small player such as Manila undertake to enhance its threatened position (see Table 3.4)? In a unified bid to capture a greater market share, the private sector together with the Department of Tourism (DOT) and the Philippine Convention and Visitors Corporation (PCVC) has been spearheading a major campaign to promote Metro Manila globally as a prime international MICE destination. The uniqueness of this campaign is its recognition of the importance of public-private partnership. It is the first time that a MICE campaign received private sector support in the Philippines (PCVC, 2001).

Australia

After several years of tremendous growth, Australia had rather disappointing years in 1998 and 1999. However, the Olympic Games in Sydney in 2000 significantly improved its position. In an attempt to capitalize on this mega-event, the Australian Tourist Commission (ATC), through its Meetings, Conventions and Incentives (MC&I) business unit implemented strategies in 1995 to promote the country as a unique and desirable MICE destination. Initiatives that focused on this high-yield business sector included

- funding assistance for 104 Australian associations to the value of AU$310,000;
- provision of promotional assistance to the Australian incentive industry;
- a review of MC&I global activities to assist in developing an MC&I global marketing strategy; and
- handling of 3,400 inquiries and conducting 120 industry interviews (ATC, 1996).

Sydney has clearly been the most successful of all Australian destinations. Even on a global scale it outperformed competitors by climbing steeply to the first rank in 2000 <http://www.icca.nl>. Emphasizing partnership and coordination of effort, the Sydney Convention and Visitors Bureau (SCVB) has candidly acknowledged that this success can be attributed to the successful bid for the 2000 Summer Olympic Games (Asher, 2000). In particular, the following were noted:

- The bid win average increased by 34 percent compared to bid wins prior to 1993. As a result, the average amount of revenue generated for the city increased by 118 percent following the 1993 decision for Sydney to host the 2000 Olympic Games.
- An essential catalyst for business is infrastructure development in hotels and venues—between 1994 and the end of the third quarter of 1999, a 53 percent increase in the number of establishments built was registered.
- The capacity of the Sydney Convention and Exhibition Centre (SCEC) increased by 12 percent following a AU$57 million expansion.
- Since Sydney was announced as the host city for the Olympics the SCVB won 210 events that were expected to attract more than 250,000 delegates and inject more than AU$940 million into the city's economy.
- The growth of the MICE industry has been significant. The segment, measured by international visitor arrivals to Australia, grew by 78 percent in the three years following the announcement; for the same period leading up to the Olympics, it grew by 17 percent.

North America

United States

The United States of America has traditionally occupied the first position in the international MICE league (see Table 3.2). Similar to Europe, after several years of troublesome performance, the United States appears to have benefited from the Asian financial crisis, with many customers having been hesitant to organize their meetings and conventions in the region. Washington, DC, is the country's leading convention destination in terms of the international meetings held by associations <www.icca.nl>, occupying the tenth position in 1999 (see Table 1.3). The new Washington, DC, convention center is the largest public works project in the District of Columbia since the city's foundation. When completed in the spring of 2003, it will contain 2.3 million square feet of space, attract 2.5 million visitors, and bring in $1.4 billion in economic stimulus a year <www.dcconvention. com>. A more detailed discussion of the development of the industry in the United States in the past decades is provided in Chapter 1.

Canada

Canada has also performed reasonably well, with the country being ranked eleventh in 1999 (see Table 3.2), and Vancouver being in the top twenty in the same year (see Table 3.3). The Canadian Tourism Commission (CTC) actively pursues partnership opportunities with organizations and individuals in the tourism sector through special programs for marketing, research, and industry and product development. Canada positions itself in the convention market as a close-in alternative to the United States—one differentiated by quality, authentic products that offer value, unique culture, service, and safety. The Meetings and Incentive Travel Program targets meetings and incentive travel decision makers with an integrated approach that has two main strategies: relationship building and advertising. These strategies include the following elements: relationship marketing, promotions and sales calls, and awareness building. The Meetings and Incentive Travel Program has been designed by an industry-led marketing committee with the primary objective of providing partnership opportunities for Canadian industry, small and large (CTC, 2000).

South Africa

South Africa is an upcoming MICE destination. It has understood the importance of partnership and destination image as a way to increase competitiveness through local uniqueness, but at the same time using joint strength and scale economies needed to compete at a global level. South Africa's big six—Durban, Cape Town, Johannesburg, Pretoria, Port Elizabeth, and Bloemfontein—have formed the South African Federation of Conference Cities (SAFCC). Paraphrasing SAFCC Chairman Keith Brebnor: "The idea is to market South Africa first, concentrating on the diversity these cities have to offer. We have the potential to fulfill a conference planner's dream" (Travel and Trade Publishing, 1998). The Internet would be at the center of the marketing thrust with the federation's Web site driving the proposed "diverse cities" theme. The site will also provide a link between all potential partners in bringing conferences to South Africa, such as South African Airways (SAA) and other inbound carriers, Southern Sun, Hilton Hotels, car rental companies, and financial institutions including MasterCard (Travel and Trade Publishing, 1998).

CONCLUSION

Planning and development are essential issues for the convention industry. It should be noted that the industry in each of the major regions is at a different stage of development. Consequently, different opportunities and distinct approaches apply with regard to the industry's planning and development. The convention industry still remains concentrated in industrialized nations, but that may change to some extent in the future due to some of the global factors that affect the industry, as discussed. The regional assessment chronicled planning and development issues and initiatives in the major regions of Europe, Asia-Pacific, and North America. There are often significant differences not only among the regions but also within them. For example, Asia is far from uniform, with some countries being very proactive in planning and development while others lag behind. The same also holds true on the national level where even within small countries such as the Netherlands and Switzerland significant differences can exist between destinations in close geographic proximity.

It seems that the challenge for the meetings and convention industry will be to develop greater flexibility to cope with more change and the diversity that characterizes nations and cultures. For planning and development, this implies that the industry will have "to embrace globalization, yet treat it with a localized focus if it is to succeed" (Go, 1996, p. 37).

The future evolution of the convention industry will continue to be marked both by uncertainty and fragmentation. While diverse in nature, no convention industry actor can escape the impact of technological innovation. It has become an essential element to global competitiveness. Paradoxically, local identity will become important again in the future for purposes of differentiation. It will require decision makers in the convention industry to capitalize on local knowledge and relationships to improve business performance through partnerships, competitiveness, and technological advancement.

Chapter 4

Marketing of Convention Tourism

Geoffrey I. Crouch
Karin Weber

INTRODUCTION

At its core, the convention tourism marketplace trades in convention destinations. As shown in Chapter 2, a destination covets convention tourism for the direct and indirect benefits it offers its residents and business community. The attractiveness of convention tourism has spurred destinations to proactively pursue the meetings and conventions market. Modern, sophisticated marketing techniques are now used by destinations to serve this segment of the travel and tourism market. The most competitive convention tourism destinations are those that understand the full potential that marketing, as a management function, has to offer the convention and visitors bureaus (CVB) and other organizations involved in attracting and serving the meetings and conventions industry.

Some destinations perceive marketing as little more than an exercise in promoting a destination. However, effective marketing involves much more than promotion alone. Marketing convention tourism requires, first, an understanding of the two main customers of the meeting and conventions industry—corporations and associations. After examining both, the principal elements of the convention destination marketing mix will be briefly reviewed. The important issue of convention site selection will then be investigated followed by a discussion of convention marketing organizations and regional case studies. The focus of this chapter is on convention destination marketing rather than the marketing of individual convention service providers (e.g., convention centers, hotels, etc.).

CONVENTION TOURISM MARKETS

Corporations

The corporate market is the largest single market segment, accounting for over 65 percent of meetings (Lawson, 2000). Nevertheless, identifying the corporate buyer for marketing purposes represents a challenge because only large corporations retain a dedicated conference management department, and job titles and responsibilities vary greatly. A professional conference organizer (PCO) is generally contracted only for larger events. Corporate meetings are essentially driven by the needs of individual businesses. They take a variety of forms, including board, management, and shareholder's meetings; training seminars; meetings with partners, suppliers, and clients; sales conferences; product launches; strategic planning retreats; and incentives. Lawson (2000) provides a detailed account of their characteristics. McCabe et al. (2000) suggest a division of the corporate sector into manufacturing, distribution and retail, and services, since each of these has unique requirements that marketers of meeting services must address to be successful.

The corporate market has a number of unique characteristics. Corporate meetings tend to be small with delegate numbers generally fewer than 100. Furthermore, they are mostly short in duration. According to System Three (1998), 50 percent of corporate conferences consisted of 100 delegates or fewer, and 40 percent of corporate conferences lasted for one day only. In Australia, corporate meetings lasting for one day account for about 55 percent of the total market and average about fifty delegates (Johnson et al., 1999). Corporate meetings are also characterized by short lead times, typically much less than a year. In the United States, the average length of time to plan corporate meetings was 6.7 months in 2000 (Meetings and Conventions, 2000). In view of the relatively small size of corporate meetings, most are typically held in hotels, with the remainder taking place in dedicated conference centers, training centers, universities, or the company's own facilities. Due to the inherent nature of incentive meetings, the venues for them are often rather unusual and of very high standards. With businesses funding delegates' attendance at corporate meetings, return on investment (cost and time) is a key priority.

Associations

The largest meetings and conventions held throughout the world each year are not conducted by individual corporations, but by the enormous number of associations that exist to present and promote the interests of their members. The association market incorporates professional and trade associations, voluntary associations and societies, charities, religious organizations, political parties, and trade unions (Rogers, 1998). Associations hold a variety of meetings, including training and development programs, networking functions, and seminars. The most visible and desirable gatherings, from a destination point of view, however, are the annual conventions that can attract thousands of delegates.

Even though associations are typically of a nonprofit nature, annual conventions often have a profit objective. The ninth annual Meeting Market Survey conducted by the Professional Convention Management Association (PCMA) in the United States found that conventions account for about one-third of associations' annual income (PCMA, 2000b). Apart from a professionally run convention, the selection of an appropriate convention destination that can boost attendance numbers is critical to achieve profit objectives. This is especially important because, in contrast to the corporate market, delegates at association conventions must cover the cost for attending themselves and may also decide to bring their families. Attractive partner and social programs in addition to pre- and posttour options are important in view of the influence family members can exert on the potential attendee's decision to participate in a convention (Oh, Roehl, and Shock, 1993).

The higher attendance numbers and longer duration for the association market are further distinguishing characteristics from the corporate sector. In the United Kingdom, for example, about 60 percent of association conferences in 1997 lasted for at least three days and more than one-third attracted more than 500 attendees (System Three, 1998). Conventions attracting several thousand delegates are common. In Las Vegas in 1999, sixty conventions attracted more than 7,000 delegates each, the largest of which was attended by more than 100,000 delegates (LVCVA, 1999). In view of the size of conventions, the diversity of member needs, associations' decision-making procedures, and the resulting complexity of association conventions, lead times can be substantial. The average lead time in the United States was 3.9 years, according to a study by one of the major industry associations (ASAE, 1992), although ten years or more is also not unusual for the largest conventions that are restricted to very few cities that can accommodate them. Finally, the complex management structures of associations influence the decision-making process and the selection of a convention site, as will be discussed in more detail later in this chapter.

Targeted Marketing

The convention tourism market segments require different marketing strategies. Table 4.1 summarizes the key attributes that characterize the corporate and association segments.

CONVENTION DESTINATION MARKETING MIX

Recognizing the significant *service* content of convention tourism, the convention destination marketing mix may be represented by the

TABLE 4.1. Corporate and Associations Market Segments – Key Differences

Corporate	Associations
Larger in number	Smaller in number
Small average meeting size	Large average meeting size
Meeting goals aligned to the needs of the firm	Meeting goals more diverse reflecting the broad needs of the membership
Limited number of players in the buying group*	Large buying group
Normally a short meeting planning time horizon	Much longer time horizon extending up to several years
Local geographic focus	More diverse geographic interests
Speedier decision making	Drawn out decision making dependent on regularity of board meetings
Likelihood of repeat buying from the same site	Often years between possibility of a return visit

*The buying group consists of the stakeholders who influence the eventual convention site decision.

"7-Ps" model (Zeithaml and Bitner, 1996, p. 25), encompassing management of the *product, place, promotion, price, people, physical evidence,* and *process.*

Product

Convention tourism involves the buying and selling of convention destination services. Corporate or association customers seek meeting and related facilities provided by alternative destination suppliers to satisfy their need for holding gatherings of various kinds. The convention tourism product, therefore, is clearly a service. More specifically, the product is the total experience that the client and its employees or members receive when a convention is held at a particular destination. Although various meeting, accommodation, and other facilities are central to this service, they are not the product per se; that is, the client does not purchase these facilities. Rather, these physical features of a convention destination provide the ability to deliver the convention tourism product (services), but they do not form part of the product itself. Hence, the convention tourism product is created from the combination of physical facilities, branding (destination image), service performance and quality, accessory services (e.g., audio-visual services), and packaging (through the local convention and visitors bureau or destination management companies). Successful convention destination marketing recognizes the product as consisting of all influences affecting the convention experience of the client.

Place

The place element of the marketing mix relates to all factors that are involved in connecting convention customers to convention products. The traditional marketing channel roles of wholesaling and retailing play no part in the meeting industry because there is little scope for the sorting, assembling, and reselling of convention services. Most transactions are handled on a direct basis between the user of convention facilities and the provider, with assistance often provided by PCOs or meeting planners, destination management companies, and convention and visitors bureaus. These intermediaries, however, do play a critical role in the selling function and can significantly influence the convention site selection decision. In this context, the reputation of the convention destination and word of mouth are critical too. Transportation is also an important place element, but in this instance, it brings the customer to the product rather than distributing the product to the customer, as occurs in many other marketing situations.

Promotion

Convention destinations engage in all forms of promotional activity. Destinations advertise their convention facilities in meeting-industry magazines, such as *Meetings and Conventions* (United States), *Meetings and Incentive Travel* (United Kingdom), *Meeting and Congressi* (Italy), *Tagungswirtschaft* (Germany), *IMA* (Singapore), *Congress and Convention* (Japan), and *Convention and Incentive Marketing* (Australia). Sales promotions are also offered to attract conventions through price discounts, subsidies, and other inducements. Public relations and publicity assist in developing a strong, positive image of a successful convention destination. However, personal selling is probably the most important promotional method used in the meetings and conventions industry. Personal contact and interaction between sales representatives of a destination and meeting planners, association executives, and professional conference organizers are vital elements of the promotional effort. Indeed, for most conventions, a site visit, including the assessment of meeting, accommodation, and other facilities, is critical. The CVB and convention center sales forces spearhead the promotional efforts of a destination.

Price

The price of a destination as a convention site is a critical marketing variable. Major convention destinations such as New York, London, Hong Kong, and Sydney are normally more expensive, as the higher cost of real estate and facilities drives up the price of meeting space, accommodations, and the cost of other services. In recent years, so-called "second-tier" cities have become more price competitive while still offering good meeting facilities in less congested but attractive environments (Braley, 1996b; Dobrian, 1998; Korn, 1998). Second-tier cities are suburbs of major cities or smaller cities that differ from first-tier cities in the hotel room inventory, the size of the convention center, and the citywide hotel rack rates (Shure, 1997).

Although clearly important, the prices of meeting and accommodation services are only one part of the total price of a destination. Marketers must also consider the accessibility and cost of transportation to the destination, local transportation, food services, etc. To attract major conventions, some destinations may subsidize the cost of the convention or offer assistance and services through the local CVB or association chapter either free of charge or at a reduced cost. Although price cannot be set and controlled by a convention destination in quite the same way as occurs in other product contexts, it is nevertheless a significant marketing variable.

People

The role of people is key in the successful marketing of services because the convention tourism product is, in essence, an experience. The experience of an association or corporation holding a convention or meeting occurs in real time simultaneously with the delivery and performance of the service by the destination. Therefore, the actions of service personnel and their interactions with customers are critical in governing overall service quality. Hence, service personnel perform a marketing function, not just an operations function. The recruitment, training, and motivation of all service personnel affecting the convention experience are therefore vital (see also Chapter 5). Service recognition and reward programs are often implemented by destinations to acknowledge the important role of people. Indeed, all human interactions, not just with employees, must be considered. For this reason the friendliness and hospitality of local residents is also important.

Physical Evidence

The convention service experience occurs in the context of an inanimate environment. The physical design and layout of the convention facilities is clearly of paramount importance, but the importance of decor, ambiance, lighting, signage, temperature control, aesthetics, equipment, employee dress, etc. should not be overlooked. Indeed, all physical evidence conveys important information about the type and level of service anticipated and perceived. This perspective can be extended beyond the meeting space itself. The whole feeling or ambiance of the city hosting the convention is also critical. The climate, perceptions of individual safety, and general attractiveness of the city are significantly shaped by all elements of physical evidence that the delegate experiences.

Process

The final element of the extended marketing mix recognizes that the delivery and operation of the convention service experience occurs through a process. A convention product is produced in the presence of the convention customer. Consequently, the convention customer's experience is not just a function of some end result. The whole flow and mix of activities from the beginning to the end of the process will govern the customer's overall experience and perception of the destination as a convention site. Indeed, this process does not begin and end with the convention itself. The selling and planning stages leading up to the convention and the postconvention activities, such as follow-up marketing research, satisfaction surveys, and resolution of any complaints, all shape the perceived quality of the experience. It is important to note that customers in this context are both the attendees and the PCOs.

CONVENTION SITE SELECTION

As previously explained, the greater flexibility in the choice of a meeting destination for the association market compared to the corporate market is a key difference between the two sectors. This section focuses specifically on associations' decision-making process in the selection of a convention site and the various factors that are considered—an understanding of which is required in the successful marketing of convention destinations. As noted by Clark and McCleary (1995), associations' site selection process is very complex due to the multitude of variables that influence the decision. These variables can be broadly divided into site-specific and association factors.

Site Selection Variables

Numerous studies have investigated the site-specific variables that influence the selection of a convention site (e.g., Alkjaer, 1976b; Benini, 1996b; Chacko and Fenich, 2000; Chon, 1991; Hiller, 1995; Oppermann and Chon, 1997; Pizam and Manning, 1982; Usher, 1991; Var, Cesario, and Mauser, 1985). Crouch and Ritchie (1998) provide a comprehensive review of the site selection literature. They found that the majority of studies are based on opinions, anecdotal evidence, and industry experience. The identification of important site selection factors is central in most publications. Yet only a small number of studies employed a rigorous approach to the task (Bonn and Boyd, 1992; Bonn, Brand, and Ohlin, 1994; Bonn, Ohlin, and Brand, 1994; Clark and McCleary, 1995; Clark, Price, and Murrmann, 1996; Fortin and Ritchie, 1977; Fortin, Ritchie, and Arsenault, 1976; Oppermann, 1996a,b; Zelinsky, 1994), and even fewer studies attempted to examine how trade-offs are made between factors (Hu and Hiemstra, 1996; Renaghan and Kay, 1987). Crouch and Ritchie (1998) then grouped the numerous variables into a set of eight primary categories along several dimensions, resulting in the identification of thirty-six convention destination attributes that govern the choice of a convention site (Figure 4.1).

Although the literature has emphasized the importance of the available meeting facilities and, to a lesser extent, aspects of the quality of accommodation facilities, it is clear from this figure that a number of additional destination attributes play critical roles. Convention destinations need to consider all potential site selection factors to avoid the pitfall of assuming that it all depends on the size and design of a convention center facility and the range and quality of accommodation available. For example, the accessibility of the convention site to the majority of attendees is often an important consideration. The offer of strong local support from a chapter of the association or the local CVB might be a highly persuasive factor favoring some sites over others. Attendees (and their accompanying families) are often persuaded to attend if the site offers attractive pre- and postconference recreational or vacationing opportunities. Hence, an attractive convention site and appealing destination image are likely to be influential. Comments by several authors also support this notion. Kingston (1995) notes that a common error made by convention planners is to

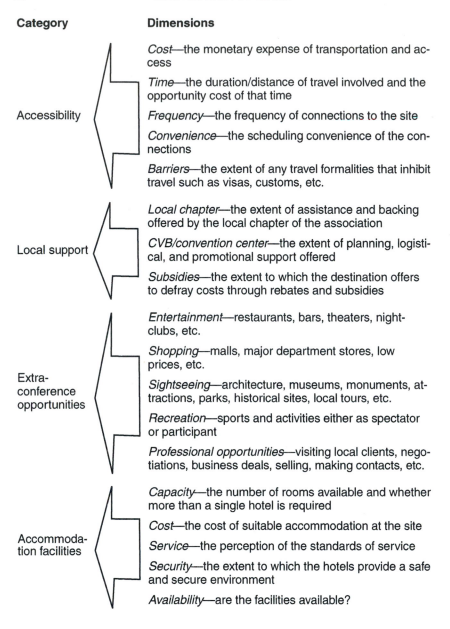

Category

Dimensions

Accessibility

Cost—the monetary expense of transportation and access

Time—the duration/distance of travel involved and the opportunity cost of that time

Frequency—the frequency of connections to the site

Convenience—the scheduling convenience of the connections

Barriers—the extent of any travel formalities that inhibit travel such as visas, customs, etc.

Local support

Local chapter—the extent of assistance and backing offered by the local chapter of the association

CVB/convention center—the extent of planning, logistical, and promotional support offered

Subsidies—the extent to which the destination offers to defray costs through rebates and subsidies

Extra-conference opportunities

Entertainment—restaurants, bars, theaters, nightclubs, etc.

Shopping—malls, major department stores, low prices, etc.

Sightseeing—architecture, museums, monuments, attractions, parks, historical sites, local tours, etc.

Recreation—sports and activities either as spectator or participant

Professional opportunities—visiting local clients, negotiations, business deals, selling, making contacts, etc.

Accommodation facilities

Capacity—the number of rooms available and whether more than a single hotel is required

Cost—the cost of suitable accommodation at the site

Service—the perception of the standards of service

Security—the extent to which the hotels provide a safe and secure environment

Availability—are the facilities available?

FIGURE 4.1. Convention Site Selection Factors

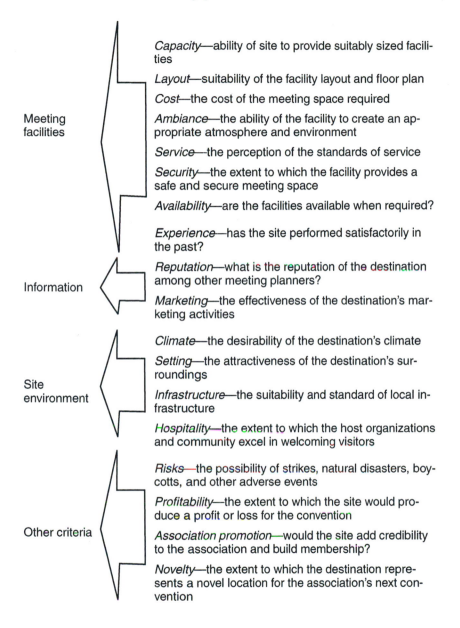

Meeting facilities

Capacity—ability of site to provide suitably sized facilities

Layout—suitability of the facility layout and floor plan

Cost—the cost of the meeting space required

Ambiance—the ability of the facility to create an appropriate atmosphere and environment

Service—the perception of the standards of service

Security—the extent to which the facility provides a safe and secure meeting space

Availability—are the facilities available when required?

Information

Experience—has the site performed satisfactorily in the past?

Reputation—what is the reputation of the destination among other meeting planners?

Marketing—the effectiveness of the destination's marketing activities

Site environment

Climate—the desirability of the destination's climate

Setting—the attractiveness of the destination's surroundings

Infrastructure—the suitability and standard of local infrastructure

Hospitality—the extent to which the host organizations and community excel in welcoming visitors

Other criteria

Risks—the possibility of strikes, natural disasters, boycotts, and other adverse events

Profitability—the extent to which the site would produce a profit or loss for the convention

Association promotion—would the site add credibility to the association and build membership?

Novelty—the extent to which the destination represents a novel location for the association's next convention

Source: Crouch and Ritchie, 1998.

assume that the convention alone is enough to attract delegates. This is the exception, not the rule. Tourist appeal is also a "central consideration for meeting planners" (Judd, 1995, p. 179).

Association Variables

Fortin, Ritchie, and Arsenault (1976) empirically assessed the relationship between the characteristics of an association and the site selection process. The results of their analysis suggested that there was indeed a relationship between the importance of site selection factors and the structure of influence for associations having different characteristics. Specifically, the influence of associations' CEOs and board members versus the meeting planners, and the power bases of committee members are critical in this context (Clark, Evans, and Knutson, 1997; Clark and McCleary, 1995; Clark, Price, and Murrmann, 1996). In addition, the scope of the association—regional, national, or international—may predetermine the range of convention locations available to the organizers, as noted by Oppermann and Chon (1997).

A conceptual model of the association site selection process (Figure 4.2) consisting of five steps was proposed by Crouch and Ritchie (1998). In Step 1, the *convention preplanning* phase, potential convention dates and budgets are established and other preliminary work is undertaken. Various antecedents shape considerations in this phase. For example, new members serving on the association's executive board may introduce different views to the process. Past experience, particularly the outcome of the association's most recent convention, is also likely to weigh heavily. Policies, for example, regarding the geographical rotation of the convention site are common. Anticipated environmental conditions leading up to and at the time of the convention could also be important. Either implicitly or explicitly, numerous site selection factors may influence this preplanning step which, in turn, could determine the relative importance of each factor when the final site decision is made. At this early stage, competing sites, too, may have already begun to exert some influence on the process by contacting the association before any shortlist of sites is prepared.

The preplanning step will also assign responsibilities either to an individual or to a committee for the second step in the process, the *analysis and recommendation* of potential sites. The focus in this

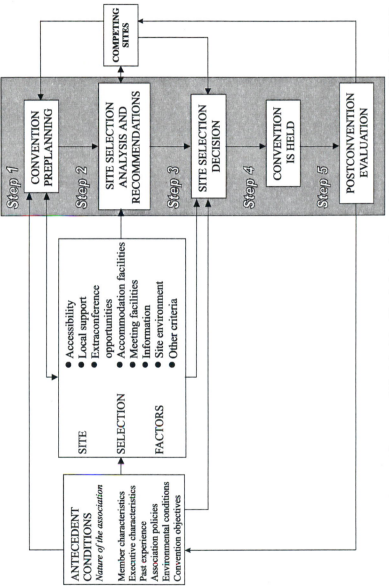

FIGURE 4.2. A General Conceptual Model of the Site Selection Process (*Source:* Crouch and Ritchie, 1998).

phase is on gathering detailed information from a number of possible sites that meet the minimum requirements, mainly through an external search combined with one or more site visits. For major conventions, a delegation from shortlisted destinations might be invited to present to the association a bid for the business. Final recommendations will be made based on the analysis and discussion of all the available information.

In view of the meeting planner's or selection committee's recommendations, the final *site selection decision* (Step 3) is then usually made by the association's executives or board of directors. Board members may weigh site selection factors differently and it is also common that they are continually lobbied by competing destinations. Antecedent conditions are also likely to shape this phase. For example, an important consideration will be the specific objectives of the convention in terms of attracting attendees and making a profit (or minimizing any loss).

Finally, the *convention is held* (Step 4), and a *postconvention evaluation* (Step 5) is undertaken which enters the site selection process as an antecedent condition for the next convention. The evaluation may also govern the potential set of competing sites for future conventions.

CONVENTION MARKETING ORGANIZATIONS

Convention destination marketing occurs at both local and national levels (Rogers, 1998). Convention and visitors bureaus represent the most prominent form of convention destination marketing organization (Morrison, Bruen, and Anderson, 1998). Their primary purpose is to "solicit and service conventions and other related group business and to engage in visitor promotions which generate overnight stays for a destination, thereby enhancing and developing the economic fabric of the community" (Gartrell, 1994, p. 21). CVBs may represent a specific city, a greater metropolitan area, a number of cities, or a regional destination. In Europe and Asia, convention bureaus representing an entire nation, supporting the efforts of individual industry players, are not uncommon (e.g., German Convention Bureau; Japan Convention Bureau).

The organizational structure of CVBs varies with the character of the destination, the quality of its product, and funding levels (Gartrell, 1994). Regardless of their geographic coverage, CVBs can be either public or private, nonprofit or for-profit organizations (Morrison, Bruen, and Anderson, 1998). Public bureaus are an integral part of the local authority structure and have a mandate to represent all suppliers in a particular geographical area. In contrast, private bureaus are membership based. According to the IACVB (1998), the majority of CVBs are independent, not-for-profit organizations. The activities of CVBs are funded by both public and private sources. The IACVB's 1998 Financial Survey revealed that public sources accounted for 82 percent of convention bureau funding, compared to 18 percent of funds being derived from private sources. The largest portion of funds was derived from hotel occupancy/transient taxes, or "room taxes" (76 percent), a public source of funding. It is important to note that room taxes as a CVB funding source are generally found in North America, especially the United States. Public funding is also derived through state matching funds and grants, and general city, county, and state taxes (Gartrell, 1994). Membership investments represent another important source of CVB funding. They are available only to private CVBs, since, as outlined above, public CVBs do not have members. Sponsorship, joint commercial activities with members, and, in some cases, commissions charged to venue members on business placed represent additional sources of funding (Rogers, 1998).

Weber (2001b) noted that despite their key role in convention destination marketing, very few academic studies have focused on CVBs, mainly in North America. Topics covered by these studies include CVBs' characteristics and their executives; roles and strategies in destination planning and product development; crisis management of CVBs; research needs; and research and Internet utilization (Fesenmaier, Pena, and O'Leary, 1992; Getz, Anderson, and Sheehan, 1998; Masberg, 1999; Morrison, Bruen, and Anderson, 1998; O'Halloran, 1992; Sims, 1990; Young and Montgomery, 1998; Yuan et al., 1999). Even fewer studies have focused on a comparison of CVBs from the various world regions (Mutschlechner, 1997; Palmer and Bejou, 1995).

Although CVBs are the principal organizations spearheading convention destination marketing activities, other city, regional, or national organizations or departments also frequently play an important role. National tourism organizations (NTOs) seek to promote the interests of the nation as a convention destination. They may take different forms in different countries—in some, they are the convention bureaus; in others, they are fully public sector organizations funded and administered by the central government structure (Rogers, 1998). State or provincial offices also play a role along with economic development agencies, major events corporations, local governments, chambers of commerce, hotel associations, and city-based retail associations.

The range of organizations and private-sector enterprises involved in this marketing effort calls for an integrated and coordinated approach. Unfortunately, this does not always occur, because the interests of each player do not necessarily converge. The reality is that political considerations often play an important role in the strategies and tactics adopted by the various convention destination marketing organizations.

CONVENTION DESTINATION MARKETING— REGIONAL INSIGHTS

Las Vegas Convention and Visitor Authority (LVCVA)

The LVCVA was created in 1955 by Nevada legislature. It is a public entity and derives its funding primarily from room taxes paid by visitors. Its operating budget, US$69 million in 2000, is the largest of any destination marketing organization in the United States, and in fact exceeds that of many NTOs. LVCVA has a thirteen-member board of directors, with representatives from both public and private sectors that oversee all its activities, while the executive staff is in charge of its daily operations. The authority also operates the Las Vegas Convention Center.

The meeting and convention market became increasingly important to Las Vegas in recent years for many reasons. Not only is it regarded by LVCVA as one of the segments with the greatest growth opportunities for new and repeat visitation, but it is also seen as critical in maintaining its traditional occupancy levels in the 90 percent range (LVCVA, 2000). The latter is a challenge in view of the tremendous growth in room supply during the 1990s, from about 74,000 rooms in 1990 to more than 120,000 in 2000. The development of new and increased air services to Las Vegas is also closely tied to this segment in view of its higher yield passenger potential for airlines. That is especially the case since the number of flights and/or seat capacity to Las Vegas, traditionally a low-yield market attracting low-cost, low-margin airfare travelers, was significantly reduced in late 1997, with several major U.S. airlines shifting their attention to high-yield markets to improve profitability (Berns, 1998). Yet that was before the city's latest transformation into a more upscale resort destination in 1998, which saw LVCVA setting out to reposition the city as the "world's leading entertainment resort destination"—getting away from its prior position as a "gaming destination with entertainment."

In that year, the first in a series of upscale megaresort openings occurred. These megaresorts are attractions in themselves and, together with the opening of exclusive shopping malls, upscale dining establishments, spa and golf facilities, and the staging of high-class entertainment, they contributed to the greater attractiveness of Las Vegas as a convention destination. As discussed previously, this is an important site selection consideration, especially for the association market. The city boasts two of the largest convention center facilities in the United States, the publicly owned Las Vegas Convention Center and the privately owned Sands Expo Center. Convention space totaled 6.1 million square feet in 1999, and in 2000, Las Vegas hosted 3,800 conventions and 3.8 million delegates, which generated US$4 billion in nongaming revenue (LVCVA, 2000). The focus of LVCVA's current marketing plan is the promotion of the expansion to the Las Vegas Convention Center that, when completed in December 2001, made it the largest convention facility in the country.

Melbourne Convention and Visitors Bureau

The Melbourne Convention and Visitors Bureau (MCVB) with an annual MICE marketing budget of AU$2.7 million and permanent staff of nine in the MICE sector, is one of the largest destination marketing organizations in Australia. It is a private, not-for-profit, membership-based, destination marketing organization. MCVB has taken a leadership role in product development, an aspect found to be neglected by CVBs in Canada, according to Getz, Anderson, and Sheehan (1998). MCVB owns and until 2000 operated the Asia-

Pacific Incentives and Meetings Expo (AIME), the largest MICE tradeshow in the Asia-Pacific region. It complements European Incentive and Business Travel and Meetings (EIBTM) Exhibition in Europe and Incentive Travel & Meetings Executive (IT&ME) Show in North America. In 2001, AIME attracted 2,400 delegates and around 300 buyers who were able to inspect products of more than 600 exhibitors from sixty-two destinations. The trade show is staged at the Melbourne Exhibition and Convention Centre every February since 1993. The event is unique in that it is owned by the MCVB. CVBs often facilitate direct sales opportunities between buyers and sellers in the form of one-day trade shows that focus on their specific city. However, MCVB operated the trade show for the entire Asia-Pacific region, offering a unique opportunity for Australian and overseas exhibitors alike to advance their position in the Asia-Pacific market. However, the fact that the event was organized and operated by MCVB lead to concerns of a potential conflict of interest. Therefore, in 1999, MCVB decided to license the organization and staging of AIME to a commercial operator. Reed International, an experienced international trade show organizer, began organizing and operating the event in 2001. It is now Reed International rather than MCVB who makes the final decision on exhibitors. Nevertheless, Melbourne will continue to derive significant economic benefits from the event. According to the AIME 2000 Economic Impact Survey, visitors attending the exhibition had the potential to book 480 business events within five years, attracting over 168,000 delegates and expenditure in excess of AU$141 million within Australia. The survey also found MICE events would boost Victoria's economy by AU$39 million over the same period (MCMB, 2000).

The Singapore Tourist Board

The Singapore Tourist Board (STB) through its Singapore Exhibition and Convention Bureau (SECB) division is responsible for the marketing of Singapore as a MICE destination. One of only few destination marketing organizations that acts both as a national tourism organization (NTO) and a convention and visitors bureau (CVB), it was founded in 1974 and has a staff of twenty-four. Testimonies to SECB's success are the numerous awards received (Singapore Tourism Board, 1999a) and the fact that Singapore is still, after sixteen years, the top convention city in Asia (Chew, 1999). The latter is of course also due to the city's advanced MICE infrastructure, an educated workforce, and an efficient administration (Singapore Trade Development Board, 1999).

The Asian financial crisis in late 1997 and the subsequent economic downturn in the region presented several problems for Singapore. Several studies found that Singapore is perceived as an expensive convention destination (Lew and Chang, 1999; Go and Govers, 1999). The city has in the past targeted its MICE industry infrastructure to the high end of the international market, resulting in difficulties to service this market in times of economic downturn, given the advantage of competitive destinations, both in Asia and other parts of the world. MacLaurin and Leong (2000a) further note that selective price reduction is not a simple solution. The fact that the city's major convention center complex, Singapore International Convention and Exhibition Centre (SICEC), is privately rather than government owned, therefore pursuing a profit orientation, also impacts any recovery measures. Yet the STB and SECB were quick to confront the crisis by implementing several strategies to preempt a rapid decline in numbers of both conventions and attendees.

In January 1998, the STB, together with the city's industry suppliers, launched the GlobalMeet program. The three-year initiative offered numerous incentives by participating members to meeting organizers, designed to increase awareness as well as reinforce and elevate the position of Singapore as the MICE destination of choice in the upcoming decade (Hurrell, 1999). Incentives included discounts, free services, and site inspections for meeting planners to confirm events, regardless of when events are held (Wee, 1999). In an attempt to encourage convention delegates to extend their stay, to bring an accompanying person, and to visit the city again within a year, the SECB initiated the "Do the Double" and "Come Visit Us Again" campaigns in August 1999 (Singapore Tourism Board, 1999b). Convention delegates who stayed in the city for at least three days and decided to extend their stay by at least two days in participating hotels were offered one of the days free of charge under the "Do the Double" promotion. Discounts worth $100 at participating food and beverage outlets, pubs, discos, and spas were also part of the program. A free night for every three nights spent in the same hotel during a repeat visit within nine months was the central feature of the

"Come Visit Us Again" campaign. This marketing approach, with its focus on price strategies, is somewhat risky due to unknown long-term effects on the city's image. However, it appears that the combination of advanced MICE marketing infrastructure, aggressive marketing strategies, and the slow recovery of economies throughout Asia have not only averted major declines in numbers of convention and delegates in Singapore, but may stimulate short- to medium-term demand (MacLaurin and Leong, 2000a).

Edinburgh Convention Bureau

The Edinburgh Convention Bureau (ECB), established in 1991, is the business tourism division of the Edinburgh and Lothians Tourist Board. With an annual marketing budget of £170,000 and four full-time staff members, it is recognized as one of the best CVBs in the country, being a runner-up in the Meetings and Incentive Travel Awards in 2001. One of the key goals of the ECB, outlined in its 1997-2001 business plan, was the objective to raise Edinburgh's position in the ICCA rankings to within the top five by 2001. To that end and in anticipation of future growth, ECB became a member of the world's first global CVB alliance—the BestCities.net alliance. The alliance, launched in February 2000, comprises, in addition to Edinburgh, of the CVBs of Boston, Massachusetts; Copenhagen, Denmark; Vancouver, Canada; and Melbourne, Australia. These cities share certain common characteristics that facilitated the formation of the alliance. They are all of similar size in terms of inhabitants, infrastructure, and meeting facilities. They are all walking cities with ease of accessibility. In terms of target marketing, all these cities focus their efforts on similar industries, namely medical, information technology, and communication industries. Furthermore, partners were selected on the basis of their commitment to improving CVB client service levels through innovation, the adoption of technology in the process, and their global perspective. The alliance has its own client service charter and leading edge operational standards known as "BestPractices." Its objective is the delivery of the world's best client service experience for the meetings industry. The alliance will guarantee to the international meeting planner excellence and consistency in the standard of service offered by each partner CVB. The bureaus, on the other hand, are able to obtain more accurate and in-depth information on particular business than is available in the various existing databases (e.g., computerized information network [CINET]). This information, shared by partner bureaus, will allow them to prepare much more targeted bids. In the future, it is envisaged to engage in multidestination bidding whereby an association's business is booked for several years into the cities of the alliance (see <http://www.bestcities. net>).

CONCLUSION

Continued economic development, world trade, and globalization will stimulate continued growth in convention tourism, spurring even greater competition among convention destinations. Cities now have to market themselves more aggressively than ever before to attract major conventions and other events. In this environment, the practice of relationship marketing and an improved cross-cultural understanding will take on critical roles.

Destinations that are consistently able to meet or exceed the expectations of their convention customers enjoy a strong reputation and positive word of mouth, which leads to repeat business and new customers that can become an important source of referral business. Many associations rotate the location of conventions to provide a variety of meeting environments. Nevertheless, convention destinations that enjoy a strong relationship with association executives and meeting planners can expect continuity and stability in their convention customers. The costs of serving the needs of repeat customers are also lower (Heskett et al., 1994), increasing the attractiveness of maintaining strong relationships. Of course, some meeting planners serve the needs of several associations; destinations that are able to develop strong relationships with these planners enjoy a competitive advantage.

The global competition among convention sites will require convention marketers to increase their sensitivity to cultural and social issues, particularly in the case of international conventions spanning diverse cultural, religious, and social groups. Convention destinations must develop cross-cultural skills in their efforts to position themselves as a major host site for international conventions.

Finally, it has been argued that the increased competition may be somewhat misguided and that the lengths taken and inducements offered to associations are sometimes so great as to bring into question the real benefits of hosting a major convention (McGee, 1993). Nevertheless, the costs and stakes of competition have never been higher.

Chapter 5

Human Resource Issues for the Convention Industry

Donald J. MacLaurin

INTRODUCTION

On any given day there are more persons attending meetings and conventions than there are in all the college and university classrooms combined.

Roy Evans, the recently retired CEO of the Professional Convention Management Association (PCMA), reiterated this famous quote on several occasions throughout his forty-year career in the meetings and convention industry. There are currently six adults in "commercial" learning environments for everyone in a traditional college or university. The "student" (who is often a convention delegate) is expecting more from the traditional delivery system and has an ever-expanding number of alternatives for lifelong learning (Association for Convention Operations Management, 1999).

The size, scope, and labor intensity of the global meetings and convention industry dictate the paramount importance of effective human resource policies and practices. The industry has grown rapidly in recent decades, supported by tremendous infrastructure and technology advancements, yet the improvements in education and professional development programs were, if evident at all, only sporadic and ad hoc. Until recently, it was mainly professional associations such as ICCA, PCMA, and IAPCO that offered education programs relevant to the industry. In the past decade, however, significant efforts have been made to rectify this situation. In view of increased globalization, attempts are also being made to create links in education programs worldwide.

The purpose of this chapter is to orient the reader to key macro business and MICE industry trends that are shaping the parameters of human resource management. The chapter will first briefly highlight employment opportunities and skill requirements before discussing the various industry trends and issues that are likely to impact the industry's human resources practices in the coming years. Finally, it will offer an in-depth review of the education and training programs offered by both industry associations and universities in Europe, North America, and the Asia-Pacific region.

EMPLOYMENT OPPORTUNITIES AND SKILL REQUIREMENTS

Despite the rapid development of the convention industry in past decades in terms of infrastructure, education and training programs have not been focused in the same systematic manner. A characteristic of employment in the MICE industry is the fact that traditionally no vocational training as such has been available and management positions are generally taken up by people from related industries (Schreiber and Beckmann, 1999). Furthermore, education and training programs offered by both national and international industry associations, and more recently by universities, have generally been of a sporadic nature. However, a more systematic approach is evolving in addition to emerging signs of cooperation between the various entities. Key programs available to MICE industry employees are detailed later in this chapter.

The MICE sector offers a wide range of employment opportunities, primarily with organizers of meetings and conventions (e.g., corporations, associations), venue operators (e.g., convention centers, convention hotels), destination marketing organizations (e.g., CVBs, NTOs), supporting service providers (e.g., technical support firms), and independent PCOs. As the convention industry is essentially a service industry, with people taking a central role, it follows that interpersonal skills are critical for those working in the MICE sector. Organizational, negotiation and communication skills, creativity, flexibility, and a team player mentality are further important requirements (McCabe et al., 2000; Montgomery and Rutherford, 1994;

Rogers, 1998), in addition to job specific competencies. To ensure that the relevant skills are imparted to new and existing industry employees, it is essential to design education and training courses with an understanding of trends and resulting challenges that face the MICE industry.

INDUSTRY TRENDS AND ISSUES

Macro and micro trends in the overall business community will drive the future of the MICE industry. This, in turn, will influence future human resource management practices within the MICE sector. Organizations and associations in the MICE industry are increasingly conducting "environmental scanning" and other forecasting techniques to ascertain where the industry will be headed in the future (e.g., PCMA, IACVB, Center for Exhibition Industry Research [CEIR], ICCA—see Chapter 12). Yet with the MICE industry being firmly embedded in the tourism and hospitality industry, trends in this broader context are also likely to affect the MICE industry.

The International Hotel and Restaurant Association (IHRA) published a report on the global hospitality industry in 2000. It noted that the focus on adding value is reshaping the management skills that have so long prevailed in the global hospitality industry. Technology, in particular, will alter the nature of the business, the skills needed to compete, the learning process, and the nature of work and the worker. A new type of manager is required in view of these changes (Aidi, 2000). A number of management trends and challenges facing the hospitality workplace of the future are outlined in the report, including the following:

- A growing shortage of qualified labor, particularly of knowledgeable workers, and the demand for higher technology skill levels among all employees
- A flattening of hierarchies, with managers developing a "first among equals" style, and leadership based on competence not seniority
- The application of technology to all aspects of human resources management, including recruiting, training, record-keeping, compensation, and performance evaluation

- A move from a heavily skills-based curriculum and hospitality education toward a general management emphasis
- An emphasis on thinking skills, decision-making capabilities and creativity, and on how hotel companies use technology to compete

Clearly, management, talent, and education are critical to the survival of the industry. It is therefore essential to address the changes in human resource practices, especially at a time when the hospitality industry is facing stiff global competition for the best of the dot-com generation workers from other sectors that offer attractive conditions and pay (Aidi, 2000).

A number of significant issues are currently impacting human resource policies and practices in the MICE industry in particular. These issues form some of the major change catalysts in human resource management within the industry. Proactive MICE organizations are developing ongoing strategic policies and practices to incorporate potential opportunities offered by ever-changing global trends. Reactive MICE organizations will be placed in a perilous situation in which they will have to "follow the leader," a potentially lethal business strategy in today's highly competitive environment.

Australia's national strategy for the MICE industry highlights several key priorities in human resource development (Commonwealth Department of Tourism, 1995) and despite being identified for a particular country, they appear to be of universal relevance. They are

- career paths and opportunities designed to develop the expertise of personnel and encourage their retention in the industry;
- industry-specific education so that the industry is able to meet the demand for qualified and trained professionals; and
- accreditation and an established code of ethics to ensure that the industry conforms to professional standards.

Addressing these issues becomes critical in an environment of increased competition among nations with highly developed infrastructure where the quality of staff is likely to offer a competitive advantage.

Staff Recruitment and Retention

McCabe et al. (2000) assert that the MICE industry, as the blue-chip end of the tourism industry, is regarded as an attractive employment area for those entering the workforce for the first time and those who seek a career change. Yet attracting and retaining the right caliber of employees still represents a key challenge to the MICE industry. Two main reasons account for this situation. First, there is the lack of status of professions in the industry (Rogers, 1998). Comments by Mr. Tan, former president of the Singapore Association of Convention and Exhibition Organizers and Suppliers, support this view. He noted that there is a perceived lack of public awareness of career opportunities in the MICE industry, fostered partly by universities and colleges that have not catered to the needs of the MICE industry by offering professional development courses to students. It is his belief that more must be done to increase the profile of the industry among potential employees (Twite, 1997). Second, the problem of a mobile workforce and high staff turnover, prevalent in the tourism and hospitality industry in general, is also apparent in and impacting the MICE industry. Results of a recent study indicated relatively high mobility rates and turnover in the convention service sector in Australia (McCabe and Weeks, 1999). In particular, the study found that the average length of time spent in a job was two to three years with many staff leaving to progress to alternative positions in the industry. This, of course, means that an organization investing in the training of its employees will not necessarily be able to reap the rewards if employees move on within a relatively short time period.

Career Progression

Rogers (1998) stresses the need to develop career structures to ensure that experience and expertise are retained within the MICE industry. Martin Kinna, former dean of Meeting Professionals International's (MPI) Certificate in Meetings Management program (CMM), noted that in addition to clear career progression opportunities, an attractive reward system must be in place to prevent employees from leaving (Twite, 1997). Rewards—both monetary and nonmonetary—are key to staff retention, as is the case in other industries. However, retaining PCOs in particular is usually more difficult since they can easily set up their own businesses once they have acquired the essential skills.

According to Rosvi Gaetos, the former Secretary General of the Asian Association of Convention and Visitors Bureaus (AACVB), national tourist organizations (NTOs) and convention and visitors bureaus (CVBs) are the best places to train new entrants into the industry, with both entities providing a broad insight into the industry. It is Gaetos's belief that a broad-based overview is essential for a successful career in the MICE industry. Following several years of employment with an NTO or CVB, an employee will have a high value and is likely to be approached by DMCs (destination management companies), convention centers, or hotels. Both NTOs and CVBs are also, usually, strong supporters and participants in MICE education programs for their employees.

Compensation in the MICE Industry

Jobs in the tourism and hospitality industry typically attract relatively low wages and salaries, and the MICE sector is not an exception. Apart from indications of wages and salaries from specific jobs advertised in the various media, only two industry associations, both U.S. based, carry out salary/compensation surveys on a continuing basis. The Professional Convention Management Association (PCMA) conducts an annual salary and compensation study among its 5,000 members. Results are published in Convene, the association's monthly publication. For its ninth annual study, covering the year 1999, PCMA surveyed individuals at more than 200 of its association members, the vast majority of which are located in the United States (PCMA, 2000a). The study found that the mean salary of meeting managers climbed dramatically from US$43,993 in 1998 to US$49,073 in 1999, reflecting associations' increased emphasis on education, the amount of nondues revenue generated by meetings and exhibitions, and the generally tight labor market. The increase in salary among meeting directors was more modest, up from US$61,562 in 1998 to US$62,448 in 1999. Meeting managers and meeting directors accounted for more than 75 percent of survey respondents. CEOs of associations earned an average salary of US$112,333, with 44 percent of the CEOs earning more than US$125,000. The mean salary for association vice presidents was US$92,333 (PCMA, 2000a).

Insights into the compensation of association executives are also provided by the American Society of Association Executives (ASAE). Its 1999 Blue Chip Association Executive Compensation and Benefits Study surveyed more than 280 associations regarding the salary and benefits provided to the highest paid executives in the organization. Trade associations reported an average total compensation of about US$260,000 per annum for CEOs, while individual membership organizations reported an average compensation package of about US$220,000 per annum. Almost a quarter of the survey respondents paid their CEO more than US$300,000 per annum. After the CEO, the highest salaries were paid to deputy chief executives, directors of environmental affairs, subsidiary heads, chief staff attorneys, and Washington, DC, office heads (ASAE, 1999).

Multiculturalism

Today's global workforce and customer base in the MICE industry is culturally diverse and striving to protect their cultural identity. The growth of global business and commerce has resulted in more international MICE attendees. Free-trade agreements and multinational corporations have furthered the world's move toward globalization. High-speed telecommunications and the Internet have encouraged the growth of commerce throughout the world. Global airline alliances make it possible for business travelers to fly from their home office to any other part of the world in twenty-four hours or less. Liberal immigration policies in many countries have encouraged the inflows of new cultures.

Line-level employees in the hospitality and tourism industry are often from a broad ethnic and cultural spectrum. This results in an instant advantage when dealing with the increasingly multicultural MICE client base. Conejo (2000) suggested four steps that an organization can follow to become truly multicultural.

> Step 1: *Identify the diversity*—Managers can start by collecting data about their workforce. This will identify cultural groups within the workforce.
>
> Step 2: *Discover the norms*—Gather detailed information on different cultures. This can be done through good reference materials at libraries or through a diversity or cultural change consultant. Employees are another good source.

    Step 3: *Discover the differences*—Different cultures gather and process information differently in a way that is unique to that culture. Sometimes logic and reason evade other cultures when they witness the actions of others. For example, there is no guilt in some Eastern cultures. This causes both a cooperation and communications barrier.

    Step 4: *Develop a plan of action*—Most businesses and even business schools are behind the times when it comes to dealing with the cultural base in the workplace. Yet the globalized economy makes an understanding of issues of gender, race, culture, norms, values, information gathering and processing, comfort zones, etc. critical.

The membership of the American Society of Association Executives (ASAE) is to a great extent made up of meeting planners and managers. The association developed a Diversity Leadership Program (DELP) in 2000. The program is designed to assist in the advance in the profession of individuals from underrepresented segments of the association community. DELP upholds the philosophies advocated in ASAE's diversity statement, which reads:

> in principle and in practice, ASAE values and seeks diverse and inclusive participation within the field of association management. ASAE will promote involvement and expand access to leadership opportunity regardless of race, ethnicity, gender, religion, age, sexual orientation, nationality, disability, appearance, geographic location or professional level. The association will provide leadership and commit time and resources to accomplish this objective while serving as a model to other associations engaged in such endeavors. (Peske, 2000a, p. 11)

Impact of Technology on Human Resource Practices in the MICE Industry

Perhaps no single issue is more dominant to current and future human resource practices in the MICE industry than the impact and uses of technology. The effect of the Internet in the past five years has been significant on all facets of business operations. Yet the expanded use of the Internet has thus far failed to slow conference attendance.

Despite the fact that online registration has become a common practice, the use of more sophisticated electronic technologies, such as videoconferencing, Webcasting and virtual trade shows, is at present still in its infancy, according to PCMA's (2000a) meetings market survey. Mistilis and Dwyer (1999) point to three main areas of concern in the adoption of information technology (IT) in the MICE industry. They note that conference organizers, in particular, middle-aged ones who are likely to occupy senior leadership roles, are often not able to adopt IT and suggest a lack of previous experience as a reason. Furthermore, the combination of the fast pace of development in IT and the time lag between budgeting and an event often prevents the acquisition of appropriate technology in a timely manner. Finally, software to coordinate the supply-side operators of the organizers had not been developed at that time. These issues must be addressed to capitalize on the potential contributions of IT to the industry.

Buhalis (1998) points to the need for research on how to best educate and train managers to develop both vision and leadership in the use of IT to gain a competitive advantage. The challenge for industry managers is to closely monitor the evolution of the various technologies and their impact on the convention market. This process will also allow MICE industry associations to better guide their members through these changes.

Fox (2000) surveyed 513 readers of the MICE industry online newsletter *EventWeb* to ascertain their interest in learning more about various MICE industry technologies and their applications. His findings have important implications for the industry's human resource development programs. The top five topics respondents were most interested in relating to the Internet were, in descending order, Internet marketing, e-mail marketing, Web-based registration, online market and competitive research, and creating Web-based revenue opportunities. In terms of technology topics in general, respondents were most interested in gaining greater insights into on-site registration; hi-tech hotels, conference centers, and convention centers; and Webcasting/videoconferencing. These topics are likely to be focused on in further training and development programs and will soon become important skill requirements for meeting professionals.

Adult Education

There is a growing realization that members of the MICE industry are more involved in the field of adult education than many had previously realized. The meetings and convention segment is primarily a purveyor of adult education and development. Convention attendees today are more geographically, culturally, and idiosyncratically diverse than in the past. These attendees have access to alternative forms of media that compete with the convention to provide them with educational and networking services. Managers in the meetings and convention industry will increasingly need to understand the fundamentals of adult education and learning to ensure an effective ROI to their customers (PCMA, 2000a).

PCMA is one of the first industry associations in the world to operate its own educational and learning facilities. It moved its headquarters from Birmingham, Alabama, to Chicago, Illinois, in 2000. Part of the inducement from the city of Chicago to lure the association was space allocation at McCormick Place convention center for the establishment of the new PCMA Learning Center. The new center occupies 4,000 square feet at McCormick Place, which is also the home for PCMA's new headquarters. The Learning Center will be used for training and executive development programs for PCMA members. Dallas-based Freeman Company, a trade show and exhibitions supplier company, made a US$500,000 contribution to the cost of opening the new PCMA Learning Center, with further MICE industry donations expected to follow (Member Digest, 2000).

EDUCATION AND TRAINING PROGRAMS FOR THE CONVENTION INDUSTRY

Education at all levels is critical to the growth of the MICE industry. The benefits of education are self-perpetuating. Businesses that are informed of increased performance levels attainable through effective conferences and meetings are more likely to invest in these activities. Education is equally important, if not more so, at a grassroots level. The demand for highly skilled employees is driven by the number of new MICE facilities being built throughout the world and the increased sophistication of the industry and its customers. Twite (1997) asserts that well-trained employees must be in place in all MICE facilities if the industry is to continue to grow and prosper. Supporting his argument are comments by Elizabeth Rich, former CEO of the Meetings Industry Association of Australia (MIAA), who stated that high-level skills and consequently high-level training are essential in the MICE industry. According to Rich, good industry professionals never stop training; they must continually train to stay abreast in a fast-changing industry.

Rogers (1998) noted that the conference industry and the education sector have been slow to develop appropriate education and training opportunities for the industry's current workforce and for potential new entrants. However, changes are taking place with both educational institutions and professional associations beginning to develop full-time, part-time, and short courses. The following sections provide information about education and training initiatives on the various continents. Not surprisingly, the pace of development in the area of education and training is reflective of the stage of development of the industry in the various regions.

Education Programs in North America— Industry Associations

North America is currently the global hub of MICE industry education and certification programs. MPI, PCMA, and IACVB are three of the largest and most powerful industry associations. Each has an educational foundation that is supported by generous financial endowments and operated at arm's length from the associations. They offer a number of industry education and certification programs, either in-house or in cooperation with each other, industry partners, or universities. Some of the key initiatives are outlined below. The following two programs have a primary focus on convention and visitors bureau operations, and destination marketing companies.

International Association of Convention and Visitors Bureaus (IACVB) Sales Academy

The education committee of the IACVB in cooperation with PCMA developed a two-day program, "Destination Selling," that addresses issues ranging from prospecting sales, qualifying leads, improving listening skills, and making initial contacts, to handling objections and follow-up. It is designed for CVB professionals with two years or less experience in destination sales, conventions, tourism, membership, services, and communications and is quickly becoming the standard for training destination marketers. IACVB unveiled a new two-day program in 2000 titled "Modern Communications Skills," which will operate simultaneously with the "Destination Selling" program. It imparts written communication skills for sales and marketing letters, and oral communication skills to be utilized during site visits and sales presentations (IACVB, 2000).

Executive Program in Destination Management

The Executive Program in Destination Management is designed and delivered by the World Tourism Management Center at the University of Calgary, Canada, and Indiana's Purdue University in the United States, and is approved by IACVB. It is targeted at senior executives and managers of destination marketing organizations (e.g., CVBs, chambers of commerce, government tourism departments) and their private sector partners in the tourism industry. The program consists of three interrelated core courses, namely "Strategic Issues in Destination Management," "Destination Marketing Planning," and "Destination Leadership." In addition to the completion of these core courses and a final exam, participants are required to complete two electives of their choice for a Certified Destination Management Executive (CDME) designation, or a total of five electives for the higher level designation of FCDME (Fellow). Awards are made jointly by the World Tourism Management Center at the University of Calgary, Purdue University, and IACVB. Participants complete the program over a two-year period on average and an ongoing recertification component is considered important to maintain current standing (University of Calgary, 2000).

The following two programs are primarily focused at MICE industry employees who serve on the supplier side of the industry, including but not limited to convention services managers (CSMs), catering managers (CMs), and auxiliary suppliers, such as audiovisual suppliers.

Learning Environment Specialist (LES)

The Learning Environment Specialist program began in 1994 as a partnership between Hyatt Hotels and PCMA. Hyatt bought the exclusive rights for the program for the first three years so that it became available to other industry organizations only in 1998. The LES program is a comprehensive and intensive learning experience devoted to a unique educational experience that encourages innovation, interaction, and practical applications. It consists of the following components:

- the evolution of adult learning and the meeting process;
- the power of the proper meeting environment; and
- business objectives, financial considerations, and best practices in event planning.

Attendees prepare several weeks in advance by taking a need assessment; they also take a final exam. Participants also submit a series of implementation reports over a two-month period after the exam. Their supervisor must approve the follow-up reports before they can graduate from the program <http://www.pcma.org/education>.

The Association for Convention Operations Management (ACOM) offered participants of their 2000 annual convention the opportunity to undertake the LES program while attending the convention. This was the first time that LES was offered to an industrywide audience and in conjunction with a regular convention (ACOM, 1999). PCMA is currently experimenting with an online version of LES.

Certified Association Sales Executive (CASE) Program

In 2000, Marriott International developed, together with PCMA, an online course, tailored specifically to the hotel chain's needs, the Certified Association Sales Executive (CASE) program. Similar to the initial LES program arrangements, Marriott has exclusive rights to the CASE program for eighteen months to allow for the training of about 120 sales managers before PCMA can adapt and sell the course to other hospitality service providers. The goal of the CASE program is to teach Marriott sales managers about associations and help them develop a more consultative approach to selling. The nine-week instructor-led course incorporates nine online training modules, three two-hour telephone conference calls, a two-day face-to-face course review and test, a follow-up two-day practicum, and a final implementation report. By structuring the course over a nine-week time frame rather than the traditional three- to five-day intensive training sessions, participants are able to schedule studies around work, family, and travel commitments. According to Chatfield-Taylor (2000), this program is a perfect illustration of the integration of online and in-person education with the potential to foster adult learning that meets corporate objectives. Furthermore, it offers significant cost advantages since, despite higher front-end costs, the online course is less expensive than offering a classroom-based program requiring participants to travel from all over the country.

Education Programs in North America—Universities

A significant number of institutions that offer programs tailored to the tourism and hospitality disciplines also include at least one MICE industry course within the existing tourism/hospitality curriculum. A growing number of institutions also offer multiple courses related to the MICE discipline. The Council of Hotel, Restaurant, and Tourism Educators International (CHRIE) (2001) membership directory lists more than 150 U.S. universities that offer hospitality and tourism degree programs. The University of Nevada, Las Vegas (UNLV), is a leader in MICE education, not only at the national but also at the international level. Its tourism and convention department offers as a concentration in the bachelor of hotel administration degree area sixteen courses that focus on various aspects of the MICE industry. Courses taught include meeting planning, destination marketing, incentive travel, association management, convention facility management, and trade show operations. An internship in the industry is also part of the program. In 1999, UNLV introduced a two-year executive master's program in the area, delivered predominantly via the Internet. For more details on both the undergraduate and graduate programs, refer to <http://www.unlv.edu/Tourism>.

The Appalachian State University, George Washington University, Georgia State University, Northeastern State University, the University of Houston, the University of New Orleans and the University of Central Florida all offer several MICE specific courses and have close links with and are supported by the industry. The University of Central Florida, Orlando, for example, recruited for a professorship in MICE in 1999 that was funded through a generous private sector donation from the Central Florida Hotel and Motel Association. Its program also recently received additional pledges of $10 million from a local hotel owner and $5 million from the Orlando Convention and Visitors Bureau. These multimillion-dollar private-sector pledges are all eligible for matching state government funding, effectively doubling the donor's financial commitments to professional MICE education (The University of Central Florida, 1999).

Education Programs in Europe—Industry Associations

The most respected education courses available to industry professionals in Europe are offered by international industry associations that are headquartered in Europe (ICCA, IAPCO), by regional associations (EFCT), and by U.S. industry associations that adapted their program to the particulars of the region (MPI).

ICCA—International Meetings Academy
(IMA) and ICCRM

ICCA offers several education and training programs under the umbrella of the International Meetings Academy, namely the Young Executive Program, Middle Management Program, and the New Executive Program (see Rogers, 1998, p. 168, for a more detailed description of these programs). In addition, it organizes the International Congress and Convention Researchers Meeting (ICCRM), a training program in research and marketing with the emphasis on international events. Initiated in 1995, it is aimed at people who conduct marketing research for national government organizations, convention and visitors bureaus, congress and convention centers, travel agents, hotels, tourism attractions, professional conference organizers or meeting planners, consulting organizations, private businesses, and college and university researchers. ICCRM enables delegates to interact by means of a variety of informal sessions, including lectures, case studies, workshops, and roundtables. Hands-on Internet workshops are held and delegates learn the best techniques for accessing and selecting vital information. They can attend ICCA DATA workshops, meet key clients face to face, and exchange new business leads with other delegates <http://www. icca.nl>.

Annual IAPCO Seminar on Professional
Congress Organization

The annual IAPCO Seminar on Professional Congress Organization (Wolfsberg Seminar) was for a long time the only further education program of significance for meeting organizers in Europe. First held in 1975, the annual seminar runs for a week in Switzerland each January and focuses on the training of executives in conference organization and international conference destination promotion in particular. Sessions in the 2002 program concentrated on relationships and future trends of the industry players, characteristics of market segments, marketing issues, cooperation with suppliers, contracts, finance, communication, technology, and sponsorships.

EFCT Annual Summer School

The Annual Summer School program was established by the European Federation of Conference Towns in 1987. It is held each year in a different European country and typically lasts three to four days. The overall intention is to demonstrate the need for and the increasing importance of a coherent marketing strategy in addition to imparting skills for better promotion of a destination, venue, or event. The program covers a wide range of topics, including destination management, the use of the Internet, and successful bidding and site inspections. It is primarily aimed at the industry's newly appointed managers, market researchers, midlevel executives, and meeting planners, in contrast to EFCT's Annual Educational Forum, which is targeted to senior industry professionals.

Certificate in Meeting Management (CMM)—MPI

The Certificate in Meetings Management was created by MPI in partnership with the Institut de Management Hôtelier in Paris, a European extension of the Cornell University School of Hotel Administration, in 1995. It was the first university-certified qualification for meeting professionals in Europe, designed for senior-level meeting professionals, at both the supply and demand side of the industry. Acceptance into the program is based on applicants' background in terms of education, experience, industry activity, employment history, responsibility, and references, all of which are subject to a scoring system and the assessment of industry evaluators. The program itself consists of three parts: participation in an MPI online learning group and prereadings, followed by an intensive weeklong residency program, and the completion of a postresidency business project. In view of its initial success, MPI decided in 1998 to adapt the CMM program for meeting professionals worldwide. Consequently, the program is now also run in the United States and Canada as part of the Global CMM program.

Numerous courses also are offered by the various national industry associations. Rogers (1998) outlines some of those offered in the United Kingdom, while Beckmann and Krabbe (1999) and Schwaegermann (1999) detail those available in Germany.

Education Programs in Europe—Universities

Universities across Europe are offering tourism and hospitality courses, and some of them also offer MICE-specific subjects, for example, Leeds Metropolitan University in the United Kingdom and the Berufsakademie in Ravensburg, Germany. At present, no comprehensive listing of universities offering MICE-related subjects in Europe is available, although efforts are being made to gather this vital information for cooperation and further development purposes.

In 2000, the European Master's in Congress Management (EMCM) was introduced. The program is a joint initiative by the European Meetings Industry Liaison Group (EMILG), the Joint Conference and Interpretation Service of the European Commission, Association for Tourism and Leisure Education (ATLAS) (network of universities that teaches tourism and leisure courses), and four European universities (Sheffield Hallam University in the United Kingdom, Universita degli Studi di Bologna in Italy, the Universidad de Deusto, Bilbao, in Spain, and the Berufsakademie in Ravensburg, Germany). It is a two-year full-time course, incorporating both general management subjects and industry-specific subjects in addition to an industry-related research project in the form of a dissertation.

Education Programs in the Asia-Pacific Region— Industry Associations

Training and education programs for the MICE industry are paramount in the Asia-Pacific region, with the rate of growth of its meetings industry being the highest in the world. The challenge to the MICE industry, especially to industry associations, is to ensure that the training of the workforce matches industry growth since at present the infrastructure is expanding faster than are the trained professionals with the necessary expertise to service the meetings market (Rich, 1996). The high and sometimes prohibitive cost of enrolling staff in globally recognized training courses is compounded in many cases by significant language barriers. The language problem in educational programs is the greatest stumbling block for Asian countries, such as Indonesia, Japan, Korea, and China, that want to avail themselves of these opportunities; most experts in the MICE industry conduct their programs in English (Twite, 1997).

Many training events in Asia are organized by national tourist offices in conjunction with local travel or MICE organizations, sometimes enlisting the support of visiting speakers from the region, with local tertiary institutions providing academic components (MacLaurin, 2000). In recent years, the major international industry associations have developed numerous educational programs with a specific regional focus.

Asia-Pacific Educational Forum (APEF)

The Asia-Pacific Educational Forum (APEF), a joint venture between AACVB and ICCA, was created in 1997 to bring the best and most relevant educational programs to Asia. Through the APEF, an international online directory of MICE education and training courses offered around the world is available in the form of an education and training calendar on ICCA's Web site. This calendar allows industry personnel in the Asia-Pacific region to identify opportunities to improve their skills. The second stage of the APEF initiative focuses on listing the various accreditation or certification programs offered by MICE associations. The importance of accreditation is amplified in Asia, where each country is presently at a different stage of industry development. In October 2001, ICCA offered its first course on "The Business of Events," in Malaysia. Designed specifically for the Asia-Pacific region, it focused on key aspects of event management, including site selection, bid preparation, program design, and budgeting.

IAPCO/AACVB

The annual IAPCO Seminar on Professional Congress Organization has a long-standing reputation as the definitive course for PCOs and others involved in international conferences either as suppliers or clients (MacLaurin, 2000). In April 2000, the first joint seminar adapted for the Asia-Pacific region was organized by IAPCO in co-operation with AACVB in Singapore. Members of the faculty from the IAPCO seminar, assisted by local and regional speakers, presented the program. As well as sharing a number of common elements with the successful Wolfsberg Seminar, it also includes elements specifically designed to address the requirements of the region and its PCO professionals. Topics covered include conference, meetings and events management, finance, general management, information technology, and marketing/sales (IAPCO Newsletter, 2000b). The second seminar was held in April 2001 in Bangkok; the third seminar took place in April 2002 in Busan, South Korea.

Some organizations offer education on a national level. These courses are also attracting interest and participants from around the Asian region. For example, the Singapore Association of Convention and Exhibition Organizers and Suppliers (SACEOS) started specific training courses for conference and exhibition organizers. SACEOS trains about sixty to seventy people a year for the conference course and another fifty for the exhibition course. Regional delegates have also been attending these courses. SACEOS also hopes to introduce diploma courses on conference and exhibition organizing soon at the local Singapore Polytechnics. The organization is also negotiating with institutions abroad for correspondence courses (Twite, 1997).

Meetings Industry Association of Australia (MIAA)

The Meetings Industry Association of Australia (MIAA) has developed short, face-to-face education sessions, one-day "Essentials for Successful Meetings" seminars for beginners, and residential meetings management courses for industry professionals with up to three years experience. Topics covered range from negotiating, leadership, and marketing, through to industry-specific issues on contracts, insurance, technology, and registration systems. A specific number of approved professional development points are allocated with each of the three options, which can contribute toward gaining industry accreditation. In addition, years of industry experience are recognized in the accreditation process. There are two types of industry accreditation, namely "Accredited Member of the Meetings Industry Association" (AMIAA—a general category covering all segments of meetings industry), and "Accredited Meetings Manager" (AMM—applicable only for meetings managers). Accredited meetings professionals must apply for reaccreditation every three years.

AuSAE—Certified Association Executive (CAE)

The Australian Society of Association Executives (AuSAE) introduced the Certified Association Executive (CAE) professional certification program into Australia and the Asia-Pacific region in 2000. This program has been adapted with the support of the American Society of Association (ASAE) which developed the original CAE certification in the United States in 1960. The CAE designation, held by approximately 2,400 association executives, indicates a commitment to excellence in association management. Its aim is to elevate professional standards and enhance individual performance (Anonymous, 1997b).

Education Programs in the Asia-Pacific Region—Universities

A number of universities and colleges in the Asia-Pacific region run tourism and hospitality courses that incorporate MICE-related subjects. It is therefore surprising that in Singapore, the leading Asian convention destination, the present investment in human capital upgrading and professional education programs for the MICE industry is significantly disproportionate to the financial capital invested within the hardware and infrastructure components of the industry (MacLaurin and Leong, 2000a). This imbalance was exacerbated by the closure of Singapore's only degree program in hospitality and tourism management at Nanyang Technological University in 2001. In contrast, the Hong Kong Polytechnic University is offering MICE subjects at both undergraduate and graduate levels, with plans to develop a dedicated stream of specialization in the area. It is also the first university in Asia to offer executive courses that are specifically designed for professionals in the MICE industry in the Asia-Pacific region.

In Australia, about thirty-five higher education institutions offer tourism and hospitality programs, though very few offer specialized subjects that focus on the MICE industry. Southern Cross University has been at the forefront of course development at both undergraduate and graduate levels in Australia. Similar to the program at the University of Nevada, Las Vegas, its undergraduate program has a concentration in MICE. Its postgraduate degree, a master's in convention and event management, incorporates broad-based subjects imparting general skills and four industry specific electives—namely MICE management, event planning and management, technological systems for conventions and events, financial analysis for hotels, conventions, and events—and an industry project. McCabe (2001a) detailed the challenges involved in the design and development of the curriculum for the university.

CONCLUSION

The MICE industry is forecast to enjoy continued growth in the future. This growth will bring continued change in human resource practices in the MICE industry. Corporate restructuring will change the nature of organizations and require employees to acquire new skills to cope with expanded job roles. This, in turn, will create additional demand for educational programming within the MICE industry. The shift to an information-based society will also bring change to the meetings industry. Advances in information technology will continue to impact the MICE industry and offer competition to the traditional delivery of MICE products and services.

MICE industry customers are also changing. Today's MICE customers are better educated and come from a broader spectrum of multicultural backgrounds. There is increased urgency in their attendance at MICE related events, as their job security and career advancement may well depend on the successful outcomes of the events they attend. Return on investment (ROI) will be a primary concern for the financial and time commitments that professionals contribute in attending an event.

Chapter 6

Research Issues and Challenges for the Convention Industry

Adele Ladkin

INTRODUCTION

In view of the wide scope of research on the MICE sector, it is easy to assume that information on the industry is readily available, and that there is little need for further research. However, this is not the case. Exploration into the existing material reveals a number of research issues and challenges. These can be broadly classified under the following themes: definitions and terminology, fragmentation of the industry, industry statistics, and primary research.

The purpose of this chapter is to closely examine these current research issues and challenges for the international MICE industry. Given its rapid expansion and the subsequent interest in the sector by tourism researchers, there is a need for an evaluation of "where we are" in terms of research as well as a need to highlight issues that must be addressed in the future. This chapter is divided into two main sections: The first section focuses on the assessment of global research issues and challenges facing the industry. The second section examines the three main sources of MICE research, namely meeting and trade associations, trade publications, and academic research. Reference is made to these sources at international, regional, and national levels, with special emphasis on the key MICE markets of North America, Europe, and the Asia-Pacific region.

GLOBAL RESEARCH ISSUES AND CHALLENGES

Definitions and Terminology

One of the key research issues in the MICE industry concerns the definitions and terms used to describe its activities. Two research challenges result from this concern over definitions and terminology. The first and most fundamental one is associated with the use of the acronym MICE, which tends to perpetuate the idea that MICE is one industry. Yet although it is convenient to use the term MICE, it hides the fact that the four industry components—meetings, incentives, conventions, and exhibitions—are actually quite separate activities. Research data and information are mostly presented as if they refer to all of these activities, but on close inspection it becomes clear that they often refer only to meetings and conventions. Despite the wide publicity of the growth and importance of the MICE industry, most data do not include incentive travel or exhibitions. This is misleading and masks the true value of the industry. The blurring of distinctions between the sectors further complicates this issue. For example, incentive rewards increasingly take the form of attendance at a conference. The question then becomes whether this is measured as "incentive travel" or "conference travel." Furthermore, a conference may also contain an exhibition. The question is, again: How should it be measured—as a conference or an exhibition?

Despite the blurring of boundaries, a wealth of sector-specific data are available. Data are provided, for example, on meetings and conventions by international associations, such as UIA and ICCA, and by convention bureaus. The Center for Exhibition Industry Research (CEIR) and the Exhibitions Venues Association (EVA) offer research on the exhibitions sector, while the Society of Incentive Travel Executives (SITE) and the Incentive Travel and Meetings Association (ITMA) focus on the incentive sector. The challenge for research is to clearly identify what specific aspect of the MICE industry is being recorded rather than using the all-encompassing acronym. The specific sectors must be precise when presenting research data if an accurate assessment of the value of the industry is to be obtained.

The second challenge in this context is the wide and varied range of definitions that are used in the MICE industry. This is particularly the case for definitions associated with meetings, conventions, and conferences. For example, a conference was defined by the British Tourist Authority in 1977 as "A meeting held in hired premises; lasting a minimum of six hours; attended by a minimum of 25 people, and having a fixed agenda or programme" (Lawson, 1981, p. 1). According to Seekings (1991, p. 265) a conference is "a large event with a hundred or thousand people, often lasting for several days and involving a social programme and exhibition with an international and national scope." More recently, the British Tourist Authority altered its definition of a conference to be "an out of office meeting of at least six hours duration, involving a minimum of eight people" (BTA, 1999, p. iii).

Similarly, a convention is defined as an assembly of persons for some common object or for the exchange of ideas, views, and information of common interest to the group. The term convention is widely used in America, Australia, and Asia to describe the traditional form of annual or total membership meetings (Lawson, 1982). To Rutherford (1990), a convention is an assembly of people for the exchange of ideas, views, and information that is periodical and often accompanied by an exhibition of products and services. Seekings (1991, p. 310) defines a convention as "an assembly, often periodical, of members or delegates, of a political, social, professional or religious group." According to the *International Meetings Industry Glossary,* a convention is defined as "a general and formal meeting of a legislative body, social or economic group in order to provide information on a particular situation and in order to deliberate and, consequently, establish consent on policies among the participants. It is usually of limited duration with set objectives, but without predetermined frequency" (Ladkin and Spiller, 2000b, p. 1).

The variety of definitions is also evident in the case of meetings. Rutherford (1990) defines a meeting as an event that brings people together for the purposes of sharing information and to discuss and solve organizational and operational problems. It is usually a small event, often involving only a few executives. It can be a corporate meeting, seminar, symposium, or training program. Seekings (1991) explains meetings as smaller group events, while conventions and conferences refer to larger events that last for several days and may involve complex social programs. More precisely, Hughes (1988) defines a meeting as an event where fifteen or more people meet on the premise for a minimum of six hours with a fixed agenda. A meeting lasts less than two days and does not include overnight accommodation. Finally, the Convention Liaison Council (CLC, 1993) in Ladkin and Spiller, 2000b, defined a meeting as "a coming together of a number of people in one place, to confer or carry out a particular activity. This can be on an ad hoc basis, or according to a set pattern" (p. 1).

It is not only the meetings and conferences/conventions sector that is plagued by varying definitions. Incentives are equally difficult to define. For example, an incentive is defined by Seekings (1991, p. 19) as "an event often held overseas and specially designed to be a 'perk' or 'reward' for attendees." The Society of Incentive Travel Executives (SITE) refers to incentive travel as "a global management tool that uses an exceptional travel experience to motivate and/or recognize participants for increased levels of performance in support of the organizational goals" (Ladkin and Spiller, 2000b, p. 2). Dwyer and Mistilis (1997, p. 220) define an incentive as a "non-cash reward given because of the achievements of a work-related goal. Incentives are used by business as a motivational tool to encourage employees to improve their productivity, sales volume or other management goals."

Specific definitions for exhibitions are also problematic. Exhibitions, also called trade shows, trade fairs, or expositions, have been defined as "presentations of products or services to an invited audience with the object of inducing a sale or informing the visitor" (Davidson, 1994a, p. 194). Goldblatt (1997) refers to an exhibition as an activity designed for targeted shareholders or suppliers of products, equipment, and services to demonstrate and promote their products to a certain market. The main advantages of exhibitions, according to Lumsdon (1997), are their potential for sales leads and contacts with influence, gathering competitor intelligence, and the opportunity for image building to the consumer. Exhibitions take the shape of 3-D advertising, where the product can be seen, handled, assessed by demonstration, or even smelled and tasted when appropriate. Exhibitors can compare their products to those of competitors, and attendees have the ability to closely examine competitive products (Montgomery and Strick, 1995).

The varying definitions of the MICE industry sectors may not seem problematic initially. It could be argued that as long as each definition is clearly stated in relation to the information that follows, it does not matter that they vary. However, it is important to realize that the variety of definitions causes problems in terms of data comparability. For example, if one hotel chain defines meetings as attracting a minimum of six people, while a competing hotel chain accounts only for meetings of twenty people minimally, figures derived for the hotel revenue generated by meetings of the two different hotel chains are not comparable.

These varied definitions are problematic for research in three additional ways. First, although the activities can be defined conceptually, in terms of measurement precise figures must be added to the definitions. Second, as measurement calls for a precise definition, inevitably this results in exclusions from data collection. For example, by deciding that a meeting needs to consist of at least fifteen people, meetings of fourteen people are omitted from data collection. The danger is that an important cohort or activity may be missed, and data are lost. Third, researchers must be aware that because of the range of definitions, they are often used interchangeably and indiscriminately. This hampers the understanding of exactly what is being measured. The definitions must be clear so that one can be certain what precisely is being measured. Only then can statistics be accurately compared. The challenge for the industry in terms of definitions is to work toward developing standard definitions for data collection purposes. If this is not achievable, at the very least clarity of definitions used in relation to the publication of data should be ensured. On a final note, these problems of definition are not surprising, given the difficulties of establishing a definition for tourism in the general sense.

Fragmentation of the Industry

The second challenge that research in the MICE industry must address relates to the complex and fragmented nature of the industry. The industry can be considered in terms of sectors (meetings, incentives, conventions, and exhibitions), buyers (corporate and association), suppliers (destinations and venues, accommodation and service providers), agencies and intermediaries, and industry organizations (trade associations, national tourism organizations, convention bureaus, industry consultants, educational institutions, and trade media). The fragmented nature of the industry can create a problem for the focus of research. It is usually impractical for research to cover the entire industry and, as a consequence, only one viewpoint or aspect of the industry can inevitably be considered in any single research project. To this effect, research does not always provide a "balanced" view but rather becomes focused on one aspect, thus simplifying the complex nature of the industry. The challenge here is to offer comparable research from the different sectors and to undertake research that explores the complex relationship among them.

The MICE industry is further fragmented in terms of geography. The state of current research varies by region. Statistics and information in North America, Western Europe, Asia, and Australia are generally of a more advanced standard than in Eastern Europe and Africa. This is a reflection of the importance of these MICE destinations and the level of business tourism development in these regions in general. Furthermore, regional statistics for international meetings and conventions tend to provide better coverage than those relating to incentive travel and exhibitions. This is largely due to the former generally receiving wider recognition and promotion through convention bureaus. However, this is likely to change in the future with the predicted growth in exhibitions and incentives. The challenge for research is for those countries with developed statistics and data collection techniques to lead the way and share best practices with developing markets.

A further fragmentation of the industry relates to size, with MICE activities varying greatly in that aspect. Meetings may be attended by as few as eight or as many as several hundred delegates, and they would still comply with the definition of a meeting. Exhibitions may include local displays contained in one room and those that require a large exhibition center with thousands of square feet of display space in numerous halls. This fragmentation by size presents a problem for research as the focus in data collection by industry bodies is often on larger events. For example, UIA and ICCA collect information only for meetings of more than 300 and 50 attendees, respectively. Consequently, smaller events are often ignored in statistics, even though they comprise the majority of MICE industry activity. The challenge for research is to develop a framework for data collection and analysis that differentiates by the size of the MICE event. It requires a concerted industry effort, with larger international and regional organizations collecting data at the international level and individual suppliers at the local level. Differentiation by size of event would greatly advance research, illustrating the value of both the small- and large-scale MICE activities.

Related to the above, it is the international rather than domestic MICE events that attract the majority of research since international events tend to generate higher expenditure (from both delegates and organizers), resulting in greater economic returns for the particular destination (see Chapter 2). For example, research undertaken in Thailand in 1998 by CSN Associates examined international conventions only. Far less is known about the domestic market, despite its importance in certain MICE destinations. Research undertaken for the British Conference Market Trends Survey 1999 (BTA, 1999) illustrates the importance of the domestic market for the country, as only an estimated 2 percent of delegates attending conferences in the United Kingdom originate from overseas (p. v).

MICE Statistics

The third global issue for research relates to the available statistics for the MICE industry. Apart from the great exhibitions of the nineteenth century and the occasional conventions that were held in the early twentieth century, the MICE industry is relatively young, stemming from the 1960s in Europe and North America, and the 1980s in Asia. As a result of this immaturity, many governments and organizations have only just begun to realize the importance of the industry, and relatively little importance has thus far been given to the collection of statistics on a national and global scale.

Furthermore, due to the fragmentation of the industry, no single body is responsible for data collection in the MICE industry. The UIA and the ICCA remain the major sources of data for international statistics on the meetings and convention industry. The various trade associations also produce statistics for the different sectors. However, without a single body for data collection, no unified method for the collection of industry statistics has been established. This lack of unified data collection methods creates enormous problems in terms of comparability over time and between sectors and countries. However, attempts are being made by the UIA and the European Union Statistics Unit (Eurostat) to develop an integrated methodology for conference sector statistics that should assist in overcoming some of these problems.

In terms of coverage, the statistics that are available for the MICE activities are dependent upon which organization is producing them. Often industry associations present data only relating to their members (e.g., ICCA and EVA). This leaves gaps in terms of data coverage. MICE activities that are not represented by a certain organization have little or no data collected on their volume and value. For example, much MICE activity takes place in individuals hotels, which are not necessarily members of any trade organization.

Related to this, coverage of the industry sectors is dissimilar, with both industry and academic research on meetings, incentives, and exhibitions lagging behind research on conventions. Furthermore, not all countries record information or have the facilities to collate data, particularly those countries that are still developing their MICE industry. As a consequence, data available from different regions vary, from comprehensive coverage for Europe, North America, and Asia to scarce data from Africa and South America.

Finally, although many venues or service providers collect statistics on their businesses, not all MICE venues have the technology, finance, or facilities to collect and record data. Information about certain activities can also be commercially sensitive and therefore may not be readily available; for example, venues are not always prepared to discuss and/or disclose sensitive financial information that is required to make assessments of the economic impact of the MICE industry. Information on incentive travel is particularly scarce, as companies will not disclose the expenditure on this type of employee benefit. The secrecy of the information unfortunately means that data are often based on estimates.

Clearly, the challenge for research is to encourage the collection of statistics at all levels and to improve the accuracy of data collection methods by developing standards or best practice for industry guidelines.

Primary Research

The final issue and challenge for MICE research relates to the collection of primary data. Due to the rapid growth of the industry and the current gaps in research knowledge, an obvious need exists to collect further information despite the wealth of existing research. Yet two main barriers are a serious hindrance to the development of detailed, comprehensive and comparable primary research studies. The first: primary research is notoriously time consuming and expensive to carry out. Even simple economic impact surveys for MICE activities require detailed information from delegates and venues. Second, primarily as a consequence of financial constraints, primary research tends to be ad hoc, thus contributing to the wealth of detailed but noncomparable research on MICE activities. However, as the industry continues to expand on a global scale, it is likely that there will be greater investments in the collection of statistical data because only then can the true value of the industry and the opportunities for profit from MICE activities be realized.

The rapid development of MICE activities combined with the clear economic benefits associated with the industry have been a driving force behind the growth in MICE research. Three different groups have primarily undertaken MICE research—the industry itself (through meetings and trade associations), trade publications, and academics. The scope of this research is international, specific to a particular region, and crosses the various sectors. It must be stated at the outset that it is not possible to explore all the research due to the volume in existence. Rather the intention is to highlight some of the key sources of research in the MICE industry.

RESEARCH SOURCES: INDUSTRY ASSOCIATIONS

Two leading industry bodies provide comprehensive data on the international convention and meeting industry. These are the Union of International Associations (UIA) and the International Congress and Convention Association (ICCA). In view of the differing criteria employed for data collection, statistics from UIA and ICCA are not directly comparable. However, both sources provide time series that allow for an assessment of long-term trends.

Since 1949, UIA's congress department has collected annual statistics on international meetings that are organized and/or sponsored by the international organizations appearing in the *Yearbook of International Organizations* and in the *International Congress Calendar.* UIA statistics also account for some national meetings with international participation organized by national branches of international associations. These latter meetings must meet the following criteria:

the minimum number of participants is 300; the minimum of foreign participants is 40 percent; the minimum number of nationalities represented is five; and the minimum duration is three days. Purely national meetings, meetings that are strictly limited in participation, and corporate and incentive meetings are the main exclusions from UIA figures.

ICCA DATA, the association's research department, has assembled information on the meetings of international associations taking place all over the world since 1972. Its extensive database is subject to strict criteria imposed upon meetings that may be included. Specifically, meetings must attract at least fifty participants, be organized on a regular basis, and rotate between at least three different countries. However, ICCA does not claim to be exhaustive in its coverage; figures refer to ICCA members only, usually on a sample basis. ICCA DATA has also been collecting profiles on corporate meeting planners who organize international events on a regular basis. The profiles contain specific information on the size (with a minimum of twenty participants) and types of events organized, as well as the services and venues they use.

In addition to UIA and ICCA, the International Association of Convention and Visitors Bureaus (IACVB), representing more than 500 CVBs of the major convention cities around the world, maintains a database that tracks historical and future records on more than 20,000 meetings profiles of associations and corporations. This database, called CINET (computerized information network), is available to only those bureaus that have subscribed to it.

As is apparent from this discussion, existing databases are to a certain extent limited because they rely on the provision of data by hundreds of CVBs, in the case of CINET, and on associations, in the case of ICCA DATA. In an effort to improve the accuracy of available data, the DOME (Data on Meetings and Events) project was initiated in 2000. DOME is an international not-for-profit foundation that is headquartered at George Washington University in Washington, DC. The premise of DOME, an online system, is to establish an accurate database of event histories, where event producers submit forecasts and actuals, and delegates must provide information relating to arrival and departure dates, and hotel and airline use before they can register for the conference. These statistics will be available to DOME subscribers. Sponsored by both ICCA and IACVB, it aims to provide more accurate data to both ICCA DATA and CINET, rather than compete with them. Furthermore, it provides CVBs and service providers with easy access to event histories and offers improved data for economic impact assessment. Benefits eventuating to event producers include improved data for budget and event forecasting and a better position for negotiations with hotels, airlines, and event venues, and greater professional credibility. DOME is expected to be available to international conventions by mid to late 2002 <http:// www.domeresearch.org>.

Several other international industry associations undertake research studies. In view of their membership, these studies are more specific to particular industry players. For example, IACVB in addition to its convention income survey conducts a CVB financial survey on a biannual basis. IACC, the International Association of Conference Centers, undertook a study on trends in the conference center industry in 1998. The Center for Exhibition Industry Research (CEIR) conducted a census of the exhibition industry in 2000, and SITE, the Society of Incentive and Travel Executives, studied the effectiveness of travel reward options in 1993. Numerous other research publications are available from the various industry associations—a listing of key industry associations at both international and regional levels, together with their Internet addresses (if available), is provided in the Appendix.

Industry organizations that collect data and conduct surveys also exist at the regional level. For example, the Asian Association of Convention and Visitors Bureaus (AACVB) collects and disseminates data on the MICE industry in Asia, in relation to capacity, expenditure, and types of events. The European Federation of Conference Towns (EFCT) and the European Meetings Industry Liaison Group (EMILG) focus on the European market. At country-level industry associations, national tourist organizations and special research entities may all engage in research pertinent to the MICE industry. In Australia, for example, the Bureau of Tourism Research (BTR) has undertaken several studies relating to the industry's economic impact and infrastructure requirements. Finally, at the local level it is individual CVBs that collect information on major conventions at the destination.

RESEARCH SOURCES: TRADE PUBLICATIONS

A further source of MICE data is generated through trade publications. Although trade publications provide a useful service in researching the market, their surveys are often confined to their own circulation and therefore are not representative of the entire industry. However, if a trade publication is international in readership, it does provide information on a global scale as well as at the destination level, perhaps as a specific destination focus for promotional purposes. The surveys produced are often ad hoc studies, do not illustrate a time series, and are primarily aimed at the marketing of a new destination or venue. However, trade publications are useful for publicizing the latest promotions and for promoting destinations and facilities. Incentive travel promotions are a main feature of trade publications, and they also occasionally provide information on the volume and value of incentive travel to particular destinations. A listing of the key industry publications, together with their Internet addresses (if available), is provided in the Appendix.

In this context it is also important to note that an increasing number of Web-based information organizations at present promote various aspects of the MICE industry. However, in the future they may well be potential sources for research. For example, <IncentiveTravel.org. uk> is a Web-based organization that brings together companies offering incentives, travel and meeting services worldwide, and buyers of corporate travel promotion programs. The Incentives and Meetings International Web site is designed for buyers and planners of international meetings and conventions, and incentive travel planners, with a focus on Europe, Africa, Asia, and the Middle East. For exhibition organizers, Exhibitions World is a single point of access to major trade show information and exhibition related services and products worldwide. Trade Fair Services is an all-in-one resource Web site and service aimed at assisting in planning for trade fair attendance.

RESEARCH SOURCES: ACADEMIC RESEARCH

A wealth of research into the MICE industry stems from academia. Although academic research is generally focused on one particular country, it is international in the sense that it is undertaken across each of the global regions. Academic research into the MICE industry has primarily occurred since the mid-1980s and has drawn from and built upon industry research. The majority of academic research to date has come from the United States, the United Kingdom, and Australia. All three regions are mature MICE destinations and have developed university disciplines in tourism, business, and marketing that fuel research into the MICE industry.

The industry's economic impacts and convention site selection issues are two topical areas that have received the greatest attention by academic researchers. The economic impacts of the MICE industry have been explored extensively in Australia by Dwyer and Forsyth (1997), Mistilis and Dwyer (1999), and Dwyer, Mellor et al. (2000, 2001). In the United States, this topic has been assessed by Braun (1992), Grado, Strauss, and Lord (1998), Fenich, (1992b, 1994, 1995, 1997, 1998b), and Rutherford and Kreck (1994). Also of relevance in this context are studies exploring the economic impacts of specific hallmark (e.g., Ritchie, 1984) or mega-events (e.g., Hiller, 1995, 1998; Long and Perdue, 1990).

Issues relating to the selection of a convention site and/or venue by meeting planners and associations have been investigated by Alkjaer (1976a), Bonn and Boyd (1992), Bonn, Brand, and Ohlin (1994), Bonn, Ohlin, and Brand (1994), Chacko and Fenich (2000), Chon (1991), Clark and McCleary (1995), Clark, Price, and Murrmann (1996), Clark, Evans, and Knutson (1997), Crouch and Ritchie (1998), Fortin and Ritchie (1977), Fortin, Ritchie, and Arsenault (1976), Hu and Hiemstra (1996), Jun and McCleary (1999), Oppermann (1996a,b, 1998), Oppermann and Chon (1997), Pizam and Manning (1982), Renaghan and Kay (1987), Upchurch et al. (1999), and Var, Cesario, and Mauser (1985).

In addition to research on convention centers (e.g., Fenich, 1995, 1998b; Foxall and Hackett, 1994), various other industry players have also received some research attention, for example, CVBs (Fesenmaier, Pena, and O'Leary, 1992; Getz, Anderson, and Sheehan, 1998; Masberg, 1999; Morrison, Bruen, and Anderson, 1998; O'Halloran, 1992; Sims, 1990; Young and Montgomery, 1998; Yuan et al., 1999; Weber, 2001a,b), and convention hotels (Bojanic and Dale, 1993; Danaher and Mattsson, 1994; Leigh and Adler, 1998; McCabe and Weeks, 1999; Montgomery and Rutherford, 1994; Shaw, Lewis, and Khorey, 1991; Schwartz, 1998; Weber, 2000, 2001a,b). Topics addressed in these publications range from services marketing issues (satisfaction, loyalty, service encounters), and human resource and planning, to policy issues.

Academic Journals and Textbooks

Given the range and diversity of academic research mentioned, the means of dissemination for this research is growing in scope and volume. Much of the research that relates to the various topic areas is disseminated through journal articles. Numerous journals publish research on the MICE industry, in particular tourism and hospitality journals. Examples are *Tourism Management, Annals of Tourism Research, Journal of Travel and Tourism Marketing, Journal of Travel Research, Tourism Economics, EIU Travel and Tourism Monitor,* the *Cornell Hotel and Restaurant Administration Quarterly,* the *International Journal of Hospitality Management,* and *Event Management* (formally *Festival Management and Event Tourism*). The selection of a journal for a research publication is largely influenced by the focus of the topic, for example, research on the economic impact of a convention center might be presented in *Tourism Economics.* However, there are no specific rules for the choice of academic journals, as the topic is relevant to many tourism, hospitality, and service industry journals and appeals to a variety of social science disciplines, such as geography, economics, sociology, and psychology.

In 1998 the *Journal of Convention and Exhibition Management* became the first journal dedicated to the publication of research in the MICE industry. To date seven issues of this quarterly journal have been published. Table 6.1 provides the titles of the articles published thus far, illustrating the diversity of topics that have been explored by academics. Due to the relative youth of the journal, it is too early to identify trends in the topics or regions where the research is based. However, clearly a wide variety of issues are currently under scrutiny.

In addition to academic journals, a number of textbooks have recently appeared, written by academics (e.g., Lawson, 2000; Montgomery and Strick, 1995; McCabe et al., 2000; Rogers, 1998; Rutherford, 1990). They provide overviews of the MICE industry and have created an awareness of the industry as a whole, which was previously neglected in industry research. Prior to their publication, textbooks focused mainly on meeting management issues (e.g., Dotson,

TABLE 6.1. Publications in the *Journal of Convention and Exhibition Management*

Volume (Issue), Year	Titles
1 (1), 1998	1. Crisis management and its impact on destination marketing: A guide for convention and visitor bureaus
	2. Economic impacts of conferences and conventions
	3. Perceptions of convention destinations: Large-half versus small-half association meeting planners
	4. Convention site selection research: A review, conceptual model, and propositional framework
	5. Convention and conference facilities: A framework of statistical predictions and judgmental adjustments for daily occupancy forecasts
1 (2/3), 1998	1. Convention center operating characteristics
	2. How a more competitive market is influencing public investments in convention centers
	3. Relationship management: Bridging internal and external quality management
	4. Group/convention cancellation policies in the U.S. hotel industry
	5. Crowd management practices
1 (4), 1998	1. Predication and reality: The development of the Australian convention industry 1976-1993, and beyond
	2. Where the world meets: Regionalism and globalization in Singapore's convention industry
	3. The Asian perspective: Which international conference destinations in Asia are the most competitive?
	4. A review of the MICE industry: Evaluation and research in Asia and Australia 1988-1998
	5. Convention services management in Sydney four to five star hotels
	6. Development of MICE tourism in Australia: Opportunities and challenges
2 (1), 1999	1. Conventions and exhibitions development in Thailand
	2. Meeting planners' perceptions of site selection characteristics: The case of Seoul, Korea

TABLE 6.1 *(continued)*

	3. From selling to relationship marketing at international trade fairs
	4. Information technology and service standards in MICE tourism
2 (2/3), 2000	1. The convention/expo summit: The first decade
	2. Profiling the hotel and conference center meeting planner: A preliminary study
	3. Determining the corporate meeting planner's role in the convention and meeting site decision: A cross-cultural perspective for sales and training
	4. Male and female compensation: A comparative analysis of male and female meeting planners and event managers
	5. A longitudinal examination of wants-out-of-life among midlife adults: Implications for event managers
	6. Measuring meeting planner satisfaction with hotel employee interactions: A pilot study
	7. Convention site selection criteria relevant to secondary convention destinations
2 (4), 2001	1. Convention planning essentials: The critical role of food safety
	2. Meeting planners' use of the Internet to plan group meetings
	3. Unusual venues as conference facilities: Current and future management issues
	4. The U.K. conference and meetings industry: Development of an inventory for attributional analysis
3 (1), 2001	1. Service quality issues for convention and visitor bureaus
	2. Association meeting planners' perceptions of five major convention cities: Results of the pre-test
	3. Taking the classroom into the real world: Teaching conference management down under
	4. Toward a conceptual framework for assessing community attractiveness for conventions
	5. Government intervention in the Australasian meetings, incentives, conventions, and exhibitions industry (MICE)

1995; Hildreth, 1990; Jones, 1984; Nadler and Nadler, 1988; Voso, 1990; Weirich, 1992; Weissinger, 1992). There are also many textbooks on the related issue of events management (e.g., Boehme, 1999; Getz, 1997; Goldblatt, 1997), with Bowdin providing a more complete bibliography on this topic at <http://www.world-of-events. co.uk>.

The Convention/Expo Summit

The Convention/Expo Summit is a research conference dedicated to the MICE industry, hosted annually by the William F. Harrah College of Hotel Administration, University of Nevada, Las Vegas (UNLV) <http://www.unlv.edu/Tourism>. A forum that brings together educators, researchers, and industry leaders, it was first convened in 1990 by Patti Shock, the chairperson of the Department of Tourism and Convention Administration at UNLV who is still the driving force behind the summit today. Roehl (2000) reflects on the research presented at the summit, noting that education, management, human resources, and marketing issues have been the dominant research topics. From his perspective as the editor of the first eight volumes of the summit's proceedings, Roehl emphasizes the need for greater consideration of validity issues, both internal and external, in MICE research.

Similarly, critics of academic research often note that it is fragmented and difficult to compare, both in spatial and temporal terms. Given the relative dearth of academic research in the MICE industry compared to other areas of tourism research, Carlsen (1999) offers a detailed proposal of future research areas for consideration. These can be broadly summarized as follows:

* Economic information at the macro- and micro-economic level
* Management structures
* Government, private-sector, and industry developments
* Tourism and products promotion and marketing
* Psychological and social dimensions of the industry
* Technology
* Training, education, and professionalism
* Globalization of the industry
* Capacity and infrastructure information

- Planning and forecasting
- Delegate and venue safety
- Financial management of venues
- Communication processes
- Hospitality issues
- Future trends

Certainly, and in line with industry research, there is a need for greater coordination and systematic research efforts. Academic research should strive to monitor industry growth and trends, and to evaluate the economic, social, and cultural benefits of the industry.

CONCLUSION

This chapter has offered a review of the main research issues and challenges in the MICE industry, and has explored the main sources of MICE research at the international level and in the three key MICE regions of North America, the Asia-Pacific region, and Europe.

The way forward for MICE research focuses on integration and diversification. On one hand, MICE research would benefit from integration in terms of methodology and data collection. The integration of methods and definitions would enable data to be compared over time and between countries and sectors. On the other hand, research would benefit from recognizing the diversity of the industry, so that the different sectors can be fully explored. A recognition of the diversity of the industry in terms of sectors (meetings, incentives, conferences, and exhibition), by size, (small and large activities) and buyers (association versus corporate), would enhance the research profile and lead to a greater understanding of the components. Finally, research should aim toward exploring the linkages between the sectors to understand the true nature and impact of the total MICE industry. Given the time and cost constraints and the range of expertise required to carry out research in the MICE industry, perhaps research partnerships would be a way forward for the collection of primary data for the international MICE industry.

Chapter 7

International Meeting Management

Catherine H. Price
Cherylynn Becker

INTRODUCTION

The number of international meetings and conventions has risen dramatically during the past decades. In the past mainly multinational companies were at the forefront of conducting international meetings, but in more recent years associations have also begun to venture overseas (Elliott, 1996c). The impetus for growth has been influenced by multiple factors. First, the expanding, untapped markets for new products and services, primarily in the exposition side of the industry, have generated an increasing number of both public and private shows that are geared toward general consumers, product distributors, and professional markets comprised largely of medical, pharmaceutical, and technological customers. Second, the increased awareness of the economic benefits accruing to the localities serving as meeting sites has resulted in government-sponsored cost incentives that enhance the attractiveness of many international sites as meeting venues. Third, as the absolute number of meetings continues to rise, the competition for attendees has increased. From this perspective, holding meetings in distant, exotic locations provides a

Special thanks to the students at the University of Southern Mississippi, Department of Hospitality Management, and to those from the Hospitality Management Program at Washington State University's Swiss Center Campus. These students in convention management classes researched the MICE industry and practices in approximately twenty-five countries around the world. They found the quantity and quality of information to be uneven and particularly absent in the area of meeting practices. Their findings have been added to the content of this chapter.

competitive advantage for increased attendance by providing meeting delegates with a simultaneous opportunity for combining business and pleasure travel. Fourth, international professional associations today find that they must provide education to international members in their own home countries or regions. In this vein, efforts to attract attendees to international meetings have generated new strategies to assist meeting attendees with the higher costs associated with these events. Finally, new technologies are erasing many marketing difficulties and communication barriers associated with hosting meetings in a country other than one's own.

Yet despite the trend toward globalization, a greater familiarity with other nations, and a convergence of consumer tastes worldwide, it is important to remember that there are still and will continue to be substantial differences that must be addressed when planning international meetings. Montgomery and Strick (1995) note that many logistic details are the same for domestic and international meetings. However, planning international meetings also requires additional considerations. Of foremost importance are differences between countries that impact negotiations, contracts, and liabilities. Shipping, customs requirements, taxes, and fees add to the complexities. Variations in language, currency, standards, and measurement units can impact the ease of communications and multiply the potential for errors.

This chapter outlines the various considerations for planning international meetings. It defines international meetings and identifies reasons for holding international meetings from various perspectives, namely the attendees, the associations/corporations, and the destinations. Most important, it highlights key issues that meeting professionals must be aware of in organizing an international meeting. The discussion is illustrated by drawing on examples from countries worldwide.

DEFINITIONS

International Meetings

International meetings have been defined in numerous ways. The Professional Convention Management Association (PCMA) regards an international meeting as synonymous with "any event that has participants from three or more countries" (Polivka, 1996, p. 642). The

International Association of Professional Congress Organizers in its publication *Meeting Industry Terminology* (2000a) and Colby's *Convention Liaison Council Manual* (1994) refer to international meetings as "meetings of an organization with multi-national membership that is available to meet on more than one continent" (IAPCO, 2000a, p. 106). The International Congress and Convention Association (ICCA), the major industry association for international meetings, defines international meetings by the number of countries in which an organization hosts its meetings. Accordingly, a sponsor's meetings must be rotated among a minimum of three different countries on a regular basis. The definition of international meetings is important particularly when interpreting statistical data that describe the size of the market and projected growth. For purposes of this chapter, the term *international meetings* will follow the criterion set forth by ICCA because it accurately reflects the professional requirements of managing international meetings held outside of the sponsor's domestic market.

PCOs and DMCs

Professional congress (conference) organizer (PCO) is the common term for European and Asian companies that offer services to inbound MICE professionals. Terms synonymous with PCO are meeting manager, planner or coordinator, conference manager, or event manager. PCO services often involve a "partnering" relationship (Bay, 1999a) and include basic logistical activities such as site selection, negotiations, and contract interpretation, as well as an ability to explain and expedite international processes, such as freight forwarding, banking, and customs. One of their most valued services is to guide the planner to reputable suppliers. A PCO normally receives a fee from the client organization and may also charge a commission to the venue (usually 8 to 10 percent of the value of the conference to the venue) (Rogers, 1998). Destination management companies (DMCs), primarily found in North America, are similar to PCOs as they provide services to inbound MICE professionals. They differ in that the types of services offered by DMCs are more social in nature than those of PCOs. The former will guide meeting planners in a direction that will enable meeting attendees to "experience" the unique attributes of a particular city or region (Price Waterhouse, 1999).

REASONS FOR STAGING
INTERNATIONAL MEETINGS

Several studies investigated the motivations of delegates to attend association conventions (Fortin, Ritchie, and Arsenault, 1976; Grant, 1994; Oppermann, 1994, 1998; Price, 1993). The desirability of the conference location emerged repeatedly as a strong reason to attend. Foreign destinations in particular do not only add to the excitement about a convention but may also be regarded as a prestige factor (Russet, 2000). Cost and time concerns associated with staging a meeting at a foreign destination are greatly alleviated with low-cost fares and convenient long-haul travel. Polivka (1996), for example, notes that in the late 1990s it could be less expensive for a U.S.-based association member to travel to a destination in Europe than to another city within the United States.

In view of increased globalization, many businesses have expanded their operations into the international marketplace and, despite advances in technology, meetings are still a necessity to facilitate the exchange of information and the finalization of business deals. Associations staging conventions in a foreign country gain an international presence and may also be able to expand their membership base in that particular region.

Destinations actively bid to host international meetings and conventions, mainly in view of expected economic benefits resulting from high spending international delegates who often combine their attendance at a convention with a holiday, especially in the case of long-haul destinations, such as Australia (Dwyer and Forsyth, 1997; Chapter 2).

CONSIDERATIONS IN INTERNATIONAL
MEETING MANAGEMENT

International Site Selection

The selection of an international meeting site requires the consideration of factors similar to the selection of a site in the home country. Accessibility, meeting and accommodation facilities, extraconference opportunities, and local support represent just some of the issues to be assessed in any site selection (Oppermann, 1996b; Chapter 4).

However, as noted by Polivka (1996), a review of international destinations and facilities must allow for the uniqueness of the site. The factors outlined in the following sections must be carefully weighted for each destination under consideration. The Internet has made the gathering of background information much easier for the meeting professional to assess a number of potential options, but a site inspection is absolutely essential before committing to a particular international destination (Bay, 1999a).

The starting point for the selection of an international site should always be the national tourist office and/or the city convention and visitors bureau. Over 400 convention bureaus may be accessed from the International Association of Convention and Visitors Bureau's Web site <www.iacvb.com> or the tourist offices worldwide directory <www.towd.com>. Services available vary depending on the economic importance placed on the MICE industry in a particular county, region, or city. Several countries have instituted special incentives to attract international meetings to their country. The Netherlands, for example, offers a "guarantee" to meeting organizers of tax-exempt organizations that they will share in any financial loss caused by a shortfall in attendance (Hill, 1997c). Meeting managers planning meetings in foreign destinations should ask about such guarantees and other types of financial assistance that allow for partial recovery of registration or exhibition revenues if there is a risk that attendance may be lower as a result of the foreign location. Such strategies might be found in countries that have made the promotion of meetings a national priority. In Japan, for example, legislation was enacted in 1997 to provide tax deductibility for contributions made by Japanese corporations or individuals to registered Japanese associations and societies for the purpose of underwriting international meetings as sponsors (Hill, 1997b). As a result of the growing competition among existing venues to host international MICE activities, opportunities to benefit from both government and corporate incentives are likely to increase, at least in the short term.

Economic and Political Climate

A careful evaluation of the economic stability of the country or region in which a proposed meeting venue is located is required. Although there are many indicators of the strength or weakness of the economy, a few readily available gauges are currency value and stability, interest rates, employment rates, and the gross domestic product. With the Internet and worldwide media coverage, it is easy to get economic information on even the most remote venue. Evaluation of a country's political environment is equally important, and often the political and economic conditions are interconnected.

Security and Safety

In recent years, safety and security issues have not only gained more prominence in the tourism industry in general (Pizam and Mansfeld, 1996), but their consideration is also critical for attracting attendees and assuring safety during an international meeting or convention. In the aftermath of the September 11, 2001, terrorist attacks in the United States, safety and security issues have become a key consideration in the selection of an international site. The political situation in parts of the Middle East, Asia, Africa, and South America in particular must be very carefully evaluated. The events of September 11, 2001, reflect the constantly changing nature of safety considerations. The U.S. Central Intelligence Agency (CIA), on its World Factbook Web site, provides maps and detailed information on the political and economic environment in almost all countries of the world <www.odci.gov/cia/publications/factbook>. Event and Security Services, an international security consulting firm specializing in the meeting industry, offers advice to the meeting industry in particular and issues a free weekly newsletter <http://www.eventsecurity. com>. Another potentially useful site for safety and security checks is <http://www. corporatetravelsafety.com>.

Yet it is not only the political situation and crime levels in a foreign country that must be evaluated, but also health, medical, and weather conditions should be carefully assessed to ensure the safety of attendees (Meyers, 1999). Updated global information on issues related to health and disease are available from both the World Health Organization <www.who.int/> and the Centers for Disease Control and Prevention in Atlanta, Georgia, <www.cdc.gov/> and the International Association for Medical Assistance for Travelers, headquartered in Guelph, Canada. Consideration of information on the Weather Channel <http://www.weather.com>, for example, may prevent a weather-related incident (e.g., hurricane in the Caribbean).

Beyond the selection of a destination, four areas in particular must be addressed relating to meeting security and safety, namely, airport security, hotel safety and security, defense against corporate espionage, and defense against corporate kidnapping. Important considerations for each of these are outlined by Carey (1999). Since September 11, 2001, meeting planners must also consider and advise on increased lead times for airport check-ins and acquisition of travel documents, as well as limitations on luggage, packing, and shipping resulting from increased security measures. The increasing trend to incorporate soft adventure options in the program of international conventions and meetings also requires meeting planners to take precautions in these areas as well (Bay, 2000a). Finally, numerous authors stress the importance of a contingency or crisis plan to ensure the safety and security of attendees in a foreign setting under all circumstances (e.g., Carey, 1999; Meyers, 1999).

Partnerships

Partners in the host country are often critical to the success of organizing foreign meetings. In some countries partners may actually be a requirement for hosting an international meeting (Polivka, 1996). Partners may include governmental agencies, professional groups, and producers of industry publications, corporations, and/or professional congress organizers or destination management companies. Partnerships are particularly valuable for explaining and expediting the activities and processes involved in planning an event at a foreign destination. Partners can provide guidance on contractual issues in addition to recommendations for reliable suppliers, currency specialists, forwarding agents, and shipping and customs brokers. The involvement of a local partner is likely to increase the negotiation clout a planner has in a foreign setting. Many meeting professionals also rely on partnerships for marketing the meeting locally. Local groups or agencies will generally have access to mailing lists and knowledge of effective marketing strategies for the local area, and they lend credibility to the event by attaching their names (Crawford, 1995).

The financial arrangements for partnerships may be fee based or based upon a percentage of the profit. A percentage-of-profit approach is recommended when the marketing of attendees is expected. If the partnership is with a related professional group, a contribution to the association may be sufficient payment. Elliott (1998c) discusses additional considerations in the revenue division for partnerships. In any case, alignment with a local partner early in the planning process can provide critical information and have significant positive effects on the meeting budget.

Numerous meeting planner associations now have initiatives in place that assist their members in organizing international meetings, for example, PCMA's International Relations Committee (Elliott, 1998a). There is also the Foundation for International Meetings (FIM), which provides advice to planners venturing overseas and has worked in the past with associations like ASAE (Elliott, 1996a).

Sponsorships

Sponsorships exist when corporate entities provide economic resources to cover traditional expenses associated with holding meetings. Sponsors may also make contributions to offset the individual costs of congress attendees by providing scholarships to attendees. The legality of using sponsors varies considerably from country to country. Sponsorships, particularly those for medical and other scientific meetings, have come under the scrutiny of governmental agencies in many regions of the world. The United Kingdom, Italy, and a large number of other European nations have instituted legislative restrictions on the goods and amounts that sponsors can contribute. In these nations, contributions by sponsors are subject to review by government agencies. In Japan, such restrictions do not apply; rather, government policy and associated tax incentives encourage corporate funding for the meetings market (Hill, 1997b). Crawford (1995) provides a good example of the benefits of multiple sponsorship.

Communication

Industry Jargon

English is a second language for most professionals in the tourism industry. Nonetheless, a false sense of security can develop, especially when verbal communication is employed. Terminology, gestures, and protocol may have different implications in different cultures, and language nuances differ even across nations that speak English as their first language. Bay (2000b) relates an incident supporting this assertion: a U.S. planner canceled food and beverage "breaks" at a meeting planned in Mexico with the result that all food and beverage functions were canceled as well as the reserved meeting space. "Breaks" is an excellent example of a term that represents commonly used meeting jargon in the United States, referring to short breaks during the daily conference program, yet has a much more nebulous definition in a traditional English usage context.

Interpretation and Translation

Translation and interpretation are required for many international and foreign meetings, both for meeting planners' relations with entities and suppliers in the host destination and for meeting attendees. Translations are necessary for promotional materials, conference handouts and schedules, and generally any type of written communication. Polivka (1996) also recommends that contracts are translated into the language of the host country to ensure that all agreements and commitments are understood. Interpreters are used as guides for the industry professional in the preplanning communications with the city, hotel, suppliers, banks, etc. During the meeting, interpreters communicate the contents of the program to delegates, using either a simultaneous or consecutive format. Simultaneous interpretation, requiring some form of voice transmission equipment, is the preferred method for most multilingual meetings; increasingly, venues interested in attracting international meetings are building facilities prewired for simultaneous interpretation in as many as five or six different languages (Elliott, 1996d). This form of interpretation avoids the time delay inherent in consecutive interpretation. It has also been found to be an extremely valuable tool in promoting high attendance numbers (Elliott, 1996d). The International Association of Conference Interpreters, based in Geneva, can provide references to professional interpreters.

In Asia, attempts to deal with jargon and other language difficulties have resulted in some creative solutions. Polivka (1996) notes that in China both an interpreter and an explainer are hired to facilitate dual-language communications. The explainer may have no second language skills but will be an expert in the technical areas for which communication is required. His or her job is to communicate with the interpreter to ensure that jargon-related miscommunications do not occur. In Japan, the National Tourist Office has created a new program called "Good Will," a complimentary service using senior citizens and students to provide guide and interpretation services for international guests. The program is in place in thirty-five cities and local districts across Japan (Hill, 1997c).

Communication Methods

Methods of communicating have become much more varied over the past few years, specifically with the use of the Internet and e-mail. Across Western Europe there appears to be a great variance in e-mail capabilities and the usage rates of venues and local suppliers. Many still prefer telephone, fax, and traditional regular/express mail options. Communications with industry professionals in the United States and Canada are becoming increasingly e-mail based, and site research is almost exclusively conducted via the Internet. Venues, properties, and services that do not have a presence on the Internet likely will not be considered as a site for international meetings of the future. Changes are occurring rapidly in this area worldwide.

Negotiations

Negotiations may be the most difficult aspect of conducting a meeting in a foreign country (Bay, 2000b). Each culture has its own unique approach to communication. Perceptions of time, proper protocol, and status vary considerably from one nation to the next (Becker, 2000). Language and industry terminology differences are evident. Some cultures make decisions quickly, without the involvement of associates, whereas others use time-consuming consensus styles of decision making. These differences impact the manner in which negotiations will be conducted and the time required to conduct them. Both market conditions and the competitive position of the destination and the properties involved will also influence the negotiation process. In some destinations, established prices may not be subject to negotiation at all and attempts to secure greater flexibility in guarantees or reductions in standard room rates will be considered offensive and inappropriate. Negotiations are one area where local partners can assist the meeting planner tremendously in understanding the local customs and the unwritten rules associated with negotiation. Because negotiations often have cultural implications, care should be taken to research each country's style of interacting in business situations. One Web site that is useful for providing cultural information in this context is <www.worldbiz.com>. Axtell's (1991; 1993) "Dos and Taboos" series on international cultures and customs is another useful source.

Contractual Details

Because contracts represent and follow the legal structures that govern a country, there are considerable differences in the format of agreements. The legal systems within the United States have encouraged the development of detailed contracts with penalties and enforcement when the terms of the contract are not met. In some venues in Europe and Asia, the agreement is a series of letters confirming different aspects of the meeting rather than the single contract format found in North America (Elliott, 1996c). Smaller-sized European hotels, especially those that are independently owned and operated, may require a deposit to reserve the guest and meeting rooms, with full payment required at a specified time prior to the meeting date. This procedure minimizes the need for contractual clauses for dealing with attrition, cancellation, and enforcement of related contract provisions. It is, however, not only crucial to carefully examine the contract details but also to be aware of the law relating to the hospitality industry in each particular country because certain codes and laws that are understood are not necessarily listed in the contract (Bay, 1999a). Although many countries provide contracts in dual languages, there are exceptions. Japan, for example, provides contracts only in Japanese. It has been suggested that theater companies have terminology most similar to the MICE industry, thus interpreters and translators from this industry can be an asset in interpreting industry jargon.

Currency, Exchange, and Payments

For each meeting, a base currency must be established and specified in all contracts that are fee based. Polivka (1996) notes that hard currency countries will mostly negotiate in their domestic currency, while negotiations in soft currency countries are predominantly in U.S. dollars. The risks inherent to both alternatives must be understood and weighted carefully. In view of currency fluctuations, it is possible and may be desirable to negotiate a fixed exchange rate as much as a year in advance by using a forward contract that locks in a predetermined rate of exchange between currencies (Elliott, 1995). When the currency in the sponsoring country is strong relative to the currency in the destination country, forward contracts may be less needed, but they are recommended as a protection against lost revenue from currency fluctuations. A second and safer option than a fixed-rate forward contract is to purchase the foreign currency of the destination on the futures market at the time the contract is negotiated (Bay, 1999a).

When using a local bank, fees may be charged for exchanging money, wiring money, making deposits and withdrawals, and preparing statements. Fees may vary considerably as compared to the standard rates in one's home country. These fees must be included in the budget. An assessment of currency restrictions and limitations, especially in developing and controlled-economy countries, is also essential to prevent money from being confiscated or impounded by a host country due to failure to observe proper limits and procedures (Polivka, 1996). Currency specialists can assist in the assessment of the best strategies in the current economic environment. When deposits are required in advance and the balance is due in full prior to the start of the meeting, a strategy that has been successful is to establish an escrow account into which a predetermined portion of revenues are held until the meeting requirements have been satisfactorily met.

The Euro

The European Monetary Union (EMU) includes twelve of the fifteen European Union (EU) members, namely, Austria, Belgium, Finland, France, Germany, Greece, Ireland, Italy, Luxembourg, Netherlands, Portugal, and Spain. The remaining three EU members—the United Kingdom, Sweden, and Denmark—have not yet joined the EMU. On January 1, 1999, the EMU member countries began the process of replacing individual currencies with one universal currency, the Euro. However, for the three years following its introduction it existed only as a unit of electronic exchange, with Euro notes and coins having been issued for daily use by individuals on January 1, 2002 <http://amue.lf.net>.

Several advantages arise for the convention industry from the introduction of the Euro. Comparative pricing is one of the key benefits. Previously when bids were received from various countries, each country's exchange rate had to be separately calculated and converted to the monetary unit of the home country. The Euro provides a common basis for evaluation and encourages hotels and suppliers in member countries to be more price competitive (Smith and Meyers, 1999; Thompson, 1999). Furthermore, the need for multiple currency conversions and associated costs is eliminated (Korn, 1999).

Meeting planners specified the conversion of all monetary arrangements to Euro if they had negotiated contracts before the introduction of the Euro, which took effect after January 1, 2002. Exchange rates, interest rates, inflation percentages, and escrow accounts are all subject to dispute if contractual terms do not specify the currency and applications of that currency in all financial matters.

Taxation

In most countries there is a flat tax on all goods and services, including hotel room charges and sales of food and beverage items. In the United States, this is called a sales tax; its European equivalent is VAT (value-added tax); other countries may refer to this tax as goods and services tax (GST). The amount of this tax ranges from 10 percent to 30 percent of the sale, depending on the city and country. Although these taxes are often fully refundable, recovery procedures are very specific and regulations must be obtained in advance to ensure that acceptable documentation and receipts are secured to facilitate the refund process (Bay, 2000a). A country's tourism board, international accounting firms, and VAT reclaim agencies can provide advice on these issues. Tax refunds can be secured for meeting expenses as well as for individual purchases. During the site selection decision process meeting planners need to investigate any potential tax liability. If negotiated in advance, some taxes may be reduced or waived completely (Polivka, 1996). This is one area where details obtained in the early stages of planning a meeting or convention may lead to a considerable reduction in expenses.

Meeting Charges/Inclusions

In the United States guest room revenues are the principal source of hotel revenue, and charges for meeting space and other public spaces are often a point of negotiation. For sizeable groups who book many room nights or contract for food and beverage functions, rates for meeting rooms may be waived entirely. In addition, a complimentary guest room policy is often in place. However, this is not true in the European hotel industry. Commonly in European hotels, and also in Japan, either a rental rate is charged for meeting room space or alternatively a daily delegate rate is established. This is a flat rate for each person and often includes several coffee breaks, lunch, room rentals, and basic audiovisual service. Alternatively, there is a twenty-four-hour rate that includes all the features of the daily delegate rate plus guest room and dinner (Bland, 1997). Complimentary guest room policies, if in place at all, are usually much less generous than they are in the United States. These differences are mainly due to hotels and meeting spaces being smaller and space being at a premium in Europe and Asia (Bay, 2000b). Furthermore, in some destinations, hotels and convention centers apply a surcharge for air conditioning, lights and other forms and uses of power, and water—items that are usually included in meeting space quotations in the United States. No assumptions should be made about commonalities of expense categories and policies from one country to another.

Passports and Visas

International meetings involve the movement of attendees across national borders. Consequently, travel documents such as passports and visas are a necessity. Passports are not only required to cross national borders but are also used as proof of identity when conducting business transactions in foreign countries and to verify citizenship when returning home. Meeting planners must advise attendees of the need for a passport not only to be current but to also be valid for six months after the date of departure.

Depending upon the meeting delegate's nationality, a visa in addition to a passport may be required to enter some foreign countries. Currently individuals holding passports from the United States, Canada, Australia, New Zealand, Japan, and countries of the European Union are often exempt from visa requirements for entering most countries if intended visits are for a duration of less than three months. However, this exception is not universal; when a meeting attracts attendees from a variety of countries, immigration requirements should be determined at the site selection stage. In addition to providing advice on any fee levied for the issuance of visas, the meeting professional also must inform delegates of the varying time requirements for obtaining a visa. The most efficient system is currently in place in Australia. Through its Electronic Travel Authority (ETA) system, the permission to enter the country is issued electronically within seconds. ETA's elimination of paperwork and speed present a competitive advantage for Australia as a meeting destination (Lambert, 1999).

Shipping/Custom Requirements

International freight forwarders and customs brokers can facilitate the shipping of goods and equipment to a foreign destination. The former transport goods and prepare the required shipping documentation, and the latter process the paperwork required by customs agencies and handle the payment of fees and tariffs when the goods reach the destination. Customs regulations vary greatly from country to country and these specialists can minimize problems, eliminate unplanned expenses, and expedite the whole shipping process. Because of shipping costs and potential delays in customs, it is recommended that the printing of conference materials, for example, is handled in the destination country—though consideration has to be given to differences in paper size, weight, and quality. Furthermore, expensive gifts and other items subject to special handling fees and/or import duties should be purchased or rented at the destination, for example, computers, video exhibit booths, and binders for printed materials (Bay, 1999a). However, goods imported for display purposes only are exempt from duty, provided they are shipped out of the host country again within a reasonable time (Polivka, 1996). Documentation accompanying any shipment must be very detailed. Furthermore, it should be clearly stated if specific material is not for resale to avoid duties (Price, 1999).

Standards and Measurements

The compatibility of hardware and software, of electrical equipment, and differences in measurements are important considerations in international meeting planning. Hardware and software vary significantly in format across countries. For example, videotapes may not be successfully interchanged between the different operating systems in Europe and North America.

Electric voltage varies around the world, with electrical systems based on 110 volts being prevalent in the Americas, while much of the rest of the world's operating systems are based on 220 to 240 volts. Furthermore, significant variations exist in sizes and designs of electrical plugs. Converters that change the voltage requirements and adapters that change the plug configuration may be used successfully for personal equipment, but neither is recommended for conference equipment, such as audiovisual items (Price, 1999).

Measurements detailing meeting space may be based either on a metric system (prevalent in most European countries) or on the imperial system (used in the United Kingdom and the United States). However, Bay (2000b) notes that the correct conversion between the two systems is only one necessity in evaluating meeting space. Apart from the total square footage/square meters, it is also crucial to assess the layout of the rooms.

Scheduling Issues

Numerous issues have to be evaluated in the scheduling of international meetings and conventions. First and foremost, as should be apparent from the review of the many considerations that go into planning international meetings, sufficient lead time should be allowed. It is generally recommended to at least double the time necessary for planning a domestic event (Elliot, 2000). Apart from the lead time, the actual dates for the convention and the timing of activities during the convention require careful attention.

Convention Dates

The peak seasons for MICE industry events are the fall and spring months for the majority of countries. October, November, March, and April are the busiest months for the industry overall; September and June are the most popular months for holding international meetings. Scheduling events in this period avoids competition with the leisure travel market, which typically registers peak activity during the summer months, and with holiday and religious functions, which abound in December. However, this also means that competition for meeting space during this period is fierce. Meeting planners should also keep in mind the seasonal differences between sites in the northern and southern hemispheres, where climatic conditions are opposite.

Holidays differ across countries and at times even within a country. Scheduling conflicts with specific national, religious, and political holidays should be avoided because a convention or meeting coinciding with a particular holiday can significantly reduce the number of attendees and prevent a smooth execution of the event (Russet, 2000).

Activity Scheduling

Scheduling activities for the convention/meeting program has to take into consideration the cultural background and preferences of attendees. For example, people from Mediterranean countries prefer to eat dinner rather late. They, like South Americans, also spend more time at lunch. In the United States, breakfast meetings are very popular, but in Europe meetings are rarely scheduled before 9:00 a.m., with most meetings beginning at 9:30 or 10:00 a.m.. The inclusion of speeches and business presentations over meals should also be carefully reviewed because such a practice may be regarded as offensive in some cultures (Bland, 1998; Russet, 2000). Furthermore, attitudes toward punctuality also vary widely, impacting the need to stay on schedule for individual sessions.

Marketing to Meeting Attendees

Elliott (1996e) asserted that marketing represents one of the major challenges for foreign/international meetings. Decisions have to be made regarding the appropriate medium, the design and content of promotional material, and the language(s) (Bay, 1999b; Elliott, 1996e; Russett, 2000). When marketing to an international audience, particularly in countries where conference attendance is not prevalent, the process may be complex. Cultural values, preferences, and protocol must be isolated for each country and marketing strategies designed accordingly. For example, in the United States, marketing is primarily done through direct mail—an effective strategy in a country where conference attendance is considered part of the lifestyle. In contrast, in Hong Kong direct mail campaigns are more difficult to implement because it is illegal to sell mailing lists (Elliott, 1997). Direct mail campaigns in Europe also present challenges, particularly in view of the logistics involved in compiling a comprehensive database for pan-European meetings and the relatively high cost of mailing materials.

CONCLUSION

International meetings at foreign destinations are a reality in the world today. The roles and responsibilities of MICE industry professionals must change as new technologies and the global environment are confronted. Knowledge areas must expand. Meeting managers, congress organizers, and exposition managers will move away from logistic-based activities to design-based activities; new knowledge and technological expertise will be required. Education will be the cornerstone but must be combined with creativity and a sense of adventure. Successful industry professionals will be those who can effectively match the purpose, audience, and topical content to the appropriate medium for delivery and select the venues that best support the overall objectives sought. This is a considerable change and requires a new vision of the industry for all who intend to confront the challenges of the future.

PART II:
CASE STUDIES

Chapter 8

Convention Center Ownership and Management: The Case of the United States

George G. Fenich

INTRODUCTION

The meetings, incentives, conventions, and exhibitions (MICE) sector is a significant part of the U.S. hospitality industry. It ranked as the twenty-second largest contributor to the U.S. gross domestic product, according to the most recent comprehensive study of MICE by the Convention Liaison Council (1995). This study further indicated that the sector's total economic impact amounted to US$80.7 billion, supports 1.57 million jobs, generates US$12 billion in taxes, and accounts for one-third of hotel revenues and for almost one-quarter of airline revenues.

MICE events, because they are gatherings of people, must be housed in some type of facility. Facilities can include colleges, universities, cruise ships, restaurants, and hotels, yet none of these have the capacity to accommodate large conventions—conventions that attract over 1,000 attendees, usually include a trade show, and generate the largest economic impacts. Regarded as the premier type of MICE event, they are typically housed in convention centers. Convention centers are facilities designed to accommodate multiple groups or extremely large groups, and incorporate exhibit halls, meeting rooms, ballrooms, banquet space, and food and beverage facilities (Polivka, 1996). The *Meetings Market Report* (Meetings and Conventions, 2000) found that 45 percent of all conventions with exhibits in the United States are held in convention centers.

This chapter focuses on ownership and management issues related to convention centers in the United States. The chapter begins by placing convention centers within the context of the MICE industry. The perspective then narrows to convention centers themselves and the questions of who owns, operates, and finances them. The chapter concludes with a discussion of the pros and cons of different management structures with the most effective approaches to organization considered.

IMPACT OF CONVENTION CENTERS

Economic Impact

Convention centers are not only an important part of the hospitality industry but also a significant contributor to both local and national economies. Fenich (2001) found that the typical (median) convention center in the United States generates convention delegate spending in its host community of approximately US$57.19 million per year. Consequently, the more than 350 convention centers in the United States (Meetings and Conventions, 2001) contribute about US$20 billion annually in direct convention spending to the U.S. economy.

In addition to conventions, these venues stage gate events such as boat shows, consumer shows, and other activities for which attendees pay an admission fee. The average center attracts 600,000 attendees to gate events with daily direct spending of US$52.70, for total spending of US$31.62 million or over US$11 billion for all U.S. centers annually (Fenich, 2001). Thus, the average convention center in the United States induces direct spending at both convention and gate events of just under US$90 million or US$31 billion for all centers. This figure does not include construction spending. When the average multiplier for U.S. cities is considered (U.S. Department of Commerce, 1998), the direct and indirect economic activity supported by convention centers in the United States doubles to US$62 billion. Thus, it is clear that convention centers are a significant segment of the hospitality industry.

Site Selection Factor

Convention centers are one of the primary site selection factors meetings planners use when choosing a city in which to hold their events (Fenich, 1992a). Although the size of the center is commonly believed to be the most important center characteristic, this author has found that the type and expertise of management at the center is equally important. The size of the center is actually a screen used to eliminate centers that are not large enough to accommodate a given convention; management is then the primary variable in choosing a center.

CONVENTION CENTER OWNERSHIP

There are two broad categories of ownership of convention centers: public and private. Sixty-three percent of the convention centers in the United States are publicly owned; the rest are privately owned (Ross, 1999a).

Public Ownership

In the public ownership model, title is held by some level of government that includes the state, regional authority, county (parish), city, or town. The largest facilities are state owned but not necessarily state operated, with the other levels of government laying claim to smaller facilities that are related in size to community population. The federal government neither owns nor operates convention facilities. Because the "public" owns these facilities, the interests of residents have to be balanced with the needs of the hospitality industry, including convention organizers and attendees. This can create a dilemma because conventions or trade shows cannot be held in convention centers at the same time as gate events such as car and home shows or other activities open to the public. For example, May is a time of good weather in much of the northern United States and is a correspondingly popular month for conventions. However, it is also a popular time for gate events, especially flower and home shows. Convention centers need to make a conscious decision whether to host conventions to bring in their commensurate outside spending, or to host the gate events for their citizenry and forego the economic benefit of conventions.

In fact, the primary role of government in the development of convention centers is to discuss and pass "enabling legislation" that makes it possible for one of the government subdivisions mentioned previously to build such a center. Based on U.S. constitutional law, this legislation is enacted at the state, not federal level. The legislation may establish an "agency" or "authority" to build and/or operate the center. The statute usually determines how the center will be financed, who will finance it, and other policies about how the center will operate.

In Louisiana, the state established a Convention Center Authority to build and operate the Morial Convention Center in New Orleans. The Convention Center Authority contracts SMG Management to run the center that, in turn, contracts with ARAMARK to provide the food service. The state issued the bonds and guarantees their payment through a portion of the hotel/motel tax.

In New York, three organizations operate the Jakob Javits Convention Center in Manhattan. The Convention Center Operating Corporation (CCOC) is a public benefit corporation of New York State. It has overall responsibility for the building as well as direct accountability for sales, marketing, finance, and public relations. Another organization, Ogden Allied Facility Management Corporation, is a private company that manages the facility under contract to the CCOC. It is responsible for all building operations, supervises the arrangements involved in setting up and dismantling trade shows, provides the custodial work, and maintains all utilities. The third partner is Service America Corporation, the exclusive food service provider. Thus, there is an arrangement in which two private management firms run the center under contract to the operating authority, which is a quasi-governmental agency. This organizational structure is intended to ensure that policy implemented by the CCOC is in the public interest yet takes advantage of the efficiencies of private enterprise in the day-to-day operations of the facility. Financing was accomplished through bonds issued by the Triborough Bridge and Tunnel Authority. They are paid in part by hotel/motel taxes, yet the state underwrites any operating deficit.

Financing of Publicly Owned Convention Centers

The means and types of financing used to fund a convention center have a significant impact on the ultimate cost of the facility. Sources of funding for centers have followed patterns similar to many government projects and much of it comes from the same capital markets that satisfy other sectors of the economy (Fenich, 1992a).

Government-issued bonds represent the most common type of finance for the construction of convention centers, followed by federal subsidies such as "block" grants from the U.S. Department of Housing and Urban Development (HUD). The bonds are commonly general obligation (GO) bonds or general revenue bonds. Sometimes a special authority such as the Triborough Bridge and Tunnel Authority in New York issues the bonds. This financing method is beneficial to the community that hosts the center since the state, rather than the local community, is responsible for repaying this debt so that the construction of the convention center is effectively free to the host community.

In the past decades there has been a shift away from GO bonds toward general revenue bonds due to federal cutbacks and rigid tax limitations. Revenue bonds are often guaranteed by special taxes, such as hotel occupancy taxes, reservation taxes, or food and liquor taxes. Sale/leaseback is still another method for repaying bonds. Convention center development bonds may require public referenda. The ability of a municipality to float a bond issue is directly related to its fiscal health.

In more recent years, additional methods for financing centers have evolved: certificates of participation (COPs), tax increment financing (TIF), and selling of naming rights, as with the TWA Dome in St. Louis or the RCA Dome in Indianapolis. Fenich (1998b) and Nelson (1998) discuss the financing of convention centers in more detail.

Private Ownership

Privately owned convention centers are held by companies or corporations with an entrepreneurial orientation. They are in business to make money and employ numerous strategies to attain their profit objectives. Other than obeying applicable government regulations, they need not be concerned with community preferences when making their business decisions. They are often tied to a hotel (e.g., Sands Expo and Convention Center in Las Vegas) and in some cases occupy former warehouse buildings in office/industrial parks (e.g., Bound Brook Convention Center in New Jersey). Although private centers generally tend to be smaller in size than public ones (Fenich, 1998b), an exception is the Sands Expo and Convention Center in Las Vegas which rivals many of the largest facilities in the world.

Financing Privately Owned Convention Centers

Privately owned convention centers must finance development through corporate sources. This takes many forms including internally generated funds, corporate bonds, or partnerships (Sands Expo and Convention Center). Although the government does not directly finance private centers, they may provide financial incentives such as tax abatements, hiring subsidies, and below-market utility rates.

CONVENTION CENTER MANAGEMENT

The management of a convention center has a significant impact on operating efficiency, economic impact, and overall success of a center (Fenich, 1995). Management is not synonymous with ownership. For example, a publicly owned convention center may contract with private management to operate the facility. Peterson (1989, p. 34) emphasized that "the quality of management and marketing influences the occupancy and financial performance of a project more than any other factor." In the United States, about 55 percent of convention centers are privately operated; the rest are operated by a division of municipal or quasi-governmental agencies (Ross, 1999a). Some of the best-known centers are quasi-governmental operations, for example, McCormick Place in Chicago, the Georgia World Congress in Atlanta, and the Las Vegas Convention Center. Privately managed (not necessarily owned) centers include the Bayfront Center in St. Petersburg, Florida, the Eastern States Exposition in Springfield, Massachusetts, the Moscone Center in San Francisco, California, and the Prairie Capital Convention Center in Springfield, Illinois. A center that is both privately owned and operated is the Sands Convention Center in Las Vegas. The Louisville Commonwealth Convention Center operates under quasi-governmental structure, and the Kentucky Fair and Exposition Center that is also located in Louisville is a department of municipal government. Similarly, in Seattle, the Civic Center is a municipal department while the Trade Center is a private operation.

Private Management

A privately managed convention center is operated like a business enterprise, with profit being its primary objective. Entrepreneurial strategies are utilized to reach the profit objective. Thus, private management seeks to bring business to the convention center that will yield the greatest revenues and profits. Competing in a field of contenders that are heavily subsidized, private facilities leverage efficient staffing, flexible booking policies, and value-added services to minimize costs and maximize revenues. "We run the Expo Center as a business," remarked Rich Heller, the Vice President and General Manager of the Sands Expo Center. "We're in it to deliver a service and make a return" (Chatfield-Taylor, 1995). These private venues are also more efficient. For example, the Textile Hall Corporation, an eighty-year-old private company that produces and manages shows for the textile industry, employs only thirty full-time staff. Even the Sands Expo Center, the country's largest private facility, has only fifty-seven full-time staff, supplemented on a need basis by a vast number of part-time workers. According to Rich Singer, manager of California's 20,000-square-foot Modesto Center Plaza, "In a small facility you want to maintain control and there is a savings to be had by privatizing"; as a result, private management is very sensitive to the needs of its tenants and will strive to accommodate their needs whenever possible. "Flexibility, efficiency and service are the tools of the trade in private facility management" (Chatfield-Taylor, 1995).

Private management tends to attract a greater proportion of consumer shows; food and beverage functions, such as proms; and gate events, such as concerts or wrestling matches. These types of events are more profitable for a center than conventions or trade shows and fit well within the generally smaller-sized private centers. Fenich (2001) found that private convention centers attracted over four times more gate events than conventions, while publicly operated facilities attracted twice as many gate events as conventions. Quasi-public facilities attracted about the same number of each. (See Table 8.1 for a summary of the advantages and disadvantages of the three management structures.)

Since privately managed centers have a profit motive, they function as competitors to hotels, restaurants, arenas, and public convention centers. Further, they are not subject to public policy constraints

TABLE 8.1. Advantages of Alternative Convention Center Management Structures

Public Management	Quasi-Public or Authority	Private
Advantages		
Financial support	Increased operating autonomy	Greatest operating autonomy
Sharing staff	Special purpose role	Efficiency incentives
Community control	Independent revenues	Care about users
	Government presence	Negotiating flexibility
	Fewer purchasing and hiring restrictions	Experienced staff
		Greater accountability
		Lower financial risk for government
Disadvantages		
Lack of incentives	Lack of incentives	Less government control
Political influence	Political influence	Profit motive
Hiring restraints	Bureaucratic	Fewer economies of scale
Comingled funds	Board versus management in decision making	
Lack of sensitivity		
Civil service hurdles		
Purchasing procedures		
Flexibility		
Operating costs		
Contract approval		
Restrictions		

and may market to and host groups that the community opposes. Problems such as these have surfaced in many locations over the past few years. For example, the city of New Orleans sued gun manufacturers over safety and liability issues. However, the Shooting, Hunting, Outdoor, and Trade (SHOT) show was scheduled to take place in New Orleans: an obvious conflict between hosting the gun manufacturers and public policy, resulting in organizers pulling the convention out of New Orleans (Phillips, 1999). Another example occurred in Colorado, where voters defeated a proposition to allow gay and lesbian marriages at a time that a gay and lesbian convention was to be held in Denver. Privately managed centers are under no obligation to set aside dates for out-of-town groups that may have a high economic impact on the community but that do not generate as much revenue for the center.

It should be noted that privately operated convention centers tend to occupy the smaller-sized strata, with many of them having fewer square feet of space than a hotel ballroom (Fenich, 1998b). Thus, if the community has other larger facilities in hotels or in convention centers, the competition problem may be mitigated and, in fact, the private center may serve to supplement the large public facilities. It is also important to note that many groups feel overwhelmed by the vastness of large centers and opt for smaller centers that more closely match their space requirements.

Public Management

At the opposite end of the spectrum from privately operated convention centers is the public form of management. In these instances, centers are operated as a branch of local government, not unlike a highway or recreation department. As a result, this type of center is very sensitive to the needs of the community; some would say it is oversensitive or politicized. Their key objective is to maximize the benefit of the center to local residents. This can be accomplished in numerous ways. They typically try to balance conventions or gate events with civic activities, such as meetings of nonprofit groups or political rallies. They may also have a policy of hiring only local residents to ensure that the economic benefits stay in the community, and employ more, rather than fewer, people relative to their size (Ross, 1999b).

Several disadvantages, however, are associated with the public style of management. These centers often act like government agencies with their bureaucracies and little if any concern for profitability. As is common in many government agencies, they may not be very sensitive to the needs of their users. Approved vendors may not offer the best prices but rather represent friends of the politicians in power. It is also not uncommon to find among the top management political appointees who may not necessarily have the required experience or expertise to run a convention center effectively. Similarly, many staff members may have gotten their jobs because of political patronage. Civil service regulations represent a hindrance to the employment process and contract requirements are often overly burdensome (Ross, 1999b). Finally, events held at publicly managed centers might reflect the hegemony of the political party in power rather than meeting the broad needs of the community.

Quasi-Public Management

The third type of management structure is the "quasi-public" or "authority" form. It is a hybrid of public and private management that tries to utilize the best aspects of each while minimizing their respective shortcomings. In most instances, quasi-public management operates a convention center that is owned by the government. The government appoints a board of directors or governors for the center that sets the policies for the operation of the center, including policies relating to employment and contract issues, and the type of events to be staged. For example, the board may decide that the mission of its center is economic development. Consequently, it sets a policy whereby the primary goal is to bring out-of-town convention delegates to the community in view of their spending habits, a policy commonly known as "putting heads in beds." This may mean that events attracting local residents are held only if there is no convention scheduled for a given time frame.

The board is empowered to hire private management to run the convention center. Some boards take a broad approach by hiring a management firm that in turn hires the general manager, key executives, and employees. Ogden Allied Facility Management Corporation, based in New York, and Philadelphia's SMG are the dominant "private" facility management companies, with Houston based LMI in a distant third position. Ogden is a Fortune 500 company with almost US$4.5 billion in assets. Its facility management division operates forty-six facilities. SMG, jointly held by the Pritzker family (Hyatt Hotels), ARAMARK, the international service company and Spectacor (Snider family), manages more than sixty facilities, including about twenty-five convention centers. Other boards take a more hands-on approach by hiring key employees themselves and being involved in the day-to-day management of the center. In the latter case, the board usually forms a public corporation that becomes the employer of record. The funding for private management is derived from center revenues, even though the coverage of costs may be guaranteed by the center owner: the state, authority, or city. For example, even though the Triborough Bridge and Tunnel Authority issued the bonds for the Jakob Javits Convention Center in Manhattan, the state of New York guarantees covering all operating costs in excess of revenues.

There are numerous advantages to the quasi-public form of management. Foremost is the fact that the management team at the center operates like businesspeople, with concerns for the bottom line, rather than operating as municipal bureaucrats. Contracts do not have to follow municipal procedures, and can be implemented more quickly and, often, at lower cost. Civil service rules do not apply and, thus, the best-qualified people are employed in the center. In fact, the most notable and famous convention center general managers all work within quasi-public management structures.

WHICH TYPE OF MANAGEMENT IS BEST?

As previously mentioned, the structure of the organization that manages a convention center has a tremendous bearing on its operational effectiveness. However, decisions concerning center management are not always based on a goal of efficiency but are often politically motivated or influenced by strong labor unions. A mayor may wish to see his political supporters or relatives hired to manage the center, or a municipal workers' union may exert enough clout to have the center run as a department of government and, thus, use its members. The choice of center objectives either to attract out-of-town spending or to provide services for local residents may also impact on the management decision. The first choice will often yield a quasi-public management structure while the latter objective is likely to result in a public or governmental structure.

Fenich (1995) surveyed over 100 convention centers in the United States, comparing key operating variables of centers with different types of management. Results indicated that the largest facilities, having an average of 350,000 square feet of space, overwhelmingly adopted the quasi-public structure. The publicly managed facilities were much smaller, averaging about 145,000 square feet. As might be expected, private centers had the least square footage, with a mean of 115,000 square feet. Quasi-public facilities, then, are about 2.5 times larger than publicly managed centers and about three times larger than private ones.

Contrary to what might be expected, revenue streams do not parallel size (Table 8.2). Quasi-public centers generated total revenues of US$6.5 million on average, an amount greater than the average US$3.4 million for the public operations and the average US$3 million of the private centers. Thus, the first group outperforms the other two on this criterion by approximately double rather than the expected 2.5 and 3 times respectively. Furthermore, quasi-public centers incur the greatest net operating loss yet the difference from the other types of management is less than expected. Quasi-public operations have net losses of US$1.5 million, which is not double but only 25 percent higher than the US$1.2 million in losses incurred by public centers. In contrast, private facilities reported losses of only US$379,000—approximately one-quarter of those of quasi-publics rather than the one-third that would be expected based on the size differential. In view of these results, one might draw the conclusion that private management teams deliver the best financial performance followed by the public, while the quasi-publicly managed facilities are the worst performers. However,

TABLE 8.2. Convention Center Operations Based on Type of Management

	Public*	Private*	Quasi-public*
Direct revenue	3,408,000	2,987,000	6,469,000
Indirect revenue	494,000	280,000	316,000
Government transfers	1,655,000	1,462,000	3,422,000
Other revenue	1,298,000	100,000	701,000
Direct expenses	4,690,000	3,412,000	8,030,000
N.O.I.	-1,169,000	-379,000	-1,456,000
Debt	-2,534,000	-2,669,000	-5,983,000

*1990 Constant U.S. dollars

the differences in size obscure such a conclusion. Therefore, these operating traits were standardized to facilitate a comparison based on each 1,000 square feet of center space.

The standardization of results, allowing a direct comparison between the different types of management, had the effect of dampening the much higher income and expense streams of the more spacious quasi-public convention centers (Table 8.3). It also revealed that the public management teams have, overall, the poorest performance, worse than both quasi-public and private facilities. The public and private facilities both bring in standardized direct revenues of about US$25,000 (per 1,000 square feet) and outperform the quasi-public centers with US$18,483 on this measure. Not surprisingly, the public convention centers have to rely on far greater levels of non-operating or indirect income than do the other two types of management. This income may be derived from concessionaires, leases, contract parking, and other activities not under direct control of public management. They are also burdened with the highest level of expenses at US$32,344 per 1,000 square feet of space compared to US$29,669 for private centers and US$22,943 for the quasi-publics. Consequently, the publicly run centers have the highest net operating losses at US$8,062 per 1,000 square feet compared to a loss of

TABLE 8.3. Standardized Performance of Convention Centers Based on Type of Management

	Public*	Private*	Quasi-public*
Direct revenue	23,503	25,973	18,483
Indirect revenue	3,406	2,435	903
Government transfers	11,413	12,713	9,780
Other revenue	8,951	869	2,003
Direct expenses	32,344	29,669	22,943
N.O.I.	-8,062	-3,296	-4,160
Debt	17,476	32,209	17,094

*1990 Constant U.S. dollars

US$4,160 for the quasi-public facilities and a loss of US$3,296 for the privates.

These findings support a very important hypothesis regarding not only the operation of convention centers, but also that of other service facilities. Those convention centers that operate as private or entrepreneurial ventures are run better, financially, than those using any other type of management structure. The privately managed centers have the highest level of direct revenues relative to size and have the best net operating income, thus suggesting the highest level of management expertise. Further supporting the concept of privatization of public facilities administration is the performance of the publicly managed centers. Although they do not generate the highest or lowest direct revenues, they have the highest level of direct expenses and the lowest net operating income. This implies that they are not operating their facilities as efficiently or effectively as either of the other two management structures.

CONCLUSION

Convention centers are a major part of the MICE industry. They provide significant economic and physical impact to the cities that host them. Convention centers are typically owned by either government or private enterprises and are financed through various debt instruments, most commonly bonds. They exhibit one of three management structures: public, quasi-public, or private. Most large centers have adopted the quasi-public structure through which they seek to balance the needs of the community with those of the hospitality industry users and suppliers. Centers with public management tend to mirror other government operations with inefficiency and bloated payrolls. Although they are the smallest in size, privately managed centers are the most profitable and the most sensitive to the needs of users.

The future for convention centers in the United States looks bright (Fenich, 2001). In spite of increased use of the Internet for communication, people still exhibit a strong need to meet face to face as occurs at conventions. Communities continue to build or expand their facilities unabated. There is some concern that this construction and expansion will cause market saturation. This concern has been raised many times in the recent past, yet it has not been borne out to date.

The most likely scenario is that the biggest centers will get bigger while the medium-sized and smaller centers will focus their attention on regional meetings or smaller meetings that desire the intimacy of a smaller center. Also, facilities are becoming more high tech to meet the demands of users. Consequently, predictions that the U.S. convention industry will grow at a faster rate than previously anticipated may well be realized.

Chapter 9

Mediterranean Convention Bureaus: The Case of Italy

Harald Pechlaner
Pier Paolo Mariotti

INTRODUCTION

The Mediterranean region is one of the world's most important tourist destinations. Due to its political, social, and economic fragmentation, this fact has partly escaped the awareness of potential markets. Nevertheless, the effects of tourism in terms of politics, economics, society, and environment are enormous not only for the Mediterranean region itself, but also for neighboring market areas. Due to economic and political differences between individual states, on the one hand, and the north-south divide, on the other, the entire region appears somehow unstable concerning economy and politics. This instability is also the reason for the lack of a clear overall prospective trend for the development of the MICE industry in the Mediterranean region. Awareness of the common grounds within the region, however, is growing, bearing enormous economic possibilities. The development of some parallel political and economic areas, such as the European Union (EU), facilitates further advancement of the region. Yet it also intensifies strong local and regional cultures, further exacerbating fragmentation.

The development of convention tourism in the Mediterranean region also confirms these dilemmas. Fragmentation of activities becomes obvious due to the strength of local tourist infrastructures and marketing activities on a local level. There is also a general lack of cooperation between the nations of the Mediterranean region, making a common appearance almost impossible. To an increasing extent, however, awareness of the need for joint advertising of the diverse offers provided by the tourist destinations within the Mediterranean region is growing. Future development, however, will strongly depend on the form that a concentration of forces and core competencies of individual regional destinations will take.

This chapter provides an insight into the management and marketing strategies employed by Mediterranean convention bureaus (CBs), in particular Italian ones. The chapter will first detail some of the major challenges faced by the Mediterranean region before briefly discussing differences among European convention bureaus and the management of Southern European CBs. It will then focus on Italy in particular, assessing the state of the country's convention industry in general before outlining the major marketing initiatives adopted by Italian CBs.

CHALLENGES IN THE MEDITERRANEAN REGION

The Mediterranean region is marked by its political, economic, social, and ecological significance. Generally, it is a very delicate region. Political instabilities in various countries, once and again marked by military conflicts, make a homogeneous political line more difficult. The region may also be considered delicate in view of the instability of its ecological system, marked by differences in national policies and the degree of development concerning measures of coping with respective problems.

In its geographical limited totality, the Mediterranean region is without any doubt one of the largest and best-known destinations worldwide. Nevertheless, in the end, its popularity is founded on individual products of the states belonging to the Mediterranean region; different initial situations of tourism in individual states lead to problems in the overall development as a homogeneous destination due to different levels of development of market-oriented products. In addition, the Mediterranean region currently is not being advertised uniformly as an overall product. Only products similar to destinations, such as cruise tourism, make a significant contribution to the development of the Mediterranean region's popularity (Pechlaner, 2000; Pechlaner and Jäger, 2000).

The definition of the geographical region and the lack of data documenting the significance of tourism in the Mediterranean region represent two key problems. This is in part due to date to the small-scale efforts of cooperation among nations in the Mediterranean region, resulting from the aforementioned different levels of development and the current indistinct identification of a single Mediterranean product.

It is rather difficult to define the Mediterranean region. In the framework of the United Nations Environment Program (UNEP), eighteen nations, all of them bordering the Mediterranean Sea, define the region: Spain, Italy, Albania, Cyprus, Israel, Tunisia, France, Malta, Greece, Syria, Egypt, Algeria, Monaco, the former Yugoslavia, Turkey, Lebanon, Libya, and Morocco. This delimitation of the Mediterranean region, however, is still inadequate to grasp the reality of the entire region. The crucial problem is that many of these countries belong only partly to the region, with only the coastline and the hinterland deserving to be called Mediterranean, whereas the remaining territory of these countries calls for other geographic—and often cultural, social, and economic—classifications. One problem of delimitation that is essential for convention tourism is based on the examination of tourist-relevant areas in the eighteen countries mentioned above. In the case of Italy, approximately 70 percent of its national territory is considered part of the Mediterranean region, mainly because coastal areas and hinterland developed rather similarly in the past. Only a small part of essential product components, which support the success of the Mediterranean region, such as cultural tourism, is touching coastal areas themselves. This means that essentially alpine-based regions and provinces (Aosta, Trentino, South Tyrol, Piedmont, Lombardy, Belluno) are not considered part of the Mediterranean.

The Mediterranean region is more than just a confederation of nations bordering the same sea. Common grounds concerning history, economy, culture, geology, climate, and vegetation are the constitutive elements really defining the Mediterranean region. They represent the region's uniqueness and facilitate a better understanding of current problems from the historical point of view (Spataro and Khader, 1993). The diversity and heterogeneity of the tourist offerings present a chance for and at the same time a hindrance to common development. Even if there are some considerable differences in terms of political, economic, cultural, and religious matters, existing connections between these subcultures are obvious and may also be useful for a common development of tourism.

Examples of the hasty mass tourism developments of the 1960s and 1970s can be found throughout the region. They affected not only the environment but were also at times recognized too late in the course of increasing changes of international tourist markets. This makes modifications more or less impossible today (Williams, 1997). Considered for many decades purely a destination of sun, sea, and beaches, today the Mediterranean is attempting to position itself more as a region for which its cultural and natural assets are the essential elements of a holiday visit—presenting a significant chance for convention tourism. Montanari (1995) estimated about 160 million arrivals in the Mediterranean area in 1990. However, due to national differences, a uniform measurement of tourist arrivals is practically impossible. It is this fact that represents one of the biggest problems for future cooperation. The basis for any useful cooperation must be a common starting point; to define such a point appears to be almost impossible due to different (statistic) conditions.

The Mediterranean region is situated at the intersection of a north-south as well as an east-west divide, with the cultural and historical links holding special attraction for tourist markets. Due to their relative political stability and economic strength, the countries of the European south have been the real engines of growth for tourism in the Mediterranean region. Demand from international tourist markets concentrates on nations such as Greece, Italy, Spain, Turkey, the former Yugoslavia, and France (Papatheodorou, 1999). Therefore, the remainder of this chapter will focus on Europe's southern nations, with special consideration of Italy.

EUROPEAN CONVENTION BUREAUS

The concept of a convention bureau originated in the United States, where the first bureau was established in 1896 in Detroit, followed by hundreds across the country in the following decades. Due to the unstable political situation and the two world wars in the first half of the twentieth century, the first convention bureaus in Europe were set up in the 1960s (a notable exception are the Swiss convention bureaus). Significant differences between Northern and Southern European CBs can be observed in terms of geographical coverage and time of establishment. In Northern Europe, CBs are often national in coverage (e.g., German convention bureau) while Southern European countries lack national CBs, instead having a large number of regional or city bureaus. Furthermore, in Northern Europe CBs were established mainly in the 1960s and 1970s (e.g., the United Kingdom in 1968, Belgium in 1970, Germany in 1973) while bureaus in Southern Europe were established only in the 1980s (e.g., CBs of Madrid, Lisbon, and Florence).

Concerning the financing of CB operations, the majority of European CBs gather funding from the local, regional, and national government in the range of about 50 percent. The remainder is collected through the associated members in the form of membership fees and to a smaller extent from self-financing activities. Table 9.1 provides an insight into the composition and annual budget (in U.S. dollars) of several major European CBs.

In order to be effective, CBs need a strong consensus from the operators of supply in the region as well as from political representatives—consensus resulting from success in the marketplace and presented to the locals. The strong presence of the political institutions is reflected in the mixed legal structure chosen: mainly private in the form of consortiums with participation of official institutions. Different economic perspectives can lead to potential conflicts between private and public issues. CBs have to mediate in these instances. The variety of different legal structures in the same country allows for the autarkical spontaneous growth of these institutions, which operators recognize as a "passe par tout" to a suitable conference destination.

MANAGEMENT OF SOUTHERN EUROPEAN CONVENTION BUREAUS

In Southern Europe, due to political instability and the lack of suitable conference centers for medium-sized events in the late 1970s, it was essential for destinations to devise appropriate strategies to increase their appeal to the international convention market. In the 1980s numerous destinations in the region developed high quality infrastructure capable of hosting international events. Combined with increasing marketing efforts of the newly established CBs, meeting planners and PCOs finally took destinations in the region into careful

TABLE 9.1. Comparative Analysis of Convention Bureaus in Europe

Name of Convention Bureau	Year	Membership	Official Institutions	Others	Budget*
Lausanne Tourism	1866	30%	35%	35% services	700,000
Swiss Congress	**1964**	**100%**			**270,000**
Salzburg Convention Bureau	1957		100% City of Salzburg		250,000
CB of the Munich Tourist Office	1959		100% City of Munich		165,000
Vienna Convention Bureau	1969		90%	10% sponsors	340,000
Direction des Congres de Monaco	1972		Government		
GCB German	**1973**	**100%**		Lufthansa + DB sponsor	**268,820**
Helsinki	1974	55%	25%	20% self-financing	500,000
Antwerp Convention Bureau	1982	33%	67%		
Birmingham CVB	1982	30%	Local government		800,000
Barcelona Convention Bureau	1983	44%	44%	12% Other services	312,500
Oslo Promotion AS	1983	67%	25%	Projects 8%	93,000
Congress Stockholm	1983	25%	75%		500,000
Madrid Convention Bureau	1984	30%	70%		573,170
Cannes Convention Bureau	1984			100% city of Cannes	400,000
Promotrieste Convention Bureau	1985	10%	50%	40% L.T.B.	60,000
Lyon Convention Bureau	1986	20%	80%		270,000

Bureau	Year				Budget*
Lisbona Convention Bureau	1987	18%-40%	70%-40%	12%-20%	638,889
San Sebastian Convention Bureau	1988	15%	85%		150,000
Belgium Convention and Incentive Bureau	1989	No membership	2 tourist offices	Sabena + 6 convention cities	240,000
Edinburgh Convention Bureau	1990	20%	80%	Project funding	
Manchester CVB	1991	5%	20%	75%	190,000
Valencia Tourist and Convention Bureau	1991	20%	80%		250,000
Sevilla Congress and Convention Bureau	1992	30%	70%		140,000
Göteborg Convention Bureau	1993	50%	50%	City of Göttenburg 50%	300,000
Wonderful Copenhagen CVB	1994	60%	40%	Membership assoc.	831,000
Prague Convention Bureau	1994	Subscription	Prague City Hall		53,636
CB della riviera di Romagna	1994			5 members	2,150,000
CB Alto Adige	1994	70%	30%		161,290
Firenze	1995	30%	70%	10% Chamber of commerce	213,978
Berlin Tourismus Marketing	1996	50%	50%	50% by Berlin Tourist Board	190,000

Source: Mutschlechner, 1997.

*Budget in U.S. dollars.

consideration. The success of these strategies is reflected in the positions of Spain, France, and Italy in the top convention destination in the late 1990s, as shown in Table 9.2. Spain, for example, where the local CBs had only been established during the 1980s, was ranked in third place in 1998. Spanish CBs not only lobbied for and promoted infrastructure developments but also provided operators with special databases and survey data on specific markets.

Therefore, the ranking of Spain partly serves as a testimony that the existence of effective CBs positively influences the expansion of conference and meeting activity. This fact is also apparent when assessing the Mediterranean region's top convention cities, presented in Table 9.3. Capital cities such as Rome, Athens, and major cities such as Istanbul have similar rankings in terms of convention activity as smaller cities like Florence and Nice: the latter two cities have a CB and the former three cities do not.

TABLE 9.2. Top Convention Destinations 1996-1998

Country	Number of Conventions Held		
	1996	1997	1998
United States	232	200	192
United Kingdom	181	170	161
Spain	129	138	160
France	148	123	132
Germany	139	139	131
Italy	126	114	114
Australia	117	125	109
Netherlands	130	121	104
Japan	122	87	104
Austria	91	66	91

Source: <www.icca.nl>.

TABLE 9.3. Ranking of Mediterranean Convention Cities

City	1996	1997	1998
Madrid	33	46	76
Paris	50	47	46
Lisbon	25	23	40
Jerusalem	46	22	39
Barcelona	51	52	38
Nice	13	6	24
Rome	24	31	19
Athens	23	23	16
Florence	14	13	14
Istanbul	16	20	12

Source: <www.icca.nl>.

CONVENTION DESTINATION MANAGEMENT IN ITALY

In Italy, competition is dominated by tourist locations at local (villages and towns), regional (areas and valleys), and provincial levels (provinces, regions), the latter holding a different position in the national tourist organization Ente Nazionale Italiano per il Turismo (ENIT). ENIT mainly represents Mediterranean products. At the same time, however, it also participates in various projects of cross-border cooperation geared to promote and develop Italy as a destination in the European context. Nevertheless, ENIT does not represent a homogeneous and integrated product of Italian regions and provinces, but rather represents individual products separately to the market (Osti and Pechlaner, 2000). Each single region promotes the entirety of offerings, leading to a situation in which potential visitors cannot see the region's core competencies. From the region's point of view, unique competitive advantages and selling positions are lost. Italian regions enter different markets with different products, resulting in a diversification without any coordination or strategic controlling. This means a significant loss of synergistic effects (Pechlaner, 1999). The lack of coordination is also apparent in Italy's convention industry.

Italy's Convention Industry

The University of Bologna conducts an official survey of Italy's meetings and conference sector on an annual basis. The survey, "Osservatorio Congressuale Italiano," is financially supported by the industry publications, *Meeting and Congressi* and the *Convention Bureau della Riviera di Romagna*. According to Osservatorio Congressuale Italiano (2000), Italy in 1999 hosted nearly 100,000 meetings in 2,500 hotels and 320 conference centers, generating a total income of around L10,000 billion. Only 6.5 percent of these meetings were of an international nature. Table 9.4 provides a detailed breakdown of the type and location of these meetings, while Table 9.5 offers insights into the income generated by the various sectors.

Italy's first CBs representing tourist destinations were established in the 1990s in Naples, Genoa, Florence, Orvieto, South Tyrol, and Rimini. These CBs mainly took the form of consortia that had to report only to their members; public bodies had no control over their opreation. Each CB has fewer than five employees. Among the country's large cities such as Milan, Rome and Turin, only Turin established a CB, in 2000, as part of the "Turin International" initiative that engaged consultants from across Europe to plan the sustainable

TABLE 9.4. Number of Meetings in Italy in 1999

Number of Participants	Hotels		Conference Centers		Total	
	Number	%	Number	%	Number	%
50-100	49,467	70.6	10,598	40.0	60,061	62.2
101-300	18,531	26.5	12,080	45.6	30,613	31.7
301-500	1,350	1.9	1,215	4.6	2,565	2.7
501-1,000	598	0.9	1,905	7.2	2,503	2.6
over 1,000	87	0.1	674	2.6	761	0.8
Total	70,033	100.0	26,472	100.0	96,503	100.0

Source: Osservatorio Congressuale Italiano, 2000.

TABLE 9.5. Income by Generating Sectors

Source	Total
1.1. Meeting rooms and basic services	L 388,520,958,745
Ancillary services (set-ups, technology, and entertainment)	L 93,273,958,660
Income generated inside the venue	
Internal catering	L 379,707,326,357
Parking, papers, and tobacco	L 124,582,083,975
Subtotal	**L 504,289,410,332**
2.2. Income generated outside the venue	
2.2.1. Travel	L 4,677,698,875,712
2.2.2. Hotel accommodation	L 2,237,769,506,843
2.2.3. Urban transport	L 295,560,765,170
2.2.4. External catering	L 835,411,102,999
2.2.5. Shopping	L 541,833,023,666
2.2.6. Leisure activities	L 100,088,127,279
Subtotal	**L 8,688,361,401,669**
TOTAL Generated Income	L 9,674,445,729,406

Source: Osservatorio Congressuale Italiano, 2000.
Note: Exchange Rate 1 US$ = 2,220 L (March 2002).

growth of the city. The Turin Convention Bureau aims to promote the image of the city as an international conference destination and to provide potential buyers with the necessary support and information. Milan, on the other hand, is lacking not only a CB but also a facility that can accommodate large conventions. However, such a facility is currently under construction in the "Milano Fiera" area, to be completed in 2003. Until then, though, the biggest convention center in Milan is West End Studios, with a total of fourteen meeting rooms. The main hall has capacity for 1,800 people and offers about 11,000 square meters of exhibition space. In recent years, Genoa and Florence have turned large city areas into attractive convention centers (Lingotto, Porto Antico, Fortezza da Basso)—Florence can host conferences with up to 13,000 attendants. Authorities have approved plans for a new convention center in Rome. The Rimini Congress

Center is presently the largest convention facility in Italy. Following the current restructuring and expansion, its capacity will be raised to accommodate 8,000 delegates in the main hall.

Hotels are also capitalizing on the increased demand and are being constructed and converted to suit clients' requirements. This has certainly led to a general increase in the quality of hospitality and conference facilities but at the same time also to a standardization of services and a consequent loss of the characteristics that are the hallmarks of success in the host nation. This phenomenon relates to international chains as well as independent hotels, since international chains are now more confident in the stable political and economic situation and therefore will invest in new structures. Italian chains as well as independent hotels have been growing at a steady pace since the Gulf War in the early 1990s. Return on investment is high, but related investments are high as well. The supply of the Italian meeting industry is now at a high standard, but coordinated and cooperative promotion must be enforced. This is necessary to enhance Italy's image, to support private investors, and to raise the professional standards so that ultimately the pressures of international competition can be effectively dealt with. Several specialist publications support the advancement of higher professional standards in addition to providing advertising opportunities for Italy's meeting industry. EDIMAN Publishing is the leader in the field with its four publications, namely *Meeting and Congressi, Incentivare, Turismo d'affari,* and *IT. IT* is the magazine for the European meeting and incentive planner presenting opportunities available in Italy.

A New Marketing Strategy: The Integrated Offer of "Meet in Italy"

It is very difficult to market Italy as a meeting destination by means of a central convention bureau due to the extraordinary power of local, regional, and provincial tourist organizations. Tourist organizations are important partners of convention bureaus. They have to guarantee close contacts with businesses at a local level for purposes of product innovation and product bundling. Political issues concerning the creation of CBs and restrictive financial conditions resulted in a certain weakness of Italy's small CBs. They could not afford the high costs for international promotional activities and were therefore looking for synergies, in particular a reduction of the costs by creating consortia. The National Italian Convention Bureau was founded in 1994 by various tourism associations with the support of the National Tourist Board, ENIT. It had a short and difficult life of only three years. Reasons for its failure included the strong cultural identity of individual regions, the fragmentation of the Italian tourist industry, and finally the necessity for many regions to improve their products before marketing to the convention and meeting segment.

However, in view of the attractiveness of the convention industry to Italy and the fact that CBs grew not only in number but also in effectiveness since the mid-1990s, new attempts were made to create partnerships that could contribute to the success of the industry. "Meet in Italy" was created in 1998 by the Italian Convention Bureaus Council and Palacongress Italia (Italian Association of Congress Centers) to promote the country as a destination for meetings, conferences, and conventions. It brings together a selection of the most popular Italian destinations organized according to international quality standards. Apart from high quality services, each location offers its own unique context of history, art, and culinary traditions: the ideal setting for successful events. This partnership of regional CBs and conference centers is acting effectively as a destination management system. With this new all-inclusive concept of the conference product, Italy can offer highly competitive services on the international conference market and, at the same time, satisfy the very specific needs of meeting planners and PCOs.

Table 9.6 lists the members of this initiative—destinations highlighted in bold represent the territorial CBs while the remainder are individual congress venues acting as engines for the development of the meeting industry. "Meet in Italy" is a nonprofit association managed by a president who ensures that policies are carried out that have been set by the board of directors, which is nominated by the general assembly. The Italian Ministry of Tourism, the National Tourist Board ENIT, PCO Italia, the Italian Association of Meeting Planners, Italcongressi and Meeting Planners International (MPI), and the Society of Incentive Travel Executives (SITE) are involved in this initiative. "Meet in Italy" focuses on both association and corporate markets, at present especially in Northern Europe with plans to expand efforts to the North American market. It is present at the national industry exhibitions such as Borsa Internationale del Turismo (BIT)

TABLE 9.6. Members of the "Meet in Italy" Initiative

City/Region	Entity
Alto Adige—Südtirol	Convention Bureau
Bologna	**Palazzo della Cultura e dei Congressi**
Cernobbio—Como Lake	**Villa Erba**
Firenze	**Centro Affari**
Genova	Convention Bureau
Genova	**Cotone Congressi Genova**
Napoli	Consorzio Napoli Convention Bureau
Palermo	**Palazzo Gamma**
Portofino	Portofino Coast Convention Bureau
Rimini	Convention Bureau della Riviera di Romagna
Riva Del Garda	**Palacongressi**
Roma	**SGM Conference Center**
San Remo	Consorzio San Remo Congressi Turismo
Sorrento	**Sorrento Palace Conference Center**
Stresa	**Palazzo dei Congressi**
Torino	**Torino Incontra**
Trentino	Trentino Incontri Convention Bureau
Trieste	PromoTrieste Convention Bure

Source: <www.meetinitaly.com>.

and Borsa Turismo Congressuale (BTC), Full Contact, and Travel Trend, and also has permanent booths at main international exhibitions such as European Incentive and Business Travel and Meetings (EIBTM) in Geneva, Confex in London and Europe. The income generated in 2000 totaled about L12,000 billion (approximately US$5.5 billion), an increase of 20 percent over the previous year. However, the initiative has so far not received the wide public recognition and public funding it desires, though projects are devised to acquire both.

CONCLUSION

European convention bureaus focus primarily on the "special interest oriented" arrangement of events and regard themselves as links between the market and those entities supporting the offer, such as hotels and convention venues. Across Europe there are regional differences. Due to strong regional cultures and identities, Europe's Mediterranean region is characterized by a fragmentation of offers and infrastructures. This process of (cultural) regionalization is particularly apparent in the peripheral regions. There is a more intensive preoccupation with individual processes and products, to the disadvantage of an examination of cultural phenomena outside of the respective regions. The need for major expenditure combined with a lack of understanding of the necessity for long-term investment are essential contributors to the fact that in Mediterranean countries there is scarcely any public financing of infrastructures for large conventions. Consequently, the region boasts a large number of small and medium-sized congress infrastructures that do not have competitive strength in international markets, neither within Europe nor abroad. An additional consequence is the establishment of convention bureaus that for the most part are private-sector initiatives, resulting in a significant number of new formations—and also closures. The fragmented management of congress activities and offers makes national and cross-border coordination of congress offers in the Mediterranean region very difficult. Yet coordination is required to compete in international markets. Strong regional identities foil the necessary integration of congress tourism at a national level. The lack of national convention bureaus in most Mediterranean countries only exacerbates this situation.

The significance of the Mediterranean region is clearly shown by the proportions of tourism. However, this region is also delicate and can be easily disturbed, by ecological systems losing their balance or by political instabilities. This underlines the significance of a (tourist-) political setting as a central prerequisite for international congress destination marketing and a common policy concerning infrastructure, based on the strong points of the respective region. The increasing significance of culture—and therefore also cultural tourism—for the Mediterranean region has coincided with the deepening crisis of the traditional beach vacation. The richness of cultural heritage is an essential part of the Mediterranean region's attractiveness as a convention destination. The convention industry can make use of buildings, relics, and traditions in the landscape and in villages and cities, and give people attending the conventions and meetings an understanding of the cultural, social, and economic development of the respective regions. This can be realized through comprehensive packages, sightseeing tours for specific target groups, and, most of all, cultural events.

Chapter 10

The Convention Industry in South Korea

Sungsoo Pyo
Yeon-Seok Koo

INTRODUCTION

Korea has steadily developed into a major convention destination in Asia in recent decades. Statistics compiled by the Convention Bureau of the Korea National Tourism Organization (KNTO) indicate that in the ten-year period from 1990 to 1999, the number of international meetings, exhibitions, and events has increased at an annual average rate of 9.8 percent (KNTO, 2000a). In 1999, a total of 505 international meetings, exhibitions, and sports events were held in Korea, with the majority of these events attracting less than 1,500 delegates each (see Table 10.1). In terms of international conventions, Korea ranked twentieth in 1999 with forty-eight international meetings; its capital, Seoul, accounted for forty of these meetings, occupying eighth rank among meeting cities <www.icca.nl>.

Research has shown that the convention and meetings market makes a positive contribution to the country's economy. According to a survey by the Korea National Tourism Organization (KNTO, 2000b), the average expenditure per international convention delegate was US$1,763.51. In contrast, the per capita expenditure for international visitors amounted to only US$1,459.23. It is therefore not surprising that the government has placed special importance on the convention industry, especially since it has been faced with a decrease in tourism receipts in recent years, despite an overall increase in tourist numbers. For example, visitor arrivals to Korea totaled 4.66 million in 1999, representing an increase of 9.6 percent over the previous year. However, tourist receipts decreased by 0.9 percent to US$6.8 billion

TABLE 10.1. Number of Conferences, Events, and Conference Participants in Korea, 1990-1999

Year	Events	Conferences	Conference Participants
1990	220	145	25,802
1991	225	110	9,226
1992	252	139	13,972
1993	276	150	24,689
1994	308	146	19,164
1995	335	184	40,437
1996	395	227	28,567
1997	428	248	30,087
1998	495	267	22,725
1999	505	287	34,038

Source: KNTO, 2000a.
Note: Events include conferences and all other events with more than ten foreign participants from at least three countries or more.

(KNTO, 2000a). In an effort to change the decreasing trend in tourist receipts, a greater focus on the convention market appears sensible.

This chapter provides an overview of the state of the convention industry in the Republic of Korea (ROK). Following a brief account of the development of the tourism industry in Korea in the past fifty years, it will identify factors that contributed to the growth of the convention industry, detail the role of the Korea Convention Bureau, and outline market segmentation strategies. Finally, industry priorities are identified and discussed.

BACKGROUND ON SOUTH KOREA'S TOURISM INDUSTRY

Tourism is a relatively recent phenomenon in Korea. The Korean War ended in 1953. However, due to the need to rebuild the country's infrastructure and the pervasive image of Korea as a war-torn country, only 15,000 foreign visitors were recorded in 1962, the first year statistics on inbound tourist arrivals were available. Despite government incentives for the tourism industry in the form of tax exemptions, financial assistance, and streamlined legal procedures, there was still a much greater focus on the manufacturing sector in the following decades. That began to change in the late 1980s when Korea hosted the 1986 Asian Games, followed by the Summer Olympics in Seoul in 1988. The Olympics especially were preceded by a massive development of tourist infrastructure, the expansion of international air service, and tremendous media coverage that substantially enhanced the country's image worldwide. Since then several policies have been implemented—some of them having positive results, others having a detrimental effect. For example, in 1989 the Korean government relaxed existing travel restrictions, leading to the complete liberalization of outbound travel. However, the resulting increase in the number of Koreans traveling abroad lead to a substantial travel deficit, a problem that the government attempted to counter with the implementation of the frugality campaign in September 1990. A change in government in 1993 saw an end to the campaign and a concurrent redirection toward encouraging greater inbound travel with 1994 being declared "Visit Korea Year." In 1997 tourist arrivals totaled 3.9 million, with tourist receipts amounting to US$5.1 billion (KNTO, 2000a). The Asian financial crisis in 1997-1998 resulted in a decrease in outbound tourism, yet the industry was seen as helping to avert more serious effects on the country, due to its potential to earn foreign exchange and create jobs. Today tourism has been classified as a national strategic industry in which even the country's president has become involved through the promotion of Korea as an attractive tourist destination for international visitors.

GROWTH FACTORS FOR THE SOUTH KOREAN CONVENTION INDUSTRY

In recent years Korea played host to some major conventions and exhibitions, including the 1993 Taejon International Exposition of Science and Technology, the 1995 Lions Club Convention, the 1997 Annual World Dental Congress, and the 2000 Asia-Europe Meeting. The country's increased capability to accommodate these major events is based primarily on the increased development of convention and accommodation facilities, a greater ease of access to and increased presence of convenient transportation, and increased government support for and involvement in the industry. The country's unique cultural heritage, natural scenic beauty, cuisine, variety of shopping, and entertainment opportunities further add to the appeal (KNTO, 2000b).

Convention Facilities and Accommodation

COEX Seoul, Korea's representative convention and trade complex, is one of the largest and most modern meeting facilities in Asia. Established in 1986 as KOEX (Korean Exhibition Center), it experienced a dramatic increase in the number of exhibitions, from 37 in 1988 to 110 in 1995, with a concurrent increase in visitor numbers from 600,000 to 1.5 million over the same period ("KOEX's Contribution Ever Increasing," 1996). Renamed COEX in 1998, the complex underwent a major expansion which was completed in May 2000 at a cost of US$500 million. Features include a 6,500-seat convention hall; a 1,800-seat ballroom; a 1,100-seat auditorium; plus more than 89 rooms, a VIP center, an exhibition hall, an office complex, 650 hotel rooms, a galleria retail area, and an urban entertainment center <http://www.coex.co.kr>. COEX is equipped with ultramodern technologies and facilities that rival those of the most sophisticated convention centers around the world. It operates at an average occupancy rate of 73 percent and accounts for 80 percent of all exhibitions held in Korea ("COEX Today," 2001). Korea International Trade Association (KITA) owns the complex and COEX, a subsidiary company of KITA, manages it.

The Sejon Cultural Center and Olympic Park are two major venues in Seoul that can also accommodate large conventions. Korea's other major purpose-built convention facilities include EXCO Daegu, Busan Exhibition and Convention Center (BEXCO), and the International Convention Center Jeju. In addition to these convention centers, five more cities (Goyang, Suwon, Daejeon, Incheon, and Seoul) are planning or building international convention centers, with joint investments between local governments and the private sectors. Once the international convention centers are completed, affiliated companies will manage the facilities.

Seventy-three world-class deluxe (tourist) hotels with convention facilities are concentrated in Seoul, Busan, Gyeongju, Jeju, Daejeon, and Daegu (see Figure 10.1). Convention facilities in these deluxe

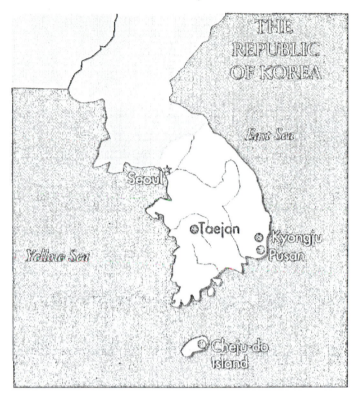

FIGURE 10.1. Major Convention Cities in Korea. Due to a recent initiative by the Korean government, the localities of Pusan, Kyongju, Cheju, and Taejon are now spelled Busan, Gyeongju, Jeju, and Daejeon, respectively.

hotels can accommodate from 300 to about 3,000 delegates, according to the Korea Hotel Association. The convention center at the Seoul Hilton, for example, has a capacity of 3,200 delegates. In terms of hotel accommodation, Korea had a total of 458 tourist hotels (48,791 guest rooms) in March 2000. About 100 of these hotels, accounting for 18,033 guest rooms, are located in the capital Seoul. In 1996, Gyeongju was host to five major convention hotels with a total of 2,000 rooms, while Busan had 56 hotels (4,600 rooms) and Jeju Island more than 4,600 rooms in 37 hotels ("Republic of Korea," 1996). Since then, several new developments have occurred in each of these locations. The criteria that are used for the grading of hotels in Korea favor hotels with convention facilities. However, Kim, Shin, and Chon (1998) also noted that the high land and construction cost make it difficult to initiate new hotel projects, and investors see little return on investment, in part also due to the high labor cost. They also point to the fact that the hotel grading system results in similar full-service facilities with a lack of alternative accommodation, such as all-suite, budget, and extended-stay properties.

Ease of Access and Convenient Transport

The quality and availability of airline services is critical to the industry, with the vast majority of international convention delegates arriving by air. Ahn and Ahmed (1994), in their analysis of South Korea's tourism industry, noted the dramatic increase in scheduled flights to and from the country, citing the Seoul Summer Olympics in 1988 and the liberalization of outbound travel in 1989 as major contributors. In March 2001 Incheon International Airport (IIA), one of the most advanced airports in the world, opened. Designed to become a major transportation hub in Northeast Asia, it can handle 27 million passengers and 170,000 flights annually. IIA is connected to downtown Seoul by an expressway, with a rail link to be completed by 2007. Gimpo Airport, until now the country's largest airport with over 780 scheduled flights per week in 2000, has been used for domestic flights only since November 2001. Two other major airports are Gimhae (Busan) and Jeju International Airport, which mainly serve Japanese and Chinese routes. Major cities are now also well connected by road and rail networks.

Government Support

Convention Promotion Law

The Korean government enacted the Convention Promotion Law in 1996 with the intention to attract meetings, conventions, and events to Korea, designate and develop "convention cities," and facilitate the construction of convention centers (KNTO, 2000a). Meant to support the local convention industry, the government's selection and development of convention cities is based on the level of advancement in infrastructure, specifically relating to convention centers, accommodation, transportation, and the existence of a convention and visitors bureau. Although no city has been designated as a convention city as yet, it is expected that several cities will receive such a designation by 2002. The Convention Promotion Law also boosts the construction of convention facilities. For example, a Tourism Promotion and Development Fund has been created to provide for convention center construction, though only very limited subsidies are currently available from this fund. Administrative procedures are simplified in the Building Act and other laws related to the building of convention centers. Classified as Social Overhead Capital Facilities, convention facilities are eligible for financial support in the form of tax exemptions, other payment reductions, and building site acquisition (KNTO, 2000a).

The Convention Promotion Law also enforces the standards for registration and responsibilities of the PCOs to maintain high quality. Fifty-two PCOs had registered with the province governments as of December 2000. Less than half of the registered PCOs also own travel agencies, and they are located in Seoul. The majority of the PCOs have about twenty employees who likely have graduate degrees. Monthly wages are expected to be greater than the average wage in related industries. Although no specific data are available, the monthly income of the entry-level positions for PCOs is probably less than US$1,500. Employees are expected to be good at English and have excellent computer skills.

Korea Convention Bureau

The Korea Convention Bureau (KCB), a nonprofit division of KNTO, was established in 1979 to promote international meetings and conventions in Korea. It has an executive director, five managers, and thirteen employees. The annual budget totals US$678,000, excluding wages. The KCB has several major tasks. These include the following: assist meeting planners in the preparation of attractive proposals, competitive bids, and presentations; coordinate site inspection visits for representatives of decision-making bodies; assist in the selection of suitable convention facilities, accommodation, and other convention suppliers; and provide a wide range of information and materials for tourism and conventions in Korea (KNTO, 2000a). Furthermore, the KCB identifies possible candidate conventions, provides one-stop services to assist PCOs and related bodies, and provides support for the organizations that hold conventions in Korea. Finally, KCB is involved in the promotion of the country's industry abroad, education and training, and data collection and provision. KNTO supports KCB's efforts by providing market intelligence that is utilized by convention professionals to attract international meetings and conventions. It is the primary information provider and promotion agent in relation to conventions and meetings; KCB is mainly responsible for the promotion of individual conventions.

Evaluation of Foreign Convention Delegates—Convention Destination Appeal

In 2000 KNTO surveyed over 700 international convention delegates to the country to determine their perceptions of Korea as a convention destination. Results indicated that delegates rated Korea very favorably. Employing a five-point scale from excellent to poor, the standard of meeting facilities and meeting operations especially received very high ratings. The price competitiveness and the kindness of people were also highly rated, as is apparent from results presented in Table 10.2.

TARGET MARKETS

More than 50 percent of conventions held in Korea in 1999 originated from Asia, as did the majority of delegates (KNTO, 2000a). About half of the conventions were organized by international associations. Data about domestic meetings and conventions are not available. To expand the market for international conventions and exhibitions, facilities still have to be improved and strong government support is needed.

Convention managers in Korea identify at least two major target markets. The first market segment is for the cooperative opportunity searchers who identify opportunities with other related bodies. The second segment is seminars that invite internationally known speakers.

Cooperative Opportunity Searchers

The target of cooperative opportunity searchers is meetings and conventions originating from international organizations. Identifying in-

TABLE 10.2. Evaluations of Foreign Convention Delegates (%)

	Excellent	Above Average	Average	Below Average	Poor
Convenient air route	22.8	50.9	20.2	5.3	0.8
Facilities	38.7	45.4	14.0	1.6	0.3
Meeting opera-tions	27.7	45.7	21.9	3.6	1.1
Travel information	11.3	40.1	38.6	8.2	1.8
Accommodation	12.3	32.2	44.7	7.9	2.9
Food and bever-age	17.2	39.4	37.0	5.3	1.1
Tour and nightlife	12.6	35.5	45.0	5.8	1.1
Attractive destina-tion	17.0	39.3	40.5	2.6	0.6
Shopping	11.8	34.3	46.3	5.7	1.9
Cultural heritage	27.4	45.0	25.3	2.2	0.1
Kindness	44.5	39.3	13.7	1.9	0.6
Price	13.1	49.1	34.5	2.5	0.8

Source: KNTO, 2000b.
Note: n = 723.

ternational opportunities and managing the process to attract these meetings and conventions are not easy tasks. In addition to the assistance from about 600 Korean organizations that are actively involved with international organizations, further systematic support is needed. To identify and attract conventions to Korea, the convention industry seeks close interindustry cooperation, covering exhibitions, events, tourism, lodging, and information providers. In an effort to maximize interindustry synergistic effects "Korea Convention and Event" (KOCE) was formed <http://koce.og.kr> and <http://www.seoulconvention.co.kr>. KOCE was created by private entities in the convention industry in July 2000. It cooperatively works and coordinates with KCB. KOCE covers marketing, public relations, and distribution while utilizing the relevant human resources and facilities to attract international conferences and exhibitions. KOCE has subpanels in charge of offering a one-stop service for international conferences. Also, human resource pools provide related personnel to PCOs at appropriate times and places. Advisory group members are engaged in consulting the management of member companies ("KOCE Dedicated to Promoting ROK Convention Industry," 2000).

Seminars

Market research is conducted periodically to identify the most recent trends in demand for advanced knowledge by industries. Personnel with experience in technology and other seminar-generating industries could be helpful in identifying the seminar market trends and demand. Most speakers at successful seminars come from the United States, Europe, or Japan. The success of the seminar is largely dependent on the invited speaker's reputation and ability to satisfy the needs of the industry, in addition to promotion. Information about reputation, affiliation, expenses, and other information about the possible candidates should be obtained, recorded, and examined to contact appropriate speakers. Fluency in the foreign language, especially for the speaker's native language, should be another consideration for the staging of successful seminars.

INDUSTRY PRIORITIES

According to KNTO (2000a), at least four priority areas for the development of the convention industry in Korea can be identified. They are the implementation of policy initiatives and supporting schemes, further construction of convention facilities, human resource development, and the establishment of independent organizations and partnerships with the stakeholders.

Policy Initiatives and Supporting Schemes

Currently two central government organizations (the Ministry of Culture and Tourism, and the Ministry of Industry and Energy) have supporting schemes for conventions and exhibitions. There are also two laws relating to promotion, namely the Convention Promotion Law and the International Trade Promotion Law. Conflicts in policies and standards between them should be avoided. Research on this issue should be carried out for efficient support for the convention industry.

Convention Facilities

More convention facilities should be built to accommodate a greater number of conventions, although financing could be a difficult task due to the low return on investment and the substantial amount of money required to build convention facilities. Incentives for investors and the private-public partnership could be encouraged, and other alternatives should be explored. Currently investments in convention centers tend to be initiated by local governments or cities with the local private sectors, and the local governments seek subsidies (matching funds) from the central government. Also, tax incentives are provided. About half of the convention facilities are located in the Seoul area and the economic impact on the local economy is not realized. Economic impact studies have until now been conducted only as part of specific convention center feasibility studies. Clearly, there is a need for more extensive economic impact studies.

Many local governments consider building convention centers. If they do go ahead with their plans, then an oversupply of facilities is a potential outcome. There is no regulatory process to prevent local governments from the construction of convention facilities. However, the designation of an official convention city through the Convention Promotion Law provides for support from the central government for the development and promotion of facilities in one particular city. There is need for feasibility studies to select a limited number of convention cities. The cities should be evaluated regarding whether they have sufficient supporting environment, infrastructures, and managerial capabilities, in addition to tourist attractions, to differentiate themselves with regional characteristics and the cooperation from stakeholders from other convention destinations.

Human Resource Development

The third important area should be human resource planning and development. At present various educational programs are available. Three universities (Hallym University, Kyung Hee University, and Kyonggi University) offer degree programs in addition to Jeju College of Tourism. Ten universities offer classes in meetings and conventions, with a larger number teaching related courses in tourism and hospitality. Furthermore, eight organizations (universities, governments, and convention- related organizations) offer training programs lasting from three weeks to one year. These programs provide an overview of the convention industry and a focus on the management and operations of meetings and convention. Professional conference organizers in Korea have limited ability in attracting foreign conventions because the industry is relatively young and PCOs have as yet not accumulated enough knowledge and experience to operate in the international market. Consequently, further advancement is needed in curriculum development, certification, forecasting the human resource demand, and schemes to develop and provide quality employees. International cooperation could be helpful in furthering human resources development.

Establishment of Independent Organizations

Establishing KCB as an independent organization from KNTO was recommended by various bodies to enhance periodical promotional activities and to organize events and related products systemically. An independent KCB could develop strategies, suggest incentives and special accommodation rates, and support public and private efforts to attract meetings and conventions. Also, local convention bureaus could coordinate chambers of commerce, local PCOs, lodging facilities, travel agencies, educational institutions, and other related stakeholders to promote conventions and boost the local economy.

CONCLUSION

The convention industry in Korea has experienced a dramatic increase in the past decade. It is becoming a major player in the Asia-Pacific region, and its future prospects are promising with expanding markets, strong government support, and constant improvements to both the infrastructure and superstructure. However, to become more competitive on a global scale it is crucial to engage in more international exchanges to gain greater insights into market trends and managerial expertise. KCB's involvement in major international convention-related organizations will be critical in that context. Furthermore, closer links with international private-sector organizations should be forged—at present they are not extensive due to limited budgets, resources, and experiences. Continuous market research is necessary for the development of medium- and long-term strategic plans, to promote and to attract conventions, to develop competitive convention products, and to conduct targeted campaigns. Finally, cities with convention centers should carefully consider convenience, a comfortable environment, and unique tour programs for convention delegates so that they can become preferred destinations.

Chapter 11

Convention Hotels in Australia: Trends and Issues

Vivienne S. McCabe

INTRODUCTION

Hotels worldwide, through the provision of accommodation, meeting and function space, food and beverage, and other associated supporting facilities are a major supplier to and key component of the MICE industry. They have recognized the monetary value and related benefits of this truly global industry, regarding it as a high yield and highly lucrative area that provides a positive revenue stream and a means to contribute to a solid profit. However, the hotel sector also recognizes that as the convention and exhibition industry grows, so too does the level of competition between destinations, their hotels, venues, and other industry suppliers (PATA, 2000). Both conference delegates and conference organizers become more discerning in their choice and requirements of a destination and its convention hotels. Therefore, convention hotels need to keep abreast of key industry trends and issues if they are to maintain and develop their business in this lucrative and desirable market.

Australian hotels have long recognized the potential benefits of the convention and exhibition industry as a key generator of income. The past ten to fifteen years have seen major developments and sustained growth within the sector as the country has increasingly become recognized as one of the world leaders in the provision of high quality facilities, its infrastructure, and for the professionalism of its service. This growth has impacted upon and influenced the construction and development of hotels that focus on the sector as a key component of their business. Particularly interesting is that this development has not followed the traditional format of its European and North American counterparts. Rather, Australia, although recognizing the achievements in these continents, developed its own approach to the operation of its convention industry.

This chapter focuses on the trends and issues that are faced by Australian convention hotels. It first provides an overview of the spatial distribution of convention hotels in Australia before offering a historical perspective on their development in the past decades and an assessment of the range of convention hotels found in the country. The continued development and expansion of facilities, the greater involvement of regional convention hotels in the business, and changes in the operation and management of conventions and meetings are just some of the key trends identified and discussed. Throughout the chapter similarities with and differences to convention hotels in the United States and Europe are highlighted.

SPATIAL DISTRIBUTION

In Australia the development of the industry and its venues has been concentrated upon state and territory capital cities and follows the distribution of the country's population. There is a concentration toward the eastern seaboard (see Figure 11.1), with all major convention destinations, except Canberra (the nation's capital) and Hobart (Tasmania), having international as well as domestic airports in addition to a range of convention hotels. These have been supported by appropriate infrastructure and facilities including a convention and visitors bureau and in many instances a dedicated purpose-built convention and exhibition center.

HISTORICAL PERSPECTIVE

Realizing its potential, Australia began to develop the convention and exhibition market in the late 1980s, with the development being sustained during the 1990s. One of the key strategies was the construction of a number of dedicated and stand-alone purpose-built convention and exhibition centers in Adelaide, Canberra, Melbourne, and Sydney. Brisbane and Cairns followed in 1995 and 1996 with extensions to the centers in Sydney, Melbourne, and Adelaide taking

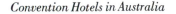

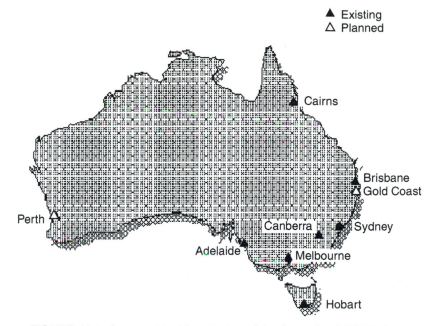

FIGURE 11.1. Geographical Distribution of the Australian MICE Industry

place in the late 1990s. This initiative was accompanied by the development of hotels that focused on the convention industry as a market sector and provided support to those stand-alone centers that operated without the traditional bedstock. In capital cities where there was no dedicated purpose-built convention and exhibition center, large hotels, often with a casino attached, provided the focus for the development of the conference and exhibition business. For example, in Tasmania the Wrest Point Hotel Casino and Conference Center in Hobart took the lead, and in Perth it was the Burswood International Resort Casino.

Convention hotels in Australia may have been victims of a number of external environmental forces that have impacted not only on their development but also on their ownership by overseas organizations and the opinion of financial institutions. The recession of 1991-1992 in Australia led to many hotels being placed in the hands of the receiver while still operating (Richardson, 1999, p. 225). Despite low occupancy levels being recorded overall, there were shortfalls in four- and five-star accommodation and facilities at certain key business periods (BTR/TFC, 1998, p. 16) together with seasonal peaks and troughs of business. Both industry and government recognized the need to develop sufficient accommodation and meeting facilities in many city centers to allow for the growth of the industry. This fact together with the need to ensure the availability of long-term finance to encourage investment in facilities were some of the key issues outlined in the Commonwealth Government's National MICE strategy produced in 1995.

Today hotels that focus on the convention business in Australia are in the majority owned by either international or national hotel chains. Many changes in the corporate structure of these groups have taken place over the past few years as they have repositioned themselves and adopted global strategies. Accor Asia Pacific, for example, is the dominant international hotel group and the largest provider of meeting and conference facilities; other companies include Six Continents; local operators include, for example, Rydges Hotels and All Seasons.

It is important to acknowledge that the convention business in Australia is predominantly domestic business, with approximately 80 percent of the market being gained from local conventions and meetings (Commonwealth Department of Tourism, 1995). As such it is subject to the external factors that may impact upon the domestic business environment. For example, in the mid-1990s, the withdrawal of the government's training guarantee scheme and support for employee training saw a downturn in the domestic conference and meeting business undertaken in the corporate and government sector attracting between twenty and sixty delegates. This particularly affected convention hotels, the main provider of meeting and conference rooms for this segment. In contrast, the announcement in late 1994 by then IOC president Juan Antonio Samaranch of the success of the Sydney Olympic bid brought the press comment, "Wham bam, thank you, Juan," as the Sydney convention market became inundated with requests to hold international and national conferences in the city. It became a catalyst for the development of infrastructure not only in Sydney but also throughout the country and foresaw a period of continued sustained growth. Hotel companies and convention destinations went into partnership to promote the quality of the venues and infrastructure and the professionalism of their operation. There was a wide representation at overseas trade shows together with associated publicity and public relations campaigns. The volume of business increased substantially, with Sydney alone having won 210 events worth AU$940 million for the city in the period from 1994 to 2000 (SCVB, 2000). In 2000, the International Congress and Convention Association (ICCA) identified Sydney as the number one convention city in the world. The Asian economic crisis of the late 1990s also had an impact on the volume of international business, yet the effect was perhaps somewhat overshadowed or dulled by pre-Olympic euphoria and the delight and interest in Australia as a destination. However, recent reports reveal that in the post-Olympic period and due to the global impact and downturn in the industry following the events of September 11, 2001, low occupancies and low volumes of convention business are being experienced in Sydney and other capital cities in Australia <www.atc.net.au>.

For the period 1991-1992 to 2000-2001, there has been an 84 percent increase in the number of rooms provided by convention hotels in the Sydney area. This has been supported by associated meeting facilities. Growth patterns have also occurred in the other capital cities, the main centers of business and population, for example, Melbourne and Brisbane. Table 11.1 provides a summary breakdown, by star rating, of the hotels providing convention facilities in the central business district (CBD) and metropolitan areas of the main cities of Australia. Sydney (no doubt influenced by the Olympics) followed by Melbourne has by far the largest hotel stock, in terms of the number of convention hotels, room accommodation, range and number of meeting rooms available, and in number of five-star hotels. Research conducted by the Sydney Convention and Visitors Bureau indicates that 79 percent of international convention delegates to the city tend to stay in four-star or five-star hotels with 37 percent using selected five- star hotels. This is in contrast to domestic convention delegates where there is a predominance to frequent four-star properties (SCVB, 1999).

Sydney, Melbourne, and Brisbane also feature the country's largest purpose-built convention and exhibition centers, often regarded as a catalyst for the encouragement of convention business to a city or area.

TABLE 11.1. Profile of Convention Hotels in Major Australian Cities

CBD and Inner-City Star Rating	Brisbane	Gold Coast	Sydney	Canberra	Melbourne	Hobart	Adelaide	Perth/ Fremantle	Cairns
3.5	1	N/A	11	3	N/A	0	N/A	N/A	2
4	8	N/A	15	7	N/A	7	N/A	N/A	7
4.5	3	N/A	13	4	N/A	2	N/A	N/A	4
5	6	N/A	14	1	N/A	0	N/A	N/A	4
Total number of hotels	**18**	**23**	**53**	**15**	**29**	**9**	**17**	**20**	**17**
Total number of accommodation rooms	3,649	6,558	15,514	2,493	6,873	985	2,732	4,420	3,717
Number of hotels 1-4 meeting rooms	4	6	20	6	14	5	6	7	10
Number of hotels 5-9 meeting rooms	9	12	19	8	9	3	7	9	6
Number of hotels 10 and more meeting rooms	5	5	14	1-Jan	6	1	4	4	1
Largest capacity of meeting rooms (theater style)	1,125	2,160	1,500	1,500	2,500	1,650	800	2,300	600
City has purpose-built convention and exhibition center	Yes	Planned	Yes	Yes	Yes	No	Yes	Planned	Yes

Source: Compilation by author of figures from convention and incentive planners/facilities guides produced by individual city convention bureaus.

RANGE OF CONVENTION HOTELS IN AUSTRALIA

Australian hotels that specialize in conventions, conferences, and meetings comprehensively cover the five categories of hotels that provide meeting facilities as identified by Lawson (2000). The country's convention hotel facilities range from large city-center business hotels with 250 to 600 rooms, medium-sized suburban and motor hotels with 100 to 250 rooms, large resort hotels and integrated resorts, airport hotels, to country house and boutique resorts. The high standards provided by these hotels and their supporting facilities have been recognized by the industry and businesses worldwide. Premier convention hotels encompass world-class accommodation, purpose-built conference and meeting rooms, separate group check-in areas, and specifically designated parking and drop-off areas. Also found are column-free ballrooms and meeting spaces, a comprehensive range of meeting rooms and breakout areas, and food and beverage facilities specifically designed to support primarily the meeting space and associated functions. Many of the properties boast not only a full and extensive list of audiovisual facilities but on-site experts who are readily available to support the meeting organizer. Numerous major hotels have convention and meeting facilities located within one area by providing dedicated floors within their properties that specifically focus on and are tailored to conventions and meetings (e.g., Hotel Intercontinental, Sydney). Unlike Europe, Australia did not have a large stock of traditional and historical hotels and consequently was able to take advantage of the latest in construction techniques to accommodate the requirements of the industry. It has been able to incorporate not only the latest in convention and meeting room design but also in the supporting infrastructure.

A key area of development for the convention industry in Australia has been the construction of a number of resort hotels and integrated resorts, as might be found in the United States but which tend to be absent in Europe. These properties and resorts range in size from up to 300 rooms plus a number of suites to integrated island resorts that encompass four hotels with a combined total of over 750 rooms plus suites. In addition, they feature extensive meeting and function rooms, a large ballroom and conference rooms, a range of swimming pools, recreation facilities, and golf courses. These integrated resorts, often focusing on the lucrative corporate and incentive markets, are an integral part of the Australian convention and meeting scene. They are found throughout the country and in a number of key locations, such as Queensland which features, for example, Hamilton Island, the Sheraton Mirage, Port Douglas, and Gold Coast, Hyatt Coolum. A number of regional areas such as Coffs Harbour on the Northern New South Wales coast and Uluru (Ayers Rock) in Central Australia have also developed either integrated resorts or resort hotels, seeing it as an opportunity to attract both the leisure and business tourist.

CURRENT TRENDS AND ISSUES

Improvement of Facilities

The continued improvement of facilities through development and upgrades as seen in the United Kingdom, United States, and Asia is also apparent in the convention hotel industry in Australia. Many venues are building new convention facilities; others undertake multi-million dollar refurbishments to expand and upgrade existing facilities. The construction of new or the expansion of existing stand-alone purpose-built convention and exhibition centers also continues (for example, in Perth, Sydney, Adelaide, and on the Gold Coast) since it is seen as a major facilitator for attracting both national and international MICE business to the area. Hotel companies have recognized that although these centers provide competition they are also a catalyst for new business. They are therefore continuing to develop new or upgrade their existing facilities to compliment such developments in an effort to increase their share of the convention market. Especially hotels that are in close proximity to the city's convention center and tourist attractions, such as Crown Towers in Melbourne and the Novotel in Sydney's Darling Harbour, possess a distinct advantage.

The construction of apartment and all-suite hotels in many of the capital cities has been a further area of development for the Australian conference market. Operated by such companies as the Mirvac Hotel Company, these venues offer studios and one- to three-bedroom apartments, often with an office. They frequently feature three to four conference rooms with capacities for 25 to 100 delegates, a restaurant, room service, and a range of leisure and supporting facilities. As such they are particularly targeted to the domestic corporate market sector.

To date the development and expansion of convention hotels has been mainly concentrated in cities. However, the desire to attract and expand business to regional areas and their venues is also evident. Regional venues want to become more involved due to the recognition of the highly lucrative and high-yield nature of the industry. This, however, is posing difficulties in some areas given the lack of quality facilities and professionalism of service. Consequently, conference organizers in regional hotels may need to use more lateral thinking as to how to overcome these problems in an area that often lacks the traditional support and infrastructure found in venues in capital cities, especially their central business district (CBD) properties.

The boutique venue, mainly situated outside capital cities, is another feature of the Australian conference scene. These individual properties, often in remote but beautiful locations, such as the Blue Mountains in New South Wales or Cradle Mountain, Tasmania, have recognized the benefit of the conference market. They provide both high levels of service and facilities such as small meeting rooms, and leisure and recreation facilities, all aimed to attract the domestic corporate business retreat market. This sector, however, may not be as well developed as in the United Kingdom where the country house hotel owner is specifically targeting the conference organizer (Greaves, 2001).

Shorter Lead Times

Shorter lead times between the booking with the venue and the actual occurrence of the conference or meeting are now commonplace. This trend, identified in a study by McCabe and Weeks (1999), has over the past few years become a fact of life and appears to be continuing. Initially, the trend was seen only within the corporate and business sectors. However, it now appears to be affecting other MICE market segments. For example, some conference hotels report association conferences with lead times of six months from initial booking to the actual event. This supports the trend reported in the United States, where lead times of twenty-four weeks for domestic training and management meetings and twelve weeks for sales meetings are being cited. An increasing number of management meetings are being planned and executed in less than a month (Swisher, 2001).

Greater Price Competitiveness

Australia is seen as a competitive and value-for-money destination. However, there is evidence of price competitiveness in the marketplace at both a national and local level. Convention hotels need to ensure that they provide value for money in the packaging of their convention product as they adjust to the peaks and troughs of business. Some city convention hotels in Australia provide a "day" and a "twenty-four hour" delegate rate for conference and meeting room hire; in other destinations, venues tend to provide "a la carte" pricing (individual costing of items such as room hire, food and beverage, audiovisual equipment, etc.). In contrast, some historical houses and castles in the United Kingdom employ a different approach to pricing. Prices are quoted for the exclusive use of the property, for example, £2,500 per twenty-four-hour period for twenty guests—this amount would cover accommodation, the use of facilities, and all food and beverages (Gosling, 2001). Venue operators using this system believe that they are providing value by quoting a total inclusive figure that will assist the potential conference buyer budget accurately for the event. Though this system has not been reported in Australia there is the potential for it to be implemented in boutique style venues in regional areas.

Price competitiveness and speed of response (often with the need to provide a firm proposal and quotation within eight hours of the initial inquiry) are frequently found to be the deciding factors for four-star CBD hotel venues to gain business, particularly in the lucrative corporate market. In the United States, Hyatt Hotels introduced a new initiative, offering "e-mmediate" group bookings that enables the conference organizer to reserve room blocks and meeting space online. This procedure, which bypasses the "request for proposal" process, will affect the whole industry (Anonymous, 2001b). The effect on price negotiation for the meeting space is still to be determined. Meanwhile, the increased use of Internet technology and e-mail facilitates communication between the convention hotel and conference organizer. However, although a conference organizer may undertake the preliminary research of the venue and a virtual tour through the hotel's Web site, the quality of service and attention to detail still remain paramount. Many convention hotels now fully recognize the importance of identifying the organizers and their delegates' needs and are totally committed to meeting those needs (PATA, 2000).

Shorter, Smaller, More Targeted Meetings

At the same time, there is evidence of a trend toward shorter meetings, and meetings and conferences that are more focused on a subsector of a particular market. As a result, events are becoming more targeted and are attracting smaller delegate numbers. If this trend continues it will impact upon the size of the conference facility and the conference plenary and breakout rooms required. The trend, experienced in the United Kingdom by some hotels—particularly country house hotels and medium-sized suburban hotel groups—to perhaps focus on one sector of the MICE market, such as the corporate training market, by providing training suites and rooms and equipment, has not occurred to date in Australia. Although there are a few residential conference centers, such as The Bardon Conference Center, Brisbane, to date no hotel chain has focused on a specific MICE product area as its main business. Many of the medium-sized suburban and motor hotels, found in the city suburbs and within regional areas, are individually owned and tend to provide general convention facilities such as a main conference room for 80 to 200 people and two to three small meeting rooms or breakout areas. These venues continue to focus mainly on the domestic corporate, government, and association markets, often within their local area.

Australian convention hotels are also keen to attract and develop the highly lucrative incentive sector. The country is seen by this sector as appealing, providing a diverse product and a unique experience. This coupled with the low exchange rate of the Australian dollar offers the incentive traveler value for money and "big bangs for corporate bucks"—a perfect reward incentive. According to Mr. Ken Boundy, ATC's managing director, from the Australian Tourist Commission, the MICE industry wants to increase its 8 percent share of the international incentive tourism industry <www.atc.net.au>. The growth to date in this sector has provided an opportunity for certain specialist convention venues to expand, develop, and promote their facilities to the incentive market—a market that has traditionally utilized resort style venues. There is now a trend for deluxe city-center properties such as the Le Meridien, Sydney, and regional areas, such as the Hunter Valley to focus on this market. Some venues such as the Park Hyatt in Melbourne have appointed specialists to develop this potential area of sales. Partnerships between convention and incentive hotels and other attractions and facilities within an area have been forged in a joint effort to attract incentive groups to a city or region.

Greater Product Differentiation

In this highly competitive environment, hotels that specialize in the convention market continue to look for ways to differentiate their product and to build relationships with their customers. New ways to tantalize the customer are being sought. There are now twenty-first century concept hotels where the image is not one of space-age décor and technology but more about practicality, comfort, and style all designed to meet the needs of the business traveler, as well as hotels featuring private offices and small soundproofed executive meeting rooms. Golf courses, health and fitness centers with ultramodern gymnasium, spa, massage, and relaxation facilities, complete with highly trained therapists, continue to be a familiar trend. So too is the opportunity for team-building seminars, motivational programs, and other incentive activities, all of which are available both on and off site.

The theming of events within convention hotels is now commonplace, with examples such as the Australian beach party—"where the bush meets the sand" being popular. Hotels are now also providing facilities such as crèches, kids clubs, and activities to accommodate and encourage the families of potential conference attendees to accompany them to the event, thereby increasing potential delegate attendance and associated revenue. This trend is also being confirmed in the United States where conference organizers are recognizing that attendance at the conference by a delegate's immediate family is becoming more commonplace. This trend has been apparent for the association market and more recently also in the corporate sector. It is in line with corporations' initiatives centering on more family-friendly work practices (Ligos, 2000).

The emphasis on the provision of quality food continues to be a key area focused upon by convention hotels. "Intelligent cuisine," light, innovative, business-style conference lunches, interesting and healthy coffee and tea breaks that provide, for example, fresh fruit platters, fresh fruit juice, and herbal and fruit teas, are now commonplace, replacing or complementing the traditional tea, coffee, and biscuits. Australian conference organizers have still to confirm the trend identified in the United States whereby the cost of providing food and beverage by hotels is found to be approximately 20 percent of an average conference budget (Anonymous, 2001c). A popular method that is being used by some Australian CBD convention hotels to expand the capacity of their venue and to achieve peak utilization of their facilities at certain times is to provide outside catering to corporate clients. This is seen as a means not only to expand the facilities and potential capacity but as an opportunity to strengthen the relationship with the client.

Changing Organizational Structures

The trends outlined so far impact upon the management and operation of the convention and exhibition facilities within convention hotels. For example, for convention hotels to become more responsive to the needs of the customer, changes in organizational structures are necessary with evidence of reengineering taking place. Changes to the operational systems and structures have occurred, particularly in international hotel groups, during the last few years. Task forces and teams have become dominating terms. There are changes to the role of convention management in hotels and to the job titles of convention management staff. For example, convention service managers (CSM) or directors within some hotel groups have now been termed events managers—a title designated to identify the many facets and changes in their role. The previous convention management team, including banquet operations, is now placed under a director of event management. In some cases, the director of event management reports directly to the director of food and beverage and then through to the hotel general manager.

"One-stop shopping" in the booking and organization of a potential event has now become commonplace with all aspects of a conference, exhibition, and event, including functions such as lunches, dinners, parties, etc., being handled by the event management team. This includes the previously separated "residential accommodation" component of a conference that was handled and managed by the reservation department. This trend was identified by McCabe and Weeks (1999).

The importance and value of yield management systems for hotels' revenue from their convention and exhibitions functions are becoming more recognized. Although yield management techniques for hotel accommodation have long been successfully employed, there is now a trend in some venues and hotel companies with specialist convention facilities to formulate, develop, and utilize more sophisticated yield management systems. These systems support moves toward a more comprehensive system of revenue management. In fact, some hotel companies appoint a director of revenue management whose role is total responsibility for yield management for the venue.

Staffing and Career Management Issues

Hotels are seen as a key recruitment and training ground for the MICE industry. This has major implications for the training and development of staff not only within a venue but also within this industry. McCabe (2001b), in a study of the career and labor mobility of managers and supervisors in the MICE industry, found a high level of mobility between the sectors of the industry. More than a quarter of the respondents indicated that at some time in their career they had worked in the convention and function areas of a hotel. However, case histories of a small number of convention service directors employed in five-star hotels revealed that their career progression had been solely within this sector of the MICE industry. It brings to the forefront the issue of career opportunities for a senior manager of convention and events—someone who is responsible for a major revenue generation area in a hotel. The average length of time at a position of convention services manager in a four- or five-star convention hotel ranges from two years in Australia (McCabe and Weeks, 1999) to four to five years in the United States (Montgomery and Rutherford, 1994). This fact poses several questions: What strategies are in place to ensure that these key managers are retained in the convention hotel? What is the potential career progression? Is it common for an individual who has specialized in this role to become a hotel general manager? Some of the major hotel groups, such as the Marriott Corporation, offer specific training. Job enrichment strategies, such as short secondments to a group-training role to assist in the delivery of new training initiatives and being given the task to develop the standards and systems for convention management for the group's hotels, are found in other establishments. In terms of long-term career aspirations, several convention services directors interviewed by McCabe (2001b) readily stated that their next move was to director of food and beverage and then hopefully to hotel general manager.

In some cities, such as Sydney, a continual lack and availability of service staff in hotels has been reported with shortages in the number of operational staff becoming acute (convention services managers, Sydney, personal communication, September 1997). This has implications for the recruitment and retention of staff within this sector of the industry and provides a challenge for convention hotels to reduce staff turnover. There are calls from the sector to the education and training providers for staff specifically trained in banqueting and convention services operation and supervision.

CONCLUSION

Australian convention hotels have progressed dramatically over the past ten years and demonstrated their commitment to the MICE industry and its development. However, to maintain a competitive advantage they will need to keep abreast of both global and national trends and address critical issues in a timely manner. The highly lucrative nature of the expanding MICE market is attracting more international competition at a time when there are indications of a slowdown in the global economy and of customers being ever more discerning. It will be crucial for Australian convention hotels to keep abreast and ahead of global trends to effectively compete in the twenty-first century.

PART III:
THE FUTURE

Chapter 12

Trends and Key Issues for the Convention Industry in the Twenty-First Century

Karin Weber
Kye-Sung Chon

INTRODUCTION

The convention and meeting market is cyclical in nature and susceptible to changes in the business environment. The current slowdown in the global economy and impending recession have the potential to decrease conference and meeting activity in the near future, given the lead times associated with the industry. Yet even in times of recession meetings and conventions are still held, albeit in fewer numbers, with the view of them representing investments rather than costs only. It is therefore likely that the increase the convention industry has experienced in the past decades is set to continue in the longer term. With the benefits of convention tourism now being recognized, destinations are interested not only in investing in the required infrastructure but in maintaining growth and obtaining a return on investments. Competition is likely to intensify, with newly developing destinations challenging the positions of the mature ones. However, the greatest changes are likely to occur in the structure of the convention industry and the role it is going to play in an information-oriented society that has embraced technology.

The turn of a century and especially the beginning of a new millennium are prominent times to take stock, reflect, and, of course, also to look toward the future. Several international convention industry associations undertook studies that focused on these very issues. For example, the Professional Convention Management Association (PCMA) commissioned an environmental scan, with the purpose of identifying trends to anticipate the needs of its members and assist them to prepare for the changes ahead. Similarly, the International Association of Convention and Visitors Bureaus (IACVB) instigated the CVB Futures Project, with a survey of the association's membership being a critical part of the study. A "Millennium Leaders Summit," initiated by the International Congress and Convention Association (ICCA) and organized on behalf of the Joint Meetings Industry Council (JMIC) brought together over 100 participants from numerous industry organizations in Kuala Lumpur in June 2000. In a series of workshops they discussed issues such as globalization, technology, standards and best practice, education and professional development, and industry recognition. Finally, several meeting industry publications also conducted studies assessing future trends.

In individual chapters, authors have outlined some of the future trends and key issues pertinent to the topical focus of their chapters. This final chapter takes a more global approach to the question of future trends and developments. The focus is not so much on the likely changes within the industry but on general trends and changes in the broader environment that will affect the industry. Key issues that have to be addressed by the industry for continued growth in the future will also be discussed.

In doing so the chapter summarizes some of the key outcomes of the major industry studies outlined preivously. In addition, it draws on the results of a study by Weber and Ladkin (2001). They utilized the Delphi technique to ascertain the opinions of industry experts in Australia and the United Kingdom on key trends, principal issues, and competitive forces the industry will face in the next five years.

BUSINESS TRENDS

There are several key trends in the business environment that will affect the convention industry and the way meetings and conventions will have to be planned and organized in the future. In particular they center on the shift toward an information-oriented society, the restructuring of businesses, and continued globalization (PCMA, 2000a). In today's economy much emphasis is placed on information and knowledge. It is imperative to be up to date. However, facilitated through technology, the shelf life of information and skills has become extremely short. Previously acceptable annual updates on industry and professional changes are now insufficient. Consequently, there is a need for continuous information sharing that may take place mainly in an online environment and may periodically be supported by face-to-face contact.

In the past decade restructuring and downsizing resulted not only in lower corporate budgets but also in a flatter management structure with middle management positions, a key target for meetings and conventions, in particular being affected. It is still open to debate whether these changes had a positive or negative effect on the industry. In favor of the former it may be argued that the funds available from downsizing benefit employees who must gather intelligence for leaner organizations. Alternatively, one may contend that the number of people attending conferences in the future will be reduced, since large firms typically accounted for a disproportionate share of conference attendees.

The restructuring and downsizing also created a workforce that increasingly identifies more with their profession rather than a particular employer. For the convention and meeting industry the question arises whether the current focus on organizing meetings for similar businesses and professions will continue or whether in the future conventions will have a more diversified audience that focuses on interrelated issues. In the same context, the issue of value for money will take on a much more prominent position, with employees increasingly having to bear the cost of conference attendance from their private funds so that more intensive and targeted programs that offer transferable skills will be a prime consideration.

Continued globalization will not only provide greater business opportunities for the industry but at the same time also require adaptations in terms of meeting management. Organizers of meetings must become more familiar with the cultural backgrounds of delegates from different countries. Similarly, an understanding of business customs is essential since the organization of international meetings requires the cooperation of professionals in other countries. Even for national meetings a greater cultural awareness will be necessary since both the population and the workforce of many developed nations, such as the United States, the United Kingdom, and Australia, is increasingly multicultural.

TECHNOLOGY TRENDS

Much discussion on the future of the industry has centered on the issue of technology, how it will affect the format and the organization of conventions and meetings, and whether these changes will overall be positive or negative for the industry. Central to this discussion is the question whether advanced technologies will eventually replace the need for face-to-face meetings. Munro (1994) offers an opinion on how effectively information may be shared through the use of technology, contrasting it with his view of how ineffective and cost inefficient traditional face-to-face meetings are. Yet despite advances in technology, especially the Internet, conference attendance has failed to slow down. Studies have repeatedly shown that even though the use of the Internet has increased for online registration and e-mail, the use of more sophisticated techniques such as videoconferencing, virtual trade shows, and Webcasting is still not widespread (e.g., PCMA, 2002). The Forbes Group, who conducted PCMA's Environmental Scan, suggested that the new technologies simply evolve slowly because the infrastructure that is needed to support them is not yet in place. Results of the study by Weber and Ladkin (2001) suggest that there is a reluctance to install state-of-the-art technology because it often comes without adequate training for staff and satisfactory backup support by IT providers in case difficulties arise. These issues, however, are likely to be resolved in the near future and the question still stands whether technology will replace face-to-face communication or whether it will remain a niche application.

Industry experts in both Australia and the United Kingdom felt that there will always be a need for face-to-face contact and technology will simply alter the frequency of that but not challenge its very existence (Weber and Ladkin, 2001). Since more information can now be exchanged via technology, there is a greater need to build relationships when getting together for face-to-face meetings. Consequently, meetings in the future will focus more on social aspects rather than on business, which may be conducted mainly via technology. A further contention was that the format of meetings will change from the current formal presentation type to a more interactive style, the latter being facilitated by connectivity to the Internet from the meeting space. Therefore, collaborative workspaces offering the possibility to access laptops will be in greater demand than rooms that accommodate presentations only.

The new technology also poses challenges to professional conference organizers (PCOs) and their role in meeting management. In adapting to the changes it is essential for PCOs to focus on the process rather than the product, i.e., they should think of themselves no longer simply as organizers of large functions and forums but rather as facilitators of industry intelligence distribution and skill development (PCMA, 2000a). In line with this, flexible thinking in the decision on the appropriate medium is required—in some instances the use of "virtual applications" is more beneficial to accomplish meeting objectives; in others, face-to-face interaction is required. Finally, it is essential to realize that the new technologies are likely to lead to changes in *what* is actually done and not only in *how* things are done.

SOCIAL TRENDS

One of the biggest issues to impact the organization of meetings in the future is that not only will different generations come together but these generations take very different approaches to communication and possess different learning styles. Meeting planners must be aware of these issues to successfully organize meetings in the coming years. Panel experts at a roundtable discussion organized by *Successful Meetings Magazine* (Anonymous, 2000) noted that Generation Nexters, having grown up and spending much time on the PC and using e-mail, to a certain extent lack the verbal communication skills Baby Boomers had to cultivate in their dealings. More specifically, one participant stated: "We found that we are not getting any feedback and interaction from Generation Next in meetings, and their input is invaluable. So we had to look at gaining interaction and excitement, by bringing collaboration software like GroupWare into our meetings" (p. 44).

Although the differences among generations are one issue, the trend toward an aging population is another that is going to affect the industry. An increasing number of people are opting for early retirement, many of whom may decide to become involved in associations. Consequently, changes in associations' membership base, convention delegate profiles, and delegate needs must be considered and addressed.

Apart from generation issues, work practice changes are also likely to affect both the frequency and the format of meetings and conventions. In recent years the number of people working from home has grown substantially. Although such a work arrangement offers significant cost savings for corporations, the social isolation of home employees can present difficulties in the longer term. Periodic face-to-face contact to meet and network at meetings and conferences is especially critical for this segment of the labor market.

The workforce in general is facing increased time pressures. The quest for a greater balance between work and leisure time becomes ever more important—an understanding of this phenomenon has to be reflected in the planning of meetings and conventions. Corporate meetings are predicted to remain short, so that people can get back to their families; association meeting planners will have to make allowances for more attendees to bring families to combine work with a short break (Anonymous, 2000).

POLITICAL TRENDS

As mentioned in previous chapters governments all over the world have recognized the importance of the convention and meeting industry. However, the level of government support provided varies among countries. Differences in government funding for national marketing campaigns, business development grants, and tax reliefs, for example, all affect the international competitiveness of individual players. Consequently, government policies and support will be a more critical success factor in the future.

Conference organizers and venues are also increasingly concerned about delegate safety so that the political stability of a host nation and safety considerations will become even more important as site selection criteria for international meetings and conventions. That is especially the case following the incidents of September 11, 2001.

KEY ISSUES

Weber and Ladkin (2001) ascertained the opinion of industry experts in Australia and in the United Kingdom on key issues that the industry in its respective country must address in the next five years to ensure continued growth and competitiveness. They utilized the Delphi technique that involved the solicitation of expert panel members from convention centers, convention and visitors bureaus, convention hotels, professional meeting organizers, industry associations, tourist organizations, destination marketing companies, and universities. The experts were chosen on the basis of their experience in the industry and their status. The following sections provide a listing of the study findings that can be classified as concerns relating to marketing and selling, business and finance, human resources, and service quality. Although these issues have been identified for specific countries they clearly are also applicable in a broader geographic context.

Marketing and Selling Issues

United Kingdom

Issues that are perceived to influence the industry in the United Kingdom and/or are critical to address in a timely manner are as follows:

- Increased competition for U.K. venues from overseas ones due to direct flights and ease of access from the United Kingdom
- Budget constraints resulting in the reduction in overseas marketing of the United Kingdom
- Fragmentation of the United Kingdom market due to regional segmentation
- A need for Web sites for promotion and online booking
- Improved representation at international exhibitions by industry representatives
- Improved industry research in the form of market research and statistics collection

Australia

In Australia the major concern was the need to capitalize on the success of the Olympic Games in Sydney in 2000, which provided a window of opportunity to become more competitive on an international scale. In particular, the following key issues were identified:

- Capitalization on the success of the Sydney 2000 Olympics in the next twelve to eighteen months to secure new international business
- More aggressive marketing of Australia as a MICE destination by the Australian Tourist Commission and convention and visitors bureaus
- Strengthening of the Team Australia marketing alliance
- Need to overcome perceptions of difficult access in terms of both great distance and high cost

Australian panel experts also identified the need for improved market research and the collection of reliable statistics. There was strong support for the establishment of a national annual research program to provide comparative and continuous statistical data on the MICE industry.

Business and Finance Issues

United Kingdom

In order to remain competitive and grow further, there are a number of business and finance issues to address, in particular:

- strength of the Pound Sterling in relation to the Euro;
- investment in facilities and transport infrastructure;
- growth of in-house conference facilities;
- sponsorship of conferences;
- decreasing hotel group margins; and
- value-for-money perceptions.

Australia

In Australia panel industry experts were especially concerned with and emphasized the need for the

- expansion/refurbishment/technology update of older convention centers;
- continued development/enhancement of facilities and infrastructure in regional areas;
- continued government lobbying on tax issues; and

- government lobbying for increased funding and support for international trade missions and general offshore MICE marketing.

Human Resource Issues

Industry experts in both Australia and the United Kingdom identified almost identical key issues to address in relation to human resources. These were

- a lack of skilled human resources in the industry;
- low rates of pay compared to other service industries;
- a need for improved education and training of staff;
- a need for better terms and conditions of employment for staff that would attract and retain higher quality of staff; and
- a need to create a career structure and professional status.

In the United Kingdom, in particular, the lack of foreign language expertise at venues was noted with resulting problems for foreign delegates, which may reduce the attractiveness of U.K. venues for international meetings.

The areas for concern outlined above are clearly interrelated. They suggest a need for the industry to evaluate educational opportunities, training for staff, skill development, and career prospects, in addition to pay conditions in and the image of the industry. Improvements in these areas would greatly contribute to the industry being able to recruit and retain high-caliber employees.

Service Quality/Professionalism

Industry experts in both the United Kingdom and Australia perceived quality as a critical means of differentiation in view of the increased level of competition. That applied to the quality of facilities and available accommodation, as well as the quality of service. For Australia, it was felt to be especially important to consistently meet the high expectations on service quality levels that were generated by the Sydney Olympics.

Weber and Ladkin's (2001) study clearly indicates that although both Australia and the United Kingdom are in positions of strength, there is a need for constant monitoring of industry trends and key issues, which must be addressed to ensure continued growth. In the current competitive environment no destination can afford to be complacent, regardless of its state of industry development. Furthermore, it is critical to recognize that each of the identified key areas is linked and cannot be considered in isolation. For example, improved marketing will not be effective unless human resources and service quality issues are also addressed. Therefore, the various key issues must be resolved in their entirety; there is no one single area where all the improvements are needed.

CONCLUSION

Despite the vulnerability of the industry to the general business climate, much of its future prospects will depend on it taking a proactive stand to deal with the challenges and environmental changes that lie ahead. To do that, better coordination among industry organizations is vital and strategic alliances may also have to be put in place by industry players. Current problems with the compilation of statistics and their consistency and comparability must also be dealt with for the industry to prosper. Initiatives to that effect are currently being developed by the industry. If successfully implemented, the MICE industry is likely to further expand on a global scale, thereby further consolidating its status as a key industry in the twenty-first century.

Addendum

Just when this book was about to go to print, the terrorist attacks of September 11, 2001, occurred in New York and Washington. Apart from the tragic human loss, the business community was also deeply affected by these events. The tourism industry in particular felt its repercussions and, due to the nature of the attacks, airlines were most immediately impacted. The resulting fear of flying in the population, combined with the fact that many corporations put restrictions on travel of their employees in the immediate aftermath, led to heavy cancellations and/or postponements of travel. In view of reduced passenger numbers, major airlines, especially U.S. airlines, were forced to reduce the frequency of services on certain routes or in some cases suspend services altogether. Following on from these measures were job losses for tens of thousands of people, not only in the airline industry but rippling through all other tourism industry sectors. In the age of globalization and the linkages among economies, these effects were not confined to the United States but were felt across the world.

The meetings and convention industry, with its heavy reliance on business travel, also felt the detrimental impacts of the September 11 attacks. The cancellations of conventions and meetings, especially in the days immediately following the attacks, were widely publicized, together with the expected loss of revenue resulting from the cancellations. However, it is likely that many of the events that were cancelled amid safety concerns will take place at a later date. Less apparent than the effects of outright cancellation or postponement, however, is the lower attendance rate reported by organizers of conventions that went ahead as scheduled. Because hotel contracts typically contain attrition clauses that impose fees on groups that fail to fill all or a set percentage of their rooms and, in many cases, food and beverage commitments, many of these conventions were faced with attrition penalties, especially as numerous hotels were not prepared to renegotiate this aspect. That causes problems especially in associations for whom the earnings of the annual convention represent a key source of income. Furthermore, construction and/or expansion of convention centers was postponed in several instances due to the expected downturn in business in the short to medium term as a result of the attacks, the consequent military action by the United States, and the reduced business confidence (Anonymous, 2001a).

The impacts on the industry appear to be unevenly distributed. It is mainly international and national meetings and conventions that have been affected by the September 11 events because they require air travel by the majority of attendees. Regional meetings, in contrast, are more likely to go ahead as planned, as modes of transportation other than air travel can be easily booked if attendees are not comfortable flying. Similarly, it is mainly first-tier convention cities rather than second- and third-tier sites that feel the downturn.

In the weeks following the terrorist attacks there was a concerted effort to support the industry, in the United States in particular. Major hotel chains such as Hilton, Marriott, and Hyatt waived their cancellation fees for a certain period to accommodate organizations and associations that had decided to cancel their events. Initiatives were also put in place to assist hotels in rebooking cancelled meeting space, with the Internet playing a key role in this industrywide effort led by the Convention Industry Council. In a special sign of support for New York, numerous associations moved previously scheduled meetings to the city. The American Society of Travel Agents, for example, decided to hold its World Travel Congress in the Jacob K. Javits Convention Center rather than in Seville, Spain, as originally planned, despite the possibility of legal action by the city of Seville. The congress took place in November 2001 and drew about 3,000 delegates <http:www.astanet.com>.

It is too early to discuss possible medium- to long-term effects on the industry at the time of writing. However, it appears likely that two issues in particular will be afforded much greater prominence in the management of meetings in the future: Safety and security considerations, although important before the September 11 events, have now taken on a much more critical role. These concerns will be reflected in both the site selection and in on-site security measures. Furthermore, videoconferencing and Webcasting technology may experience a much more rapid adoption as a result of the September 11 events than previously anticipated. As an alternative to on-site attendance the use of these technologies has increased dramatically in the past months (Lessin, 2001). Whether this trend will continue, though, remains to be seen.

Appendix

MICE Industry Associations

Alliance of Meeting Management Consultants: <http://www.ammc.org/>
American Society of Association Executives (ASAE):
 <http://www.asaenet.org/>
Asia Pacific Exhibition and Convention Council (APECC):
 <http://apecc.org/>
Asian Association of Convention and Visitor Bureaus (AACVB):
 <http://aacvb.org/>
Association for Conference and Events Executives—International
 (ACE-I)
Association for Conferences and Events, The (ACE), United Kingdom:
 <http://www.martex.co.uk/ace/index.htm>
Association for Convention Marketing Executives (ACME):
 <http://www.acmenet.org/>
Association for Convention Operations Management (ACOM):
 <http://www.acomonline.org/>
Association of Australian Convention Bureaux (AACB):
 <http://www.aacb.org.au/>
Association of British Professional Conference Organisers (ABPCO):
 <http://www.abpco.org.uk/>
Association of Collegiate Conference and Events Directors—International
 (ACCED-I): <http://acced-i.colostate.edu/>
Association of Destination Management Executives (ADME):
 <http://www.adme.org/>
Association of Exhibition Organisers (AEO), United Kingdom:
 <http://www.aeo.org/>
British Association of Conference Destinations (BACD):
 <http://www.bacd.org.uk/>
Center for Exhibition Industry Research (CEIR): <http://www.ceir.org/>
Convention Industry Council (CIC): <http://www.c-l-c.org/>
Europäischer Verband der Veranstaltung-Centren e.V. (EVVC):
 <http://www.evvc.org/>

Internet addresses current in February 2002.

European Association of Event Centers (EVVC): <http://www.evvc.org>
European Federation of Conference Towns (EFCT):
    <http://www.efct.com>
European Meetings Industry Liaison Group (EMILG)
European Major Exhibition Centres Association (EMECA):
    <http://www.emeca.com/>
European Society of Association Executives (ESAE):
    <http://www.esae.org>
Exhibit Designers and Producers Association (EDPA):
    <http://www.edpa.com/>
Exhibition and Event Association of Australia (EEAA):
    <http://www.eeaa.com.au>
Exposition Services and Contractors Association (ESCA):
    <http://www.esca.org>
Federation of International Trade Associations (FITA):
    <http://www.fita.org>
Historic Conference Centres of Europe (HCCE):
    <http://www.historic-centres.com/>
Incentive Travel and Meetings Association (ITMA):
    <http://www.itmasonline.org/>
Incentive-Travel.org.uk: <http://www.martex.co.uk/itma/jitmafr.htm>
International Association for Exhibition Management (IAEM):
    <http://www.iaem.org>
International Association of Assembly Managers (IAAM):
    <http://www.iaam.org/>
International Association of Association Management Companies
    (IAAMC): <http://iaamc.org/>
International Association of Conference Centers (IACC):
    <http://www.iacconline.org/>
International Association of Conference Interpreters (AIIC):
    <http//www.aiic.net/>
International Association of Congress Centers (AIPC):
    <http://www.aipc.org/>
International Association of Convention and Visitor Bureaus (IACVB):
    <http://www.iacvb.org/>
International Association of Fairs and Expositions (IAFE):
    <http://www.fairsandexpos.com/>
International Association of Professional Congress Organizers (IAPCO):
    <http://www.iapco.org/>
International Congress and Convention Association (ICCA):
    <http://www.icca.nl/>
International Congress and Convention Researchers Network (ICCRN):
    <www.icca.nl>

International Exhibition Logistics Associates (IELA):
    <http://www.iela.org>
International Exhibition Statistics Union (CENTREX):
    <http://www.centrexstat.org/>
International Federation of Exhibition Services (IFES):
    <http://ifesnet.org/>
International Festivals and Event Association (IFEA):
    <http://www.ifea.com/>
International Society of Meeting Planners:
    <http://www.iami.org/ismp.html>
International Special Events Society (ISES): <http://www.ises.com/>
Joint Meetings Industry Council (JMIC)
Meetings Industry Association (MIA), United Kingdom:
    <http://www.meetings.org/>
Meetings Industry Association of Australia (MIAA):
    <http://www.miaanet.com.au/>
Meeting Professionals International (MPI): <http://www.mpiweb.org/>
Professional Convention Management Association (PCMA) :
    <htttp://www.pcma.org>
Society of Corporate Meeting Professionals (SCMP):
    <http://www.scmp.org/>
Society of Event Organizers (SEO), United Kingdom:
    <http://www.seoevent.co.uk/>
Society of Government Meeting Professionals (SGMP):
    <http://www.sgmp.org>
Society of Incentive and Travel Executives, The (SITE):
    <http://site-intl.org/>
Trade Show Exhibitors Association (TSEA): <http://www.tsea.org/>
Union of International Associations (UIA): <http://www.uia.org/>
Union of International Fairs (UFI) : <http://www.ufinet.org/>
Venue Management Association (Asia Pacific) Limited:
    <http://www.vma.org.au/>
World Council for Venue Management (WCVM): <http://venue.org/>
World Trade Center Association: <http://iserve.wtca.org/>

MICE Industry Publications

Association Executive (United Kingdom)
Association Manager (United Kingdom)
Association Management Magazine (ASAE): <http://www.asaenet.org>
Association Meetings (United States)
Association Meetings in Asia

Association Meetings International—CAT (United Kingdom): <http://www.cat-publications.com/indexframe.htm>
Australasian Special Events
CAT Conference and Travel Publications: <http://www.cat-publications.com/indexframe.htm>
CIM Online
Conference and Incentive Management (Germany)
Conference and Incentive Travel (United Kingdom)
Congresos, Convenciones e Incentivos (Spain)
Congress and Convention (Japan)
Convene Magazine (PCMA): <http://www.pcma.org >
Convention and Incentive Marketing (Australia)
Corporate and Incentive Travel (United States)
Corporate Meetings and Incentives Magazine
EventWeb Newsletter
EventWorld Magazine (ISES)
Exhibition Bulletin (United Kingdom)
Exhibitions Bulletin Venues Directory
Exhibitions and Events Asia
Exhibitor Magazine
EXPO Magazine : <http://www.expoweb.com/>
Incentive Magazine : <http://www.incentivemag.com>
Incentive and Meetings Asia (IMA): <http://www.ima.com.sg>
Incentive Travel and Corporate Meetings (United Kingdom)
Incentives and Meetings Europe Magazine
Incentives Today (United Kingdom)
m+a Newsline: <http://www.m-averlag.com>
m+a report: <http://www.m-averlag.com>
Meeting and Congressi (Italy)
Meeting Planner International (United Kingdom)
Meeting Professional (MPI): <http://www.mpiweb.org>
Meetings and Conventions Online: <http://www.meetings-conventions.com/>
Meetings and Conventions in Asia
Meetings and Incentive Travel
Meetings and Incentive Travel—CAT (United Kingdom): <http://www.cat-publications.com/indexframe.htm>
Meetings News Magazine: <http://www.meetingnews.com/>
Meetings Today Magazine
Quorum (Australia)
Special Events Magazine: <http://www.specialevents.com>
Successful Meetings Magazine: <http://www.successmtgs.com/>

Tradeshow Week: <http://www.tradeshowweek.com/>
TW Tagungswirtschaft (Germany) <http://www.tw-media.com>

Major International MICE Events

Confex—London, United Kingdom (February): <http://www.interna-tional-confex.com/>

AIME (AsiaPacific Incentives & Meetings Expo)—Melbourne, Australia (February): <http://www.aime.com.au/>

EIBTM (European Incentive & Business Travel & Meeting Exhibition) Geneva, Switzerland (May): <http://www.eibtm.ch/page.cfm>

Meetings & Incentive Travel Show—London, United Kingdom (June): <http://www.cat-publications.com/>

IT&CMA (Incentive Travel & Conventions, Meetings Asia)—Location in Asia varies (October/November): <http://www.itcma.com.sg>

IT&ME (Incentive Travel & Meeting Executives Show)—Chicago, United States (October)

Bibliography

Abbey, J. R. and Link, C. K. (1994). The convention and meetings sector—Its operation and research needs. In J. R. B. Ritchie and C. R. Goeldner (Eds.), *Travel, tourism and hospitality research: A handbook for managers and researchers,* Second edition (pp. 273-284). New York: John Wiley and Sons, Inc.

Ackerman, A. M. (1994). Privatization of public assembly facility management. *Cornell HRA Quarterly,* (April), 72-83.

Ahn, J. Y. and Ahmed, Z. U. (1994). South Korea's emerging tourism industry. *Cornell Hotel and Restaurant Administration Quarterly, 35*(2), 84-89.

Aidi, O. (2000). Tip for the top. *Hotels,* (September), 50.

Alkjaer, E. (1974). *The Bournemouth Centre development in the international convention market.* Copenhagen: Institute for Transport, Tourism and Regional Science.

Alkjaer, E. (1976a). A convention centre of the future. Paper presented at the 18th Congress of the International Hotel Association, Sydney.

Alkjaer, E. (1976b). Images and realities in congress tourism. *Journal of Travel Research, 14*(4), 14-15.

Alkjaer, E. and Erikson, J. (1967). *Location and economic consequences of international congresses.* Copenhagen: Institute for Transport, Tourism and Regional Science.

Allen, J. (2000). *Event planning.* Toronto: John Wiley and Sons, Inc.

American Society of Association Executives (ASAE) (1992). Association meeting trends 1992. Washington, DC: ASAE.

American Society of Association Executives (ASAE) (1999). *The 1999 Blue Chip Association Executive Compensation Study.* Washington, DC: ASAE.

Anonymous (1997a). The MICE industry in Australia. *Convention and Incentive Marketing,* (August), 3.

Anonymous (1997b). New worlds link arms: AuSAE to adopt American certification. *Incentives and Meetings Asia,* November/December. Available online: <http://www.ima.com.sg>.

Anonymous (1998). Construction progress of total exhibit space in new facilities and expansions. *Tradeshow Week, 21*(September), 4-5.

Anonymous (1999a). Events that shaped our MICE industry. *Convention and Incentive Marketing,* (December), 12.

Anonymous (1999b). Follow-up: Convention center technology. *Convene,* (February), 41.

Anonymous (2000). Now what? *Successful Meetings, 49*(1), 43-52.

Anonymous (2001a). Altered status: How major projects have been revised. *Meetings and Conventions,* (December), 49.

Anonymous (2001b). The big trends. *Successful Meetings, 50*(1), 82-83.

Anonymous (2001c). Booming budgets. *Successful Meetings, 50*(1), 77-78.

Archer, B. (1982). The value of multipliers and their policy implications. *Tourism Management,* (December), 236-241.

ASAE (1997). *1998 Meetings Outlook Survey:* Washington, DC: ASAE/MPI.

Asher, J. (2000). *Effect of Olympics on business tourism sector.* The Sydney Convention and Visitors Bureau. Available online: <http://www.scvb.com.au/nm_ff_olympic.html>. Accessed March 23, 2001.

Association for Convention Operations Management (ACOM) (1999). *ACOM 2000: Bridging Ideas into Actions.* Atlanta, GA: ACOM.

Australian Association of Convention and Visitor Bureaux (1994). *Statistical report on the scope of the meeting industry.* Sydney: AACB.

Australian Tourist Commission (ATC) (1988). *Global marketing plan for conventions and incentive travel.* Woolloomooloo, NSW: Australian Tourist Commission.

Australian Tourist Commission (ATC) (1990). *Convention Delegate Expenditure Study,* full report, Sydney. February.

Australian Tourist Commission (ATC) (1996). *Annual Report 1995.* Sydney: ATC.

Axtell, R. E. (Ed.) (1991). *Gestures: The do's and taboos of body language around the world.* New York: John Wiley and Sons, Inc.

Axtell, R. E. (Ed.) (1993). *Do's and taboos around the world,* Third edition. New York: John Wiley and Sons, Inc.

Baratta, A. (1995). CVBs offer one-stop shopping. *Travel Weekly,* July 13, 6.

Bay, H. W. (1999a). The insiders' guide to international meetings. *Successful Meetings,* July/Supplement, 16-24.

Bay, H. W. (1999b). Marketing to the world. *Successful Meetings,* July/Supplement, 2-6.

Bay, H. W. (2000a). Adventures abroad. *Successful Meetings,* July/Supplement, 20-26.

Bay, H. W. (2000b). A global game plan. *Successful Meetings,* July/Supplement, 12-18.

Becker, C. (2000). Service recovery strategies: The impact of cultural differences. *Journal of Hospitality and Tourism Research, 24*(4), 526-538.

Beckmann, K. and Krabbe, D. J. (1999). Aus-und weiterbildung in der tagungs-, kongress- und messewirtschaft. In M. T. Schreiber and K. Beckmann (Eds.), *Kongress und Tagungsmanagement* (pp. 549-564). Muenchen: Oldenbourg.

Benini, C. (1996a). Lost in space. *Meetings and Conventions, 31*(10), 61-63.

Benini, C. (1996b). Site Selection. *Meetings and Conventions, 31*(4), 40.

Benini, C. (1997). Getting there. *Meetings and Conventions, 32*(6), 61-64.

Berkman, F. W., Dorf, D. C., and Oakes, L. R. (1978). *Convention management & service*. East Lansing, MI: Educational Institute of the American Hotel and Motel Association.

Berns, B. (1998). Is the strip on the skids? *Hotel and Motel Management, 213,* 36-37.

Bland, G. (1997). Recognize differences "across the pond." *Convene,* December 1, 47.

Bland, G. (1998). Multiple venues present logistical challenges. *Convene,* April 1, 23.

Bloom, H. (1981). Marketing to meeting planners: What works? *Cornell HRA Quarterly, 21*(August), 45-50.

Blythe, J. (1999). Visitor and exhibitor expectations and outcomes at trade exhibitions. *Marketing Intelligence and Planning, 17*(2), 100-108.

Blythe, J. and Rayner, T. (1996). The evaluation of non-selling activities at British trade exhibitions: An exploratory study. *Marketing Intelligence and Planning, 14*(5), 20-24.

Board, E. T. (1974). *Report on a survey of conference venue selection*. London: ETB.

Board, E. T. (1991). Market profile: Conference hotels. *ETB Insights* (November), B39-B46.

Boehme, A. J. (1999). *Planning successful meetings and events*. New York: AMACOM, American Management Association.

Boger, C. A., Abbott, J. A., Lin, L. C., and Heinemann, A. (2000). Rate integrity in convention cities. *Journal of Hospitality and Tourism Research, 24*(1), 20-35.

Boisclair, M. (1995). Industry questions CVB role in event planning. *Meetings and Conventions, 30*(8), 21.

Bojanic, D. C. and Dale, E. A. (1993). A survey of convention sales career opportunities. *Hospitality and Tourism Educator, 5*(4), 41-43.

Bond, W. (1996). Conventions—more than a meeting. *Marketing,* (June), 30-36, 38-41.

Bonn, M. A. and Boyd, J. N. (1992). A multivariate analysis of corporate meeting planner perceptions of Caribbean destinations. *Journal of Travel and Tourism Marketing, 1*(3), 1-23.

Bonn, M. A., Brand, R. R., and Ohlin, J. B. (1994). Site selection for professional meetings: A comparison of heavy-half vs. light-half association and corporation meeting planners. *Journal of Travel and Tourism Marketing, 3*(2), 59-84.

Bonn, M. A., Ohlin, J. B., and Brand, R. R. (1994). Quality service issues: A multivariate analysis of association meeting planner perceptions of Caribbean destinations. *Hospitality Research Journal, 18*(1), 29-48.

Boyers, K. (1995). A new spin on travel and tourism. *Association Management,* (February), 60-64.

Braley, S. J. F. (1996a). Attention shoppers. *Meetings and Conventions, 31*(5), 80-84.

Braley, S. J. F. (1996b). Small cities are battling for business. *Travel Weekly, 35*(June 3), 38.

Bramwell, B. and Rawding, L. (1994). Tourism marketing organizations in industrial cities: Organizations, objectives and urban governance. *Tourism Management, 15*(6), 425-435.

Braun, B. M. (1992). The economic contribution of conventions: The case of Orlando, Florida. *Journal of Travel Research, 30*(3), 32-37.

British Association of Conference Destinations (1997). *British Conference Destinations Directory.* London: BACD.

British Tourist Authority (BTA) (1998). *International conferences in Britain 1998-2008.* London: BTA.

British Tourist Authority (BTA) (1999). *The British Conference Market Trends Survey 1999.* London: BTA.

Brummer, A. (1998). Don't fall for fool's gold. *The Guardian,* August 29, 28.

Buhalis, D. (1998). Information technology in tourism: Implications for the tourism curriculum. In D. Buhalis, A. Tjoa, and J. Jafari (Eds.), *Information and communication technologies in tourism 1998: Proceedings of the International Conference in Istanbul, Turkey, 1998* (pp. 289-297). New York: Springer Verlag.

Burns, J. P. A., J. Hatch, and T. Mules (Eds.) (1986). *The Adelaide Grand Prix: The impact of a special event.* Adelaide: The Centre for South Australian Economic Studies, University of Adelaide.

Burns, J. P. A. and Mules, T. J. (1989). An economic evaluation of the Adelaide Grand Prix. In G. J. Syme, B. J. Shaw, P. M. Fenton, and W. S. Mueller (Eds.), *The planning and evaluation of hallmark events* (pp. 172-185). Aldershot, England: Avebury.

Cairncross, F. (1997). *The death of distance.* London: Orion.

Callan, R. J. and Hoyes, M. K. (2000). A preliminary assessment of the function and conference service product at a UK stately home. *Tourism Management, 21*(6), 571-581.

Canadian Tourism Commission (CTC) (2000). *Partner Programs.* Available online: <http://www.canadatourism.com/en/ctc/ctx/partnerships/index.cfm>. Accessed March 23, 2001.

Carey, R. (1999). Out of harm's way. *Successful Meetings, 48*(May), 65-72.

Carlsen, J. (1995). Gathering information: Meetings and conventions sector research in Australia. *Journal of Tourism Studies, 6*(2), 21-29.

Carlsen, J. (1999). A review of MICE industry evaluation and research in Asia and Australia 1988-1998. *Journal of Convention and Exhibition Management, 1*(4), 51-66.

Catin, M. (1995). Economies d'agglomeration. *Revue d'Economie Regionale et Urbaine, 4*, 1-20.

CEC (1996). *Business and conference tourism in the European economic area.* Brussels: European Commission.

Chacko, H. E. and Fenich, G. G. (2000). Determining the importance of US convention destination attributes. *Journal of Vacation Marketing, 6*(3), 211-220.

Chatfield-Taylor, C. (1995). Privatization. *Expo Magazine,* July/August. Available online: <http://www.expoweb.com/expomag/BackIssues/1995/0895_privatization.htm>.

Chatfield-Taylor, C. (2000). *E-learning with Marriott and PCMA: Hybrid program integrates online and off line learning.* September 19. EventWeb. Available online: <http://www.eventweb.com/091900.html>.

Chen, K.-C. and LaLopa, J. M. (1999). Conventions and exhibitions development in Thailand. *Journal of Convention and Exhibition Management, 2*(1), 1-13.

Chew, M. (1999). Singapore is again top Asia venue for global meetings. *Business Times,* August 12, p. 4.

Chon, K. S. (1991). *Meetings management and hospitality/tourism industry.* Aix-en-Provence: Centre des Hautes Etudes Touristiques, Universite de Droit.

Chon, K. S. and Feiertag, H. (1990). The essence of meetings management. *Cornell Hotel and Restaurant Administration Quarterly, 31*(August), 95-97.

Chon, K. S. and Sparrowe, R. T. (1995). *Welcome to hospitality: An introduction.* Cincinnati, OH: South-Western Publishing Co.

CHRIE (2001). *CHRIE membership directory and resource guide.* Washington, DC: Council on Hotel, Restaurant and Institutional Education.

Clark, J. D. (1993). *A study of situational variables in an organizational marketing scenario.* Unpublished doctoral dissertation, Virginia Polytechnic Institute, Blacksburg, VA.

Clark, J. D., Evans, M. R., and Knutson, B. J. (1997). Selecting a site for an association convention: An exploratory look at the types of power used by committee members to influence decisions. *Journal of Hospitality and Leisure Marketing, 5*(1), 81-93.

Clark, J. D. and Knutson, B. J. (1995). A proposed model of the organizational buying process for the hospitality industry. *Journal of Hospitality and Leisure Marketing, 3*(3), 21-33.

Clark, J. D. and McCleary, K. W. (1995). Influencing associations' site selection process. *Cornell Hotel and Restaurant Administration Quarterly, 36*(April), 61-68.

Clark, J. D., Price, C. H., and Murrmann, S. K. (1996). Buying centers: Who chooses convention sites? *Cornell Hotel and Restaurant Administration Quarterly, 37*(August), 72-76.

Clark, L. (1997). Mega centre in the making. *Meetings and Conventions: Asia/Pacific, 4*(October), 34, 36.

COEX today (2001). *Convention and Incentive Marketing,* (January), 16.

Colby, L .H. (Ed.) (1994). *The Convention Liaison Council manual: A working guide for effective meetings and conventions, Sixth edition.* Washington, DC: Convention Liaison Council.

Commonwealth Department of Tourism (1992). *Australia's passport to growth: A National Tourism Strategy.* Canberra: AGPS.

Commonwealth Department of Tourism (1995). *A national strategy for the meetings, incentives, conventions and exhibitions industry.* Canberra: AGPS.

Conejo, C. (2000). Managers must become multicultural. *ASAE News,* September 12, 4-14.

Convention Liaison Council (1993). *The economic impact of conventions, expositions, meetings and incentive travel: A study by Deloitte and Touche.* Washington, DC: Convention Liaison Council.

Convention Liaison Council (1995). *Economic impact study.* Wheat Ridge, CO: Convention Liaison Council.

Cooper, M. (1976). *A convention centre for Sydney.* Sydney: Report to the Minister for Tourism, New South Wales State Government.

Cooper, M. (1977). *The convention industry and Sydney.* Armidale: University of New England.

Cooper, M. (1999). Prediction and reality: The development of the Australian convention industry 1976-1993 and beyond. *Journal of Convention and Exhibition Management, 1*(4), 3-15.

Council on Hotel, Restaurant, and Tourism Education (1999). *CHRIE membership directory and resource guide.* Washington, DC.

Crawford, J. (1995). Finding a partner to share the load. *Convene,* July 1, 25.

CRC (2000). *The Melbourne convention delegate study 1999.* Melbourne: CRC.

Crocker, M. (1990). Picking a place: What matters most. *Meetings and Conventions, 61*(Supplement), 52-55, 61.

Crompton, J. (1999). *Measuring the economic impact of visitors to sports tournaments and special events.* Ashburn, Virginia: National Recreation and Park Association.

Crompton, J. L. and McKay, S. L. (1994). Measuring the economic impact of festivals and events: Some myths, misapplications and ethical dilemmas. *Festival Management and Event Tourism, 2*(1), 33-43.

Crouch, G. I. and Ritchie, J. R. B. (1998). Convention site selection research: A review, conceptual model, and propositional framework. *Journal of Convention and Exhibition Management, 1*(1), 49-69.

CSN and Associates (1998). *Survey on international convention, incentive travel and exhibitions in Thailand, 1998.* Tourism Authority of Thailand.

Danaher, P. J. and Mattsson, J. (1994). Cumulative encounter satisfaction in the hotel conference process. *International Journal of Service Industry Management, 5*(4), 69-80.

Davidson, R. (1994a). *Business Travel.* London: Pitman Publishing.

Davidson, R. (1994b). European business travel and tourism. In A. V. Seaton (Ed.), *Tourism: The state of the art* (pp. 377-382). Chichester: John Wiley and Sons, Inc.

Davidson, R. (1998). *Travel and tourism in Europe,* Second edition. Harlow, Essex: Longman.

Day, G. S. (1990). *Market driven strategy: Processes for creating value.* New York: Harper and Row.

Delpy, L. and Li, M. (1998). The art and science of conducting economic impact studies. *Journal of Vacation Marketing 4*(3), 230-254.

Department of Export Promotion and Thailand Exhibition Association (1997). *1996 convention and exhibition survey.* Bangkok: Tourism Authority of Thailand.

Dobrian, J. (1997). 2nd tier—not 2nd class. *The Meeting Professional,* (September), 26-35.

Dobrian, J. (1998). Second-tier cities: Venues with value. *The Meeting Professional,* (December), 58-67.

Dobrian, J. (1999). Conference centers: Corporate and campus alternatives. *The Meeting Professional,* (February), 26-34.

Dotson, P. C. (1995). *Introduction to Meeting Management* (Second Edition). Birmingham, AL: PCMA.

DTI (1997). *The future of the British exhibitions industry.* London: Department of Trade and Industry.

Duarte, A. (1992). Hanging in there. *Meetings and Conventions, Supplement,* (March), 93-95.

Dube, L. and Renaghan, L. M. (2000). Marketing your hotel to and through intermediaries: An overlooked best practice. *Cornell Hotel and Restaurant Administration Quarterly, 41*(1), 73-84.

Dwyer, L. and Forsyth, P. (1996). *MICE tourism to Australia: A framework to assess impacts, proceedings of the Australian Tourism and Hospitality Research Conference* (pp. 313-323). Canberra: Bureau of Tourism Research.

Dwyer, L. and Forsyth, P. (1997). Impacts and benefits of MICE tourism: A framework for analysis. *Tourism Economics, 3*(1), 21-38.

Dwyer, L., Forsyth, P., Madden, J., and Spurr, R. (2000). Economic impacts of inbound tourism under different assumptions about the macroeconomy. *Current Issues in Tourism, 3*(4), 325-363.

Dwyer, L., Mellor, R., Mistilis, N., and Mules, T. (2000). A framework for assessing "tangible" and "intangible" impacts of events and conventions. *Event Management, 6*(3), 175-189.

Dwyer, L., Mellor, R., Mistilis, N., and Mules, T. (2001). Forecasting the economic impacts of events and conventions, *Event Management, 6*(3), 191-204.

Dwyer, L. and Mistilis, N. (1997). Challenges to MICE tourism in the Asia-Pacific region. In M. Oppermann (Ed.), *Pacific Rim Tourism* (pp. 219-230). Wallingford: CABI.

Dwyer, L., Mistilis, N., Forsyth, P., and Rao, P. (2001). International price competitiveness of Australia's MICE industry. *International Journal of Tourism Research, 3*(2), 123-139.

Echtner, C. M. and Ritchie, J. R. B. (1993). The measurement of destination image: An empirical assessment. *Journal of Travel Research, 31*(4), 3-13.

Elliott, S. (1995). Foreign currency market is no place for speculation. *Convene,* October 1, 23.

Elliott, S. (1996a). Apprenticeship program provides U.S. meeting managers with tools of overseas trade. *Convene,* September 1, 70.

Elliott, S. (1996b). Even the most professional interpreters require support staff. *Convene,* November 1, 23.

Elliott, S. (1996c). Profiting from the experience of multinational companies. *Convene,* September 1, 35.

Elliott, S. (1996d). Simultaneous translation promotes AAO's international surge. *Convene,* April 1, 27-28.

Elliott, S. (1996e). Understanding how Europeans respond to promotional materials. *Convene,* October 1, 31.

Elliott, S. (1997). Customized seminar series propel APA's Far East expansion. *Convene,* September 1, 59.

Elliott, S. (1998a). Don't overlook your most important resource. *Convene,* May 1, 31.

Elliott, S. (1998b). Global partnerships enhance meeting success. *Convene,* February 1, 47.

Elliott, S. (1998c). Structuring a global partnership: How the money is divided. *Convene,* March 1, 60.

Elliott, S. (2000). Experience of others is best teacher for first-time planner of overseas event. *Convene,* March 1, 64.

Elman, L. G. (1998). The state of CVBs. *The Meeting Professional,* (April), 28-44.

Elsayed-Elkhouly, S. M. and Lazarus, H. (1995). Business meetings in North America, Asia, Europe, and the Middle East. *American Journal of Management Development, 1*(4), 15-22.

European Federation of Conference Towns (1997). *A report on Europe in 1997.*

Evans, M. R. and Dave, D. S. (1999). The thorny question of automatic service charges: Policies at prominent U.S. resorts. *Cornell Hotel and Restaurant Administration Quarterly, 40*(4), 78-83.

Falk, E. T. and Pizam, A. (1991). The United States' meetings market. *International Journal of Hospitality Management, 10*(2), 111-118.

Falkner, D. E. and Berberoglu, H. (1987). *Convention and banquet management.* Toronto: Ryerson Polytechnical Institute.

Faulkner, B. and Bonnett, G. (1993). The conventions/meetings industry: Statistical and research requirements. Paper presented at the national conference on tourism research: Building a research base in tourism, Sydney.

Feiertag, H. (1996). Work closely with local convention bureaus. *Hotel and Motel Management, 211*(August 12), 14.

Fenich, G. G. (1992a). Convention center development: Pros, cons and unanswered questions. *International Journal of Hospitality Management, 11*(3), 183-196.

Fenich, G. G. (1992b). *The dollars and sense of convention centers.* Unpublished doctoral dissertation, Rutgers University, New Brunswick, NJ.

Fenich, G. G. (1994). An assessment of whether the convention centre in New York is successful as a tool for economic development. *Economic Development Quarterly,* (August), 245-255.

Fenich, G. G. (1995). Convention center operations: Some questions answered. *International Journal of Hospitality Management, 14*(3/4), 311-324.

Fenich, G. G. (1997). Conventions, centres and meetings: An analysis of the past decade. *Visitors in Leisure and Business. 16*(4/winter), 4-13.

Fenich, G. G. (1998a). Convention center operating characteristics. *Journal of Convention and Exhibition Management, 1*(2/3), 1-25.

Fenich, G. G. (1998b). Conventions, centers, and meetings: Analysis of the past decade. *Visions in Leisure and Business, 16*(4), 4-13.

Fenich, G. G. (2001). Using New Orleans as a predictor for the convention industry. *Journal of Convention and Exhibition Management.* Forthcoming.

Fesenmaier, D. R., Pena, C., and O'Leary, J. (1992). Assessing information needs of visitor bureaus. *Annals of Tourism Research, 19*(3), 571-574.

Fortin, P. A. and Ritchie, J. R. B. (1977). An empirical study of association decision processes in convention site selection. *Journal of Travel Research, 15*(4), 13-20.

Fortin, P. A., Ritchie, J. R. B., and Arsenault, J. (1976). *A study of the decision process of North American associations concerning the choice of a convention site.* Quebec City: Quebec Planning and Development Council.

Fox, D. (2000). *Survey Results: Technology, 5*(46). November 17. EventWeb newsletter. Available online: <http://www.eventweb.com>.

Foxall, G. and Hackett, P. (1994). Customer satisfaction with Birmingham's international convention centre. *The Service Industries Journal, 14*(3), 369-380.

Gartrell, R. B. (1991). Strategic partnerships for convention planning: The role of convention and visitor bureaus in convention management. *International Journal of Hospitality Management, 10*(2), 157-165.

Gartrell, R. B. (1992). Convention and visitor bureau: Current issues in management and marketing. *Journal of Travel and Tourism Marketing, 1*(2), 71-78.

Gartrell, R. B. (1994). *Destination marketing for convention and visitor bureaus,* Second edition. Dubuque, IA: Kendall/Hunt Publishing.

Getz, D. (1994). Event tourism: Evaluating the impacts. In J. R. B. Ritchie and C. R. Goeldner (Eds.), *Travel, tourism and hospitality research: A handbook for managers and researchers,* Second edition (pp. 437-450). New York: John Wiley and Sons, Inc.

Getz, D. (1997). *Event management and event tourism.* New York: Cognizant Communication.

Getz, D., Anderson, D., and Sheehan, L. (1998). Roles, issues, and strategies for convention and visitors' bureaux in destination planning and product development: A survey of Canadian bureaux. *Tourism Management, 19*(4), 331-340.

Ghitelman, D. (1995). Convention center development: Never enough. *Meetings and Conventions,* (February), 48-58.

Ghitelman, D. (1996). Are CVBs going too far? *Meetings and Conventions, 31*(2), 39-47.

Go, F. M. (1996). A conceptual framework for managing global tourism and hospitality marketing. *Tourism Recreation Research, 21*(2), 37-43.

Go, F. M. (1997). Asian and Australasian dimensions of global development. In F. M. Go and C. L. Jenkins (Eds.), *Tourism and economic development in Asia and Australasia* (pp. 3-34). London: Pinter.

Go, F. M. and Appelman, J. (2001). Achieving global competitiveness in SMEs by building trust in interfirm alliances. In S. Wahab and C. Cooper (Eds.), *Tourism in the age of globalisation* (pp. 183-197). London: Routledge.

Go, F. M. and Govers, R. (1997). The Asian perspective: Which international conference destinations in Asia are the most competitive? *CEMS Business Review,* *2*(1), 57-65.

Go, F. and Govers, R. (1999). The Asian perspective: Which convention destinations in Asia are the most competitive? *Journal of Convention and Exhibition Management 1*(4), 37-50.

Go, F. and Zhang, W. (1997). Applying importance-performance analysis to Beijing as an international tourist destination. *Journal of Travel Research, 35*(4), 42-49.

Goel, P. and Haghani, A. (2000). Model for determining airline fares for meeting or convention demand. *Journal of Transportation Engineering—ASCE, 126*(2), 107-114.

Goldblatt, J. J. (1997). *Special events: Best practices in modern event management,* Second edition. New York: Van Nostrand Reinhold.

Gosling, J. (2001). Lasting attractions. *Conference and Incentive Travel,* April, 23-24, 27, 29.

Govers, R., Go, F. M., and Jansen-Verbeke, M. (2000). Virtual tourist destinations: Their effectiveness in the communication with and through foreign intermediaries. In D. R. Fesenmaier, S. Klein, and D. Buhalis (Eds.), *Proceedings of the International Conference on Information and Communication Technologies in Tourism (ENTER 2000)* (pp. 93-103). Wien: Springer Verlag.

Grado, S. C., Strauss, C. H., and Lord, B. E. (1998). Economic impacts of conferences and conventions. *Journal of Convention and Exhibition Management,* *1*(1), 19-33.

Grant, Y. N. J. (1994). Factors that contribute to the selection process of meetings from the perspective of the attendee. Virginia Polytechnic and State University.

Graveline, D. (1984). Convention centers. *Urban Land, 43*(7), 2-5.

Greaves, S. (2001). New style venues make their mark. *Marketing,* July 5, 29-30.

Greco, J. (1998a). Convention centers: Revamp, rebuild, revitalize. *The Meeting Professional,* (May), 20-22, 27-35, 38.

Greco, J. (1998b). Courting minority meetings: A new focus for CVBs. *The Meeting Professional,* (November), 22-26.

Greco, J. (1998c). One-stop shopping. *The Meeting Professional,* (March), 26-35.

Greenblat, A. (1993). Three keys to booking a citywide convention. *Association Management,* (July), 62-104.

Grimaldi, L. (1997). Both sides now. *Meetings and Conventions, 32*(2), 65-68.

Hansen, K. (1996). The dual motives of participants at international trade shows: An empirical investigation of exhibitors and visitors with selling motives. *International Marketing Review, 13*(2), 39-53.

Hansen, K. (1999). From selling to relationship marketing at international trade fairs. *Journal of Convention and Exhibition Management, 2*(1), 37-53.

Harris, R. and Manincor, J. D. (1998). *The Australian and international meetings industry: A bibliography.* Sydney: Meetings Industry Association of Australia.

Hartley, J. S. and Witt, S. F. (1990). Hotel cancellation policies in respect of conference and function bookings. *International Journal of Hospitality Management,* *9*(4), 335-346.

Hartley, J. S. and Witt, S. F. (1994). Increasing the conversion rate of conference and function enquiries into sales. *International Journal of Hospitality Management, 5*(2), 13-16.

Harvey, D. (1985). *The urbanization of capital.* Baltimore: The John Hopkins University Press.

Heskett, J. L., Jones, T. O., Loveman, G. W., Sasser Jr, W. E., and Schlesinger, L. A. (1994). Putting the service-profit chain to work. *Harvard Business Review,* (March-April), 165-174.

Hildreth, R. A. (1990). *The essentials of meeting management.* Englewood Cliffs, NJ: Prentice Hall.

Hill, D. (1997a). International briefs. *Convene,* December 1, 48.

Hill, D.(1997b). International briefs. *Convene,* February 1, 33.

Hill, D. (1997c). International briefs. *Convene,* May 1, 25.

Hill, R. A. (1996). Small is sometimes best. *HSMAI Marketing Review, 13*(2): 45-46.

Hiller, H. H. (1995). Conventions as mega-events: A new model for convention-host city relationships. *Tourism Management, 16*(5), 375-379.

Hiller, H. H. (1998). Assessing the impact of mega-events: A linkage model. *Current Issues in Tourism, 1*(1), 47-57.

Hinkin, T. R. and Tracey, J. B. (1998). The service imperative: Factor driving meeting effectiveness. *Cornell Hotel and Restaurant Administration Quarterly, 39*(5), 59-67.

Hofstede, G. (1984). *Culture's consequences: International differences in work-related values.* Beverly Hills, CA: Sage.

Hong Kong Tourist Association (HKTA) (2000). *Annual Report 1999.* Hong Kong: HKTA.

Horwarth Axe Consultants (1996). *Business and congress tourism in the European economic area.* Paris: Author.

Hu, C. and Hiemstra, S. J. (1996). Hybrid conjoint analysis as a research technique to measure meeting planners' preferences in hotel selection. *Journal of Travel Research, 35*(2), 62-69.

Hughes, C. G. (1988). Conference tourism—a salesman's dream. *Tourism Management, 9*(3), 235-237.

Hunn, C. and Mangan, J. (1999). Estimating the economic impact of tourism at the local, regional and state or territory level, including consideration of the multiplier effect. In *Valuing Tourism: Methods and Techniques.* Bureau of Tourism Research Occasional Paper Number 28, Canberra.

Hunt, J. (1989). The conference industry in Asia. *Travel and Tourism Analyst, 6,* 56-75.

Hurrell, A. (1999). Singapore maintains its status as a top convention venue. *Convention and Incentive Marketing, 30*(June), 32-34.

Hutchinson, J. (1997). *Tourism—getting it right for the millennium.* Sydney: SCVB.

IACVB (1998). 1998 IACVB Foundation CVB Financial Survey. Washington, DC, IACVB.

Infratest Burke. (1996). *The German meetings market 1994/95.* Frankfurt: German Convention Bureau.

International Association of Convention and Visitors Bureaus (IACVB) (2000). The IACVB Sales Academy. Available online: <http://www.IACVB.org/salesacad.html>. September 1.

International Association of Professional Congress Organizers (IAPCO) (2000a). *Meeting industry terminology, Fourth edition.* Brussels: International Association of Professional Congress Organizers.

International Association of Professional Congress Organizers (IAPCO) (2000b). Newsletter, April. Available online: <http://www.iapco.org/>.

International Hotel & Restaurant Association (IHRA) (2000). *Leading hospitality into the age of excellence: Expansion competition and vision in the multinational hotel industry 1995-2005.* Paris: IHRA.

Johnson, L., Foo, M., et al. (1999). *Meetings make their mark: Characteristics and economic contribution of Australia's meetings and exhibitions sector.* Bureau of Tourism Research Occasional Paper No. 26, Canberra.

Jones, J. E. (1984). *Meeting management: A professional approach,* Second edition. Stamford, CT: Bayard Publications.

Judd, D. R. (1995). Promoting tourism in US cities. *Tourism Management, 16*(3), 175-187.

Jun, J. and McCleary, K. W. (1999). Classifying US association meeting planners based on international destination selection criteria: A case study of South Korea. *International Journal of Hospitality Management, 18*(2), 183-199.

Jung, H. S. and Baker, M. (1998). Assessing the market effectiveness of the World-Wide-Web in national tourist offices. In D. Buhalis, A. M. Tjoa, and J. Jafari (Eds.), *Proceedings of the International Conference on Information and Communication Technologies in Tourism (ENTER'98)* (pp. 94-102). Wien: Springer Verlag.

Jusko, J. (1994). Partner in tourism. *Hotel and Hotel Management, 209,* 16-17.

Kim, W.G., Shin, H. J., and Chon, K. S. (1998). Korea's lodging industry: Problems, profitability and regulations. *Cornell Hotel and Restaurant Administration Quarterly, 39*(1), 60-67.

Kingston, A. (1995). Locale Heroes. *Report on Business Magazine,* (February), 72-78.

KNTO (1996). *KOREA meeting and incentive planner's guide 1996.* Seoul: KNTO.

KNTO (1997a). *97 International Convention Seminar.* Seoul: KNTO.

KNTO (1997b). *The present state of international meetings in Korea.* Seoul: KNTO.

KNTO (2000a). *Conventions in Korea.* Seoul: KNTO.

KNTO (2000b). *Survey of international convention delegates.* Seoul: KNTO.

"KOCE dedicated to promoting ROK convention industry" (2000). *Korea Times,* September 28.

"KOEX's contribution ever increasing" (1996). *Business Korea, 13*(7), 65.

Koh, W. A. M. (1996). *An evaluation of convention development in Singapore from a tourism perspective.* Unpublished master's thesis, University of Surrey, Guildford, Surrey.

Korn, I. (1998). Second tier, first choice. *Association Meetings,* (June), 57-68.

Korn, I. (1999). The invisible Euro. *Successful Meetings, 48*(March), 24.

Kotler, P., Haider, D. H., and Rein, I. (1993). *Marketing places: Attracting invest-ment, industry, and tourism to cities, states, and nations.* New York: The Free Press.

KPMG Peat Marwick (1993). *The economic impact of the Adelaide convention in-dustry.* Adelaide: Adelaide Convention and Tourism Authority.

Kraal, C. (1996). Suntech Centre: Past, present and future. *Meetings and Conven-tions: Asia/Pacific, 4*(April), 44-46.

Ladkin, A. and Spiller, J. (2000a). Market segments: The European exhibition mar-ket. *Travel and Tourism Analyst* (2), 49-63.

Ladkin, A. and Spiller, J. (2000b). *The meetings, incentives, conferences, and exhi-bitions industry: An international research report.* London: Travel and Tourism Intelligence.

Lambert, J. (1999). Business visas under fire. *Convention and Incentive Marketing:* 2.

Lash, S. and Urry, J. (1994). *Economies of signs and space.* London: Sage.

Las Vegas Convention and Visitors Authority (LVCVA) (1999). *Marketing Bulle-tin 1999, 27*(112).

Las Vegas Convention and Visitors Authority (LVCVA) (2000). *Annual Report 1999.* Las Vegas, NV: LVCVA.

Law, C. M. (1993). *Urban tourism: Attracting visitors to large cities.* London: Mansell.

Lawson, F. (1981). *Conference, convention and exhibition facilities: A handbook of planning, design and management.* London: The Architectural Press.

Lawson, F. R. (1980). Congresses, conventions, and conferences: Facility, supply, and demand. *Tourism Management, 1*(3), 184-188.

Lawson, F. (1982). *Conference and convention centres.* London: Routledge.

Lawson, F. (2000). *Congress, convention and exhibition facilities: Planning, de-sign and management.* London: Architectural Press.

Leask, A. and Spiller, J. (2001). *UK conference venues—past, present and future.* Paper presented at the IX Convention/Expo Summit, Las Vegas, NV.

LeBlanc, G. (1992). Factors affecting customer evaluation of service quality in travel agencies: An investigation of customer perceptions. *Journal of Travel Re-search,* (spring), 10-16.

Lee, M. H. and Weaver, P. A. (1994). What do meeting planners want? A compari-son between corporate and association meeting markets. *Journal of Hospitality and Tourism Research, 5*(1), 1-14.

Leemans, H. (1994). *Het Veelvormige Boek: Informatiegebruik bij de aankoop van een hedonistisch product.* Delft: Eburon.

Leigh, S. K. and Adler, H. (1998). Group/convention cancellation policies in the U.S. hotel industry. *Journal of Convention and Exhibition Management, 1*(2/3), 57-118.

Leiper, N. (1990). *Tourism systems: An interdisciplinary perspective.* New Zealand: Department of Management Systems, Massey University.

Lenhart, M. (1998a). Affordable cities. *Meetings and Conventions, 33*(6), 78-81.

Lenhart, M. (1998b). Building a better bureau. *Meetings and Conventions, 33*(2), 53-57.

Lenhart, M. (1998c). Yours for the booking. *Meetings and Conventions, 33*(3), 72.

Lessin, M. (2001). Travel concerns prompt national organizations to hold meetings via live Internet and satellite technology. Available onnline: <http://www.connectlive.com>. Accessed September 24.

Lew, A. A. and Chang, T. C. (1999). Where the world meets: Regionalism and globalization in Singapore's convention industry. *Journal of Convention and Exhibition Management, 1*(4), 17-36.

Lewis, R. (1983). The incentive travel market: How to reap your share. *Cornell HRA Quarterly, 24*(May), 19-27.

Ligos, M. (2000). The great escape. *Successful Meetings, 49*(3), 33-39.

Listokin, D. (1985). The convention trade: A competitive economic prize. *Real Estate Issues, 10*, 43-46.

LLP, P. W. (1997). *1997 convention and congress center annual report.* Tampa, FL: Author.

Long, P. T. and Perdue, R. P. (1990). The economic impact of rural festivals and special events: Assessing the spatial distribution of expenditures. *Journal of Travel Research 29*(spring), 10-14.

Lumsdon, L. (1997). *Tourism marketing: Tourism and hospitality management series.* London: International Thomson Business Press.

MacLaurin, D. J. (2000). The importance of human capital. Available online: <http://www.ima.com.sg/feb_mar2002/index.html>.

MacLaurin, D. J. and Leong, K. (2000a). Strategies for success: How Singapore attracts and retains the convention and trade show industry. *Event Management, 6*(2), 93-103.

MacLaurin, D. J. and Leong, K. (2000b). *Strategies for success: How Singapore attracts and retains the convention and trade show industry.* Paper presented at the Convention Expo Summit, Las Vegas, NV.

Masberg, B. A. (1998). Defining the tourist: is it possible? A view from the convention and visitors bureau. *Journal of Travel Research, 37*(1), 67-70.

Masberg, B. A. (1999). What is the priority of research in the marketing and promotional efforts of convention and visitors bureaus in the United States? *Journal of Travel and Tourism Marketing, 8*(2), 29-40.

McCabe, V. (1998). The D.D.C. landscape: A snapshot of the management and operation of dedicated convention centres in the UK, US and Australasia. Paper presented at the Australian Tourism and Hospitality Research Conference, Gold Coast, Australia.

McCabe, V. S. (2001a). Educating MICE in Australia: An exploration of issues relating to the curriculum design, development and delivery of meetings, incentives, conventions and exhibitions (MICE) management course within a regional university in Australia. Working paper. Council of Australian Universities Tourism and Hospitality Educators Conference (CAUTHE), Canberra. February.

McCabe, V. S. (2001b). MICE career paths and labor mobility. In keynote presentation, "Love'em or lose'em." MIAA National Conference, Canberra. April.

McCabe, V., Poole, B., Weeks, P., and Leiper, N. (2000). *The business and management of conventions.* Milton, Qld: John Wiley and Sons, Inc.

McCabe, V. and Weeks, P. (1999). Convention services management in Sydney four to five star hotels. *Journal of Convention and Exhibition Management, 1*(4), 67-84.

McCleary, K. W. (1977). *Factors influencing the marketing of meeting facilities: An empirical study of the buying/selling relationship for corporate group meetings.* Unpublished doctoral dissertation, Michigan State University, East Lansing.

McCleary, K. W. (1978). The corporate meetings market: Components of success in attracting corporate group business. *Cornell Hotel and Restaurant Administration Quarterly, 19*(August), 30-35.

McGee, R. (1993). Convention centers: Bright hope or big hoax for America's cities? *Association Meetings, 5*(4), 20-24.

McGuiness, D. (1982). Convention centers: Too much of a good thing? *Planning, 48*(November), 13-15.

MCMB (Melbourne Convention and Marketing Bureau) (2000). *AIME 2000 Economic Impact Survey.* Melbourne: MCMB.

McNulty, and Wafer, P. (1990). Transnational corporations and tourism issues. *Tourism Management, 11*(4), 291-295.

Meetings and Conventions (2000). Meetings market report. Secaucus, NJ: Cahners Business Information.

Meetings and Conventions (2001). An international guide to facilities and services. *Meetings & Conventions,* April.

Meetings Industry Association (1998). *UK conference market survey 1998.* Broadway: Meetings Industry Association.

Member Digest (2000). Freeman companies donate $500,000 to PCMA learning center. *Professional Convention Management Association,* Birmingham AL: July, p. 2.

Meyers, C. (1999). On alert. *Successful Meetings,* July/Supplement: 8-14.

Migdal, D. (1993). Getting the best from your bureau. *Meetings and Conventions, 28*(2), 51-52, 70.

Mistilis, N. and Dwyer, L. (1998). Information technology and service standards in MICE tourism. *Journal of Convention and Exhibition Management, 2*(1/December), 55-65.

Mistilis, N. and Dwyer, L. (1999). Tourism gateways and regional economies: The distributional impacts of MICE. *International Journal of Tourism Research, 1*(6), 441-457.

Montanari, A. (1995). The Mediterranean region: Europe's summer leisure space. In A. Montanari and A. M. Williams (Eds.), *European tourism* (pp. 41-65). Chichester: John Wiley and Sons, Inc.

Montgomery, R. J. and Rutherford, D. G. (1994). A profile of convention-services professionals. *Cornell HRA Quarterly* (December), 47-57.

Montgomery, R. J. and Strick, S. K. (1995). *Meetings, conventions, and expositions—An introduction to the industry*. New York: Van Nostrand Reinhold.

Morgan, R. (1999). A novel, user-based rating system for tourist beaches. *Tourism Management, 20*(4), 393-410.

Morrison, A. M., Bruen, S. M., and Anderson, D. J. (1998). Convention and visitor bureaus in the USA: A profile. *Journal of Travel and Tourism Marketing, 7*(1), 1-19.

Mules, T. (1999). Estimating the economic impact of an event on a local government area, region, state or territory. In *Valuing tourism: Methods and techniques*. Bureau of Tourism Research Occasional Paper Number 28, Canberra.

Munro, D. (1994). Conference centers in the 21st century. In A. V. Seaton (Ed.), *Tourism: The state of the art* (pp. 58-65). London: John Wiley and Sons, Inc.

Muqbil, I. (1997). Market segments: The Asian conferences, meetings and incentives market. *EIU Travel and Tourism Analyst* (2), 38-56.

Murphy, P.E. (Ed.) (1997). *Quality management in urban tourism*. Chichester: New York: John Wiley and Sons, Inc.

Murray, M. (1995). When will the balloon burst for convention centres? *Hospitality,* (February/March), 16-18.

Mutschlechner, C. (1997). *Comparative analysis of convention bureaux in Europe*. Amsterdam: ICCA.

Nadler, L. and Nadler, Z. (1988). *The comprehensive guide to successful conferences and meetings*. San Francisco: Jossey-Bass Publishers.

Nelson, R. R. (1996). Emerging concerns about the use of convention centres as catalysts for local economic development. Paper presented at the Advances in Hospitality and Tourism Research. Proceedings of the Conference on Graduate Education and Graduate Student Research, Houston, TX.

Nelson, R. R. (1998). How a more competitive market is influencing public investments in convention centers. *Journal of Convention and Exhibition Management, 1*(2/3), 27-37.

Office for National Statistics (1997). *International Passenger Survey—Overseas Conference Visitors to the UK 1996*. London: Office for National Statistics and BTA/ETB Statistical Research.

Oh, H., Roehl, W. S., and Shock, P. (1993). Family decision-making in convention participation. Paper presented at the Convention/Expo Summit IV, Las Vegas, NV.

O'Halloran, R. M. (1992). Tourism management profiles: Implications for tourism education. *FIU Hospitality Review, 10*(1): 83-91.

O'Neill, J. W. (1998). Effective municipal tourism and convention operations and marketing strategies: The cases of Boston, San Antonio, and San Francisco. *Journal of Travel and Tourism Marketing, 7*(3), 95-125.

Oppermann, M. (1994). *Modelling convention location choice and participation decision making process: A review with emphasis on professional associations.* Aix-en-Provence: Centre des Hautes Etudes Touristiques, Universite de Droit.

Oppermann, M. (1996a). Convention cities—Images and changing fortunes. *Journal of Tourism Studies, 7*(1), 10-19.

Oppermann, M. (1996b). Convention destination images: Analysis of association meeting planners' perceptions. *Tourism Management, 17*(3), 175-182.

Oppermann, M. (1998). Perceptions of convention destinations: Large-half versus small-half association meeting planners. *Journal of Convention and Exhibition Management, 1*(1), 35-48.

Oppermann, M. and Chon, K.-S. (1997). Convention participation decision-making process. *Annals of Tourism Research, 24*(1), 178-191.

Osservatorio Congressuale Italiano (2000). Annual survey financed by Meeting & Congressi and Convention Bureau della Riviera di Romagna, University of Bolgna.

Osti, L. and Pechlaner, H. (2000). *Organizzazione turistica regionale in Italia—Quo vadis?* Bolzano-Bozen: Quaderni dell' Accademia Europea Bolzano.

Ovechka, G. (1993). Partners in marketing: How convention and visitor bureaus can make a hotelier's day. *Lodging,* (October), 46-51.

Pacific Asia Travel Association (PATA) (2000). Issues and trends: New trends in planning meetings. *Pacific Asia Travel Association, 5*(12), December.

Pakistan Ministry of Culture and Tourism (1987). *Convention tourism in Pakistan.* Islamabad: Pakistan Ministry of Culture and Tourism.

Palmer, A. and Bejou, D. (1995). Tourism destination marketing alliances. *Annals of Tourism Research, 22*(3): 616-629.

Papatheodorou, A. (1999). The demand for international tourism in the Mediterranean region. *Applied Economics, 31*(5), 619-630.

PCMA (2000a). *Environmental scan, non-conventional behaviors: Long-range trends influencing the demand for meetings and conventions.* Birmingham, AL: PCMA.

PCMA. (2000b). Freeman companies donate $500,000 to PCMA Learning Center. *Members Digest,* July 2.

PCMA (2002). *11th meetings market survey.* Chicago: PCMA.

PCVC (Philippine Convention and Visitors Corporation) (2001). *Major MICE campaign unfolds.* Available online: <www.dotpcvc.gov.ph/mmm.html>. Accessed March 20.

Pechlaner, H. (1999). Alpine destination management and marketing in Italy—Trans-regional cooperation as a factor of competition. Paper presented at the Turistica: Economia—Management—Marketing, VIII, Firenze.

Pechlaner, H. (2000). Cultural heritage and destination management in the Mediterranean. *Thunderbird International Business Review, 42*(2), 409-426.

Pechlaner, H. and Jäger, B. (2000). Cultural tourism as competitive factor in Mediterranean tourism—A comparative study of the Japanese and the German source markets for the Italian cultural heritage. *Tourism and Hospitality Management, 5*(1/2), 229-242.

Perth Convention Bureau (1994). *Western Australian convention delegate expenditure study.* Prepared by Tourism Research Services. May.

Peske, T. (2000a). ASAE selects executives for diversity leadership program. *ASAE News,* August 1, 11.

Peske, T. (2000b). MPI, PCMA foundations to co-sponsor high-level educational forum. *ASAE News,* November 28, 1.

Peterson, D. C. (1989). *Convention centers, stadiums and arenas.* Washington, DC: Urban Land Institute.

Phillips, G. (1999). Association boycotts: Social agendas make site selection a political decision. *Convene,* 05/01, 42.

Pizam, A. and Manning, P. B. (1982). The impact of inflation on convention site selection. *International Journal of Hospitality Management 1,* 65-66.

Pizam, A. and Mansfeld, Y. (Eds.) (1996). *Tourism, crime, and international security issues.* New York: John Wiley and Sons, Inc.

Polivka, E. G. (Ed.) (1996). *Professional meeting management.* Birmingham, AL: Professional Convention Management Association.

Port of Singapore Authority (PSA) (1998). *WTC Exhibition and Convention Centre.* Singapore: PSA.

Porter, M. E. (1998). Clusters and the new economics of competition. *Harvard Business Review,* (November-December), 77-90.

Porter, M. V. (1997). The rise of third-party housing services. *Association Management, 49*(13), 51-53.

Price, C. (1993). An empirical study of the value of professional association meetings from the perspective of attendees. Virginia Polytechnic and State University.

Price, C. H. (1999). *The complete guide to professional meeting and event coordination.* Washington, DC: George Washington University.

Price Waterhouse (1999). *Convention Centre Annual Report.*

Pruyn, A. T. H. (1994). Imago: Een analytische benadering van het begrip en de implicaties daarvan voor onderzoek. In C. B. M. Riel (Ed.), *Corporate Communication geselecteerde artikelen voor het hoger onderwijs* (pp. 139-175). Bohn Stafleu Van Loghum: van, Houten.

Publishing, T. T. (1998). *Conference cities link into "Big Six"* (September issue). Southern Africa Tourism Update. Available online: <http://www.tourismupdate. co.za/>. Accessed March 23, 2000.

Qu, H., Li, L., and Chu, G.K.T. (2000). The comparative analysis of Hong Kong as an international conference destination in Southeast Asia. *Tourism Management, 21*(6), 643-648.

Quain, W. J., Render, B., and Hermann, P. W. (1991). A multi-variate approach towards marketing decisions in the convention segment. *International Journal of Hospitality Management, 10*(2), 147-155.

Quain, W. J., Render, B., and Higgins, J. M. (1990). Using decision theory for strategic decision making in the convention industry. *International Journal of Hospitality Management, 9*(3), 237-246.

Queensland Travel and Tourism Corporation (1997). *Queensland convention industry: Delegate expenditure and characteristics study.* Brisbane: QTTC.

Renaghan, L. M. and Kay, M. Z. (1987). What meeting planners want: The conjoint-analysis approach. *The Cornell Hotel and Restaurant Administration Quarterly, 28*(May), 67-76.

"Republic of Korea" (1996). *Successful Meetings,* April, 7-8.

Rich, E. (1996). Handling industry growth through training and education. *Meetings and Conventions, Asia-Pacific,* October, 79.

Richardson, J. I. (1999). *A history of Australian travel and tourism.* Melbourne: Hospitality Press.

Richison, S. H. (1989). A descriptive analysis of convention and visitor bureaus in North Carolina and surrounding states. *Visions in Leisure and Business, 8*(3), 41-60.

Riezebos, H. J. (1994). *Brand-added value: Theory and empirical research about the value of brands to consumers.* Delft: Eburon.

Right Solution, The (1997). *The UK Conference Market Survey 1996.* Eastcote: The Right Solution Ltd.

Riley, M. and Perogiannis, N. (1990). The influence of hotel attributes on the selection of a conference venue. *International Journal of Contemporary Hospitality Management, 2*(1), 17-22.

Ritchie, J. R. B. (1984). Assessing the impact of hallmark events: Conceptual and research issues. *Journal of Travel Research, 23*(1/summer), 2-11.

Rockett, G. and Smillie, G. (1994). Market segments: The European conference and meetings market. *EIU Travel and Tourism Analyst* (4), 36-50.

Roehl, W. S. (2000). The convention/expo summit: The first decade. *Journal of Convention and Exhibition Management, 2*(2/3), 1-10.

Rogers, T. (1998). *Conferences: A twenty-first century industry.* Harlow, Essex: Addison Wesley Longman.

Ross, J. R. (1999a). Who's minding the store? The case for private management. *Convene,* (October), 43.

Ross, J. R. (1999b). Who's minding the store? The case for public management. *Convene,* (October), 42.

Russet, M. (2000). One meeting, one world. *Successful Meetings,* July/Supplement, 3-10.

Rutherford, D. (1990). *Introduction to the conventions expositions and meetings industry.* New York: Van Nostrand Reinhold.

Rutherford, D. G. and Kreck, L. A. (1994). Conventions and tourism: Financial add-on or myth? *Journal of Travel and Tourism Marketing, 3*(1), 49-63.

Rutherford, D. G. and Umbreit, W. T. (1993). Improving interactions between meeting planners and hotel employees. *Cornell Hotel and Restaurant Administration Quarterly, 34*(1), 68-80.

Sanders, H. T. (1992). Building the convention city: Politics, finance and public investment in urban America. *Journal of Urban Affairs, 14,* 135-159.

Schreiber, M. T. and Beckmann, K. (1999). *Kongress und Tagungsmanagement.* Muenchen: Oldenbourg.

Schwaegermann, H. (1999). Verbaende der kongresswirtschaft: Professionale interessenvertretungen. In M. T. Schreiber and K. Beckmann (Eds.), *Kongress und tagungsmanagement* (pp. 533-548). Muenchen: Oldenbourg.

Schwartz, Z. (1996). A dynamic equilibrium pricing model: A game theoretic approach to modelling conventions' room rates. *Tourism Economics, 2*(3), 251-263.

Schwartz, Z. (1998). Convention and conference facilities: A framework of statistical predictions and judgmental adjustments for daily occupancy forecasts. *Journal of Convention and Exhibition Management, 1*(1), 71-88.

Schweitzer, C. (1997). One hundred years of CVB experience. *Association Management, 49*(February), 67-68.

Seekings, D. (1991). *How to organize effective conferences and meetings,* Sixth edition. London: Kogan Page Ltd.

Selin, S. (1993). Collaborative alliances: New interorganizational forms in tourism. *Journal of Travel and Tourism Marketing, 2*(2/3), 217-227.

Shaw, M. (Ed.) (1990). *Convention sales: A book of readings.* East Lansing: Educational Institute of the American Hotel and Motel Association.

Shaw, M., Lewis, R. C., and Khorey, A. (1991). Measuring meeting planner satisfaction with hotel convention services: A multi-variate approach. *International Journal of Hospitality Management, 10*(2), 137-146.

Shinnar, R. S. and Montgomery, R. J. (1998). The impact of change on the Hong Kong convention and exposition business. *Visions in Leisure and Business, 16*(4), 14-27.

Shone, A. (1998). *Business of conferences: A hospitality sector overview for the UK and Ireland.* Oxford: Butterworth-Heinemann.

Shure, P. (1997). The tracks of tiers. *Convene,* (February), 44.

Shure, P. (1998). Room rate hikes, availability squeeze altering association's rotating patterns. *Convene,* (February 1), 41.

Sims, L. and Shaw, M. (1994). Current perspectives and practices in meeting planning. *HSMAI Marketing Review,* (fall), 44-49.

Sims, S. L. (1990). Educational needs and opportunities for personnel in convention and visitor bureaus. *Visions in Leisure and Business, 9*(3), 27-32.

Singapore Convention and Exhibition Bureau (SCEB) (2000). *Statistics on the meetings, incentives, conventions and exhibitions industry in Singapore 1999.* Singapore: SCEB.

Singapore Tourism Board (1999a). PATA gold awards cap series of wins for Singapore Tourism Board. Press release, April 15.

Singapore Tourism Board (1999b). Singapore Tourism Board goes after exhibition and convention visitors with a one-two combination campaign. Press release, September 1.

Singapore Tourism Board (2000). *Annual report 1999*. Singapore: STB.

Singapore Trade Development Board (1999). Exhibiting the right stuff. *Singapore Trade News 3*(3), 10-13.

Smith, G. (1989). The European conference market. *EIU Travel and Tourism Analyst* (4), 60-76.

Smith, G. (1991). Professional organizations in the European meetings industry. *International Journal of Hospitality Management, 10*(2), 119-126.

Smith, G. and Meyers, C. (1999). Are you Euro-ready? *Successful Meetings,* 48, 11.

Spataro, A. and Khader, B. (1993). *Il Mediterrane—Popoli e risorse verso uno spazio economico commune.* Roma: Edizioni Associate.

Spiller, J. E. and Ladkin, A. (2000). The growth and trends of conference centres: A case study of the UK. Paper presented at the Conference Proceedings, Sheffield Hallum.

Stavro, L. and Beggs, T. (1984). Attributes of significance a priori and during the meeting. Paper presented at the World Hospitality Congress II, Boston, MA.

Stavro, L. and Beggs, T. G. (1986). Buyer behavior and the meeting planner: An exploratory study. In R. C. Lewis, T. J. Beggs, M. Shaw, and S. A. Croffoot (Eds.), *The practice of hospitality management II* (p. 521). Westport, CT: AVI Publishing Company.

Strick, S. K., Montgomery, R. J., and Gant, C. (1993). Does service sell the site: A meeting planner's perspective. *Journal of Travel and Tourism Marketing, 2*(1), 87-93.

Swisher, P. (2001). Meeting now! *Successful Meetings, 50*(7), 16.

Sydney Convention and Visitors Bureau (SCVB) (1996). *Sydney convention delegate study 1995.* Prepared by MARC.IT. February.

Sydney Convention and Visitors Bureau (SCVB) (1997). *Sydney convention delegate study 1996.* Prepared by MARC.IT. February.

Sydney Convention and Visitors Bureau (SCVB) (1998). *Sydney convention delegate study 1997.* Prepared by SCVB. May.

Sydney Convention and Visitors Bureau (SCVB) (1999). *Sydney convention delegate study 1998.* Prepared by SCVB. May.

Sydney Convention and Visitors Bureau (SCVB) (2001). *Sydney convention delegate study 2000.* Prepared by SCVB.

System Three (1998). *Conference Delegate Expenditure Research 1998.* London: BTA.

Tasmanian Convention Bureau (1996). *Research on the impact of delegates on the Tasmanian economy.* Hobart: Tasmanian Convention Bureau.

Teale, K. (2001). *ETC foresees growth in 2001; Launches expanded Visiteurope. com TV promotion.* European Travel Commission. Available online: <http://www. visiteurope.com/pressroom/>. Accessed March 23.

Teye, V. B. and Diffenderfer, P. (1988). The impact of a convention boycott on metropolitan Arizona. *Visions in Leisure and Business, 7*(2), 34-45.

Thompson, D. (Ed.) (1995). *The concise Oxford dictionary of current English,* Ninth edition. Oxford: Clarendon Press.

Thompson, M. (1999). Embracing the Euro. *Successful Meetings* (July/Supplement), 26-28.

Tourism Authority of Thailand (1998). *Convention and exhibition calendar 1997-2001.* Bangkok: Tourism Authority of Thailand.

Tourism Research and Marketing (1999). *British conference market trends survey: Annual report 1998.* London: Tourism Research and Marketing.

Travel Industry Association of America (TIA) (1999). *Survey of business travelers 1999.* Washington, DC: TIA.

Travel and Trade Publishing (1998). Conference cities link into "Big Six." *Southern Africa Tourism Update.* Available online: <http://www.tourismupdate.co.za/>. September. Accessed March 23, 2000.

Twite, P. (1997). Learning the ropes. *Incentive and Meetings Asia,* (January-February), 7-10.

University of Bologna (2000). *Osservatorio Congressuale Italiano.* Bologna: University of Bologna.

University of Calgary (2000). Executive program in destination management. <http://www.fp.ucalgary.ca:8030/tour/programs/iacvb.html>. Accessed December 19.

University of Central Florida (1999). *Central Florida Hotel and Motel Association professorship: Department of hospitality management, faculty position announcement.* Orlando, FL. October.

University of Nevada Las Vegas (2000). *Tourism and convention administration department, convention courses.* Available online: <http://www.unlv.edu/Tourism/conv.html>.

Upchurch, R. S., Jeong, G.H., Clements, C., and Jung, I. (1999). Meeting planners' perceptions of site selection characteristics: The case of Seoul, Korea. *Journal of Convention and Exhibition Management, 2*(1), 15-35.

U.S. Department of Commerce (1998). *R.I.M.S. II.* Washington, DC: U.S. Department of Commerce.

Usher, C. M. (1991). Las Vegas: The key to increased convention attendance. Unpublished professional paper, University of Nevada, Las Vegas.

Var, T., Cesario, F., and Mauser, G. (1985). Convention tourism modelling. *Tourism Management, 6*(3), 194-204.

Vogt, C. A., Roehl, W. S., and Fesenmaier, D. R. (1994). Understanding planners' use of meeting facility information. *Hospitality Research Journal, 17*(3), 119-130.

Voso, M. (1990). *The convention and meeting planner's handbook.* Lexington, MA: Lexington Books.

Waarts, E. (1996). *Analysing competitive links in marketing: A three-level perspective.* Rotterdam: Erasmus Universiteit.

Walshak, H. (1998). Great tech'xpectations: High-tech centers creating the next wave of convention networking. *Convene,* (October), 38.

Weber, K. (2000). Meeting planners' perceptions of hotel chain practices and benefits: An importance/performance analysis. *Cornell Hotel and Restaurant Administration Quarterly, 41*(4), 32-38.

Weber, K. (2001a). Association meeting planners' loyalty to hotel chains. *International Journal of Hospitality Management, 20*(3), 259-275.

Weber, K. (2001b). Meeting planners' use and evaluation of convention and visitor bureaus. *Tourism Management, 22*(6), 599-606.

Weber, K. and Ladkin, A. (2001). The Convention Industry in Australia and the United Kingdom: Key Issues and Competitive Forces: Manuscript under review.

Weber, K. and Roehl, W. S. (2001). Service quality issues for convention and visitor bureaus. *Journal of Convention and Exhibition Management, 3*(1), 1-19.

Wee, A. (1999). More meet added to Globalmeet campaign. *Incentives and Meetings Asia,* (May/June), 32.

Wei, Z. and Go, F. M. (1999). The meetings, conventions, and expositions industry in Beijing: Problems and strategies. *Journal of Travel and Tourism Marketing, 8*(1), 101-110.

Weirich, M. L. (1992). *Meetings and conventions management.* Albany, NY: Delmar.

Weissinger, S. S. (1992). *A guide to successful meeting planning.* New York: John Wiley and Sons, Inc.

White, S. (1995). Battle of the UK destinations. *Conference and Incentives Travel,* (September), 27-32.

White, S. (1996). Upturn in business. *Conference and Incentives Travel,* (September), 11.

Williams, A. (1997). Tourism and uneven development in the Mediterranean. In R. King, L. Proudfoot, and B. Smith (Eds.), *The Mediterranean—Environment and Society* (pp. 208-226). London: Arnold.

Williams, A. and Teare, R. (1990). The client perspective on hotel conference organizations. *International Journal of Contemporary Hospitality Management, 2*(1), i-ii.

Witt, S. F., Dartus, M., and Sykes, A. M. (1992). Forecasting, modeling and recall bias: Modeling conference tourism. Paper presented at the 23rd Annual Travel and Tourism Research Association Conference, Minneapolis.

Witt, S. F., Sykes, A. M., and Dartus, M. (1995). Forecasting international conference attendance. *Tourism Management, 16*(8), 559-570.

Woods, R. H. and Berger, F. (1988). Making meetings work. *Cornell Hotel and Restaurant Administration Quarterly, 29*(2), 101-105.

Wootton, G. and Stevens, T. (1995). Business tourism: A study of the market for hotel-based meetings and its contribution to Wales' tourism. *Tourism Management, 16*(4), 305-313.

Wright, M. (2000). MICE money. *Panorama (Ansett Australia's Magazine),* (April), 74-79.

Young, W. B. and Montgomery, R. J. (1998). Crisis management and its impact on destination marketing: A guide for convention and visitors bureaus. *Journal of Convention and Exhibition Management, 1*(1), 3-18.

Yuan, Y. and Fesenmaier, D. (2000). Preparing for the new economy: The use of the Internet and intranet in American convention and visitor bureaus. *Information Technology and Tourism, 3*(2).

Yuan, Y. Y., Fesenmaier, D. R., Xia, L., and Gratzer, M. (1999). The use of Internet and intranet in American convention and visitors bureaus. In D. Buhalis and W. Schertler (Eds.), *Information and communication technologies in tourism 1999* (pp. 365-375). Wien: Springer Verlag.

Zeithaml, V. A. and Bitner, M. J. (1996). *Services Marketing.* The McGraw-Hill Companies, Inc.

Zelinsky, W. (1994). Conventionland USA: The geography of a latterday phenomenon. *Annals of the Association of American Geographers, 84*(1), 68-86.

Index

AACVB. *See* Asian Association of
Convention and Visitors
Bureaus (AACVB)
Academic journals and textbooks, as
research sources, 114-117
Accredited Meetings Manager (AMM),
98
Accredited Member of the Meetings
Industry Association of
Australia (AMIAA), 97-98
ACOM, 91
Ahmed, Z. U., 176
Ahn, J. Y., 176
AIME, 74
Airfares, 27-28
American Society of Association
Executives (ASAE), 85, 86,
98
American Society of Travel Agents
(ASTA), 214
AMIAA, 97-98
AMM, 98
Anderson, D., 73
Annihilation of space by time, 39
APEC, 16
Archer, B., 31
Arsenault, J., 68
ASAE, 85, 86, 98
ASEAN Free Trade Area, 16
Asian Association of Convention and
Visitors Bureaus (AACVB),
17, 51, 84, 96-97, 111
Asian financial crisis, 75
Asia-Pacific Economic Cooperation
(APEC), 16
Asia-Pacific Educational Forum
(APEF), 96
Asia-Pacific Incentives and Meetings
Expo (AIME), 74
Asia-Pacific region, 16-19. *See also*
Australia
convention centers in, 16-17

Asia-Pacific region *(continued)*
education and training programs in,
95-98
globalization and, 40
improved infrastructure in, 16-17
performance ratings for Asian
convention destinations, 49-51
regional planning and development
initiatives in, 49-52
solutions for communication
difficulties in, 127-128
Association for Convention Operations
Management (ACOM), 91
Association for Tourism and Leisure
Education (ATLAS), 95
Association market, 59-60
Association of Southeast Asian Nations
(ASEAN) Free Trade Area,
16
ASTA, 214
ATC, 19, 27, 51, 195
ATLAS, 95
Auditorium, 3
AuSAE, 98
Australia. *See also* Asia-Pacific region
business and finance issues in,
210-211
convention hotels in, 185-199
historical perspective, 186-190
improvement of facilities, 192-193
lead times, 193
organizational structures, 197-198
predominance of domestic
business, 188-189
price competitiveness, 194-195
product differentiation, 196-197
range of, 191-192
spatial distribution, 186
staffing and career management
issues, 198-199
targeted meetings, 195-196

245

THE HAWORTH HOSPITALITY PRESS®
Hospitality, Travel, and Tourism
K. S. Chon, PhD, Editor-in-Chief

CONVENTION TOURISM: INTERNATIONAL RESEARCH AND INDUSTRY PERSPECTIVES edited by Karin Weber and Kye-Sung Chon. (2002). "This comprehensive book is truly global in its perspective. The text points out areas of needed research—a great starting point for graduate students, university faculty, and industry professionals alike. While the focus is mainly academic, there is a lot of meat for this burgeoning industry to chew on as well." *Patti J. Shock, CPCE, Professor and Department Chair, Tourism and Convention Administration, Harrah College of Hotel Administration, University of Nevada–Las Vegas*

CULTURAL TOURISM: THE PARTNERSHIP BETWEEN TOURISM AND CULTURAL HERITAGE MANAGEMENT by Bob McKercher and Hilary du Cros. (2002). "The book brings together concepts, perspectives, and practicalities that must be understood by both cultural heritage and tourism managers, and as such is a must-read for both." *Hisashi B. Sugaya, AICP, Former Chair, International Council of Monuments and Sites, International Scientific Committee on Cultural Tourism; Former Executive Director, Pacific Asia Travel Association Foundation, San Francisco, CA*

TOURISM IN THE ANTARCTIC: OPPORTUNITIES, CONSTRAINTS, AND FUTURE PROSPECTS by Thomas G. Bauer. (2001). "Thomas Bauer presents a wealth of detailed information on the challenges and opportunities facing tourism operators in this last great tourism frontier." *David Mercer, PhD, Associate Professor, School of Geography & Environmental Science, Monash University, Melbourne, Australia*

SERVICE QUALITY MANAGEMENT IN HOSPITALITY, TOURISM, AND LEISURE edited by Jay Kandampully, Connie Mok, and Beverley Sparks. (2001). "A must-read. . . . a treasure. . . . pulls together the work of scholars across the globe, giving you access to new ideas, international research, and industry examples from around the world." *John Bowen, Professor and Director of Graduate Studies, William F. Harrah College of Hotel Administration, University of Nevada, Las Vegas*

TOURISM IN SOUTHEAST ASIA: A NEW DIRECTION edited by K. S. (Kaye) Chon. (2000). "Presents a wide array of very topical discussions on the specific challenges facing the tourism industry in Southeast Asia. A great resource for both scholars and practitioners." *Dr. Hubert B. Van Hoof, Assistant Dean/Associate Professor, School of Hotel and Restaurant Management, Northern Arizona University*

THE PRACTICE OF GRADUATE RESEARCH IN HOSPITALITY AND TOURISM edited by K. S. Chon. (1999). "An excellent reference source for students pursuing graduate degrees in hospitality and tourism." *Connie Mok, PhD, CHE, Associate Professor, Conrad N. Hilton College of Hotel and Restaurant Management, University of Houston, Texas*

THE INTERNATIONAL HOSPITALITY MANAGEMENT BUSINESS: MANAGEMENT AND OPERATIONS by Larry Yu. (1999). "The abundant real-world examples and cases provided in the text enable readers to understand the most up-to-date developments in international hospitality business." *Zheng Gu, PhD, Associate Professor, College of Hotel Administration, University of Nevada, Las Vegas*

CONSUMER BEHAVIOR IN TRAVEL AND TOURISM by Abraham Pizam and Yoel Mansfeld. (1999). "A must for anyone who wants to take advantage of new global opportunities in this growing industry." *Bonnie J. Knutson, PhD, School of Hospitality Business, Michigan State University*

LEGALIZED CASINO GAMING IN THE UNITED STATES: THE ECONOMIC AND SOCIAL IMPACT edited by Cathy H. C. Hsu. (1999). "Brings a fresh new look at one of the areas in tourism that has not yet received careful and serious consideration in the past." *Muzaffer Uysal, PhD, Professor of Tourism Research, Virginia Polytechnic Institute and State University, Blacksburg*

HOSPITALITY MANAGEMENT EDUCATION edited by Clayton W. Barrows and Robert H. Bosselman. (1999). "Takes the mystery out of how hospitality management education programs function and serves as an excellent resource for individuals interested in pursuing the field." *Joe Perdue, CCM, CHE, Director, Executive Masters Program, College of Hotel Administration, University of Nevada, Las Vegas*

MARKETING YOUR CITY, U.S.A.: A GUIDE TO DEVELOPING A STRATEGIC TOURISM MARKETING PLAN by Ronald A. Nykiel and Elizabeth Jascolt. (1998). "An excellent guide for anyone involved in the planning and marketing of cities and regions. . . . A terrific job of synthesizing an otherwise complex procedure." *James C. Maken, PhD, Associate Professor, Babcock Graduate School of Management, Wake Forest University, Winston-Salem, North Carolina*

Order a copy of this book with this form or online at:
http://www.haworthpressinc.com/store/product.asp?sku=4718

CONVENTION TOURISM
International Research and Industry Perspectives

_____in hardbound at $49.95 (ISBN: 0-7890-1283-9)

_____in softbound at $29.95 (ISBN: 0-7890-1284-7)

COST OF BOOKS_____

OUTSIDE USA/CANADA/
MEXICO: ADD 20%_____

POSTAGE & HANDLING_____
(US: $4.00 for first book & $1.50
for each additional book)
Outside US: $5.00 for first book
& $2.00 for each additional book)

SUBTOTAL_____

in Canada: add 7% GST_____

STATE TAX_____
(NY, OH & MIN residents, please
add appropriate local sales tax)

FINAL TOTAL_____
(If paying in Canadian funds,
convert using the current
exchange rate, UNESCO
coupons welcome.)

❏ **BILL ME LATER:** ($5 service charge will be added)
(Bill-me option is good on US/Canada/Mexico orders only;
not good to jobbers, wholesalers, or subscription agencies.)

❏ Check here if billing address is different from
shipping address and attach purchase order and
billing address information.

Signature_____

❏ **PAYMENT ENCLOSED: $_____**

❏ **PLEASE CHARGE TO MY CREDIT CARD.**

❏ Visa ❏ MasterCard ❏ AmEx ❏ Discover
❏ Diner's Club ❏ Eurocard ❏ JCB

Account # _____

Exp. Date_____

Signature_____

Prices in US dollars and subject to change without notice.

NAME_____

INSTITUTION_____

ADDRESS_____

CITY_____

STATE/ZIP_____

COUNTRY_____ COUNTY (NY residents only)_____

TEL_____ FAX_____

E-MAIL_____

May we use your e-mail address for confirmations and other types of information? ❏ Yes ❏ No
We appreciate receiving your e-mail address and fax number. Haworth would like to e-mail or fax special
discount offers to you, as a preferred customer. **We will never share, rent, or exchange your e-mail address
or fax number.** We regard such actions as an invasion of your privacy.

Order From Your Local Bookstore or Directly From
The Haworth Press, Inc.
10 Alice Street, Binghamton, New York 13904-1580 • USA
TELEPHONE: 1-800-HAWORTH (1-800-429-6784) / Outside US/Canada: (607) 722-5857
FAX: 1-800-895-0582 / Outside US/Canada: (607) 722-6362
E-mail: getinfo@haworthpressinc.com
PLEASE PHOTOCOPY THIS FORM FOR YOUR PERSONAL USE.
www.HaworthPress.com

BOF02